Abraham Lincoln
The Author's Spiritual Guide

Going Back to Gettysburg

Autobiography of a Corrupt Indian

M.B. LAL

PARTRIDGE

A Penguin Random House Company

To order additional copies of this book, contact
Partridge India
000 800 10062 62
www.partridgepublishing.com/india
orders.india@partridgepublishing.com

Acknowledgements

I am grateful to the following persons and institutions for their inputs and contributions to this book in various ways.

Rajiv Godial, Monika Lal, Anmol Lal, Dr. G. Ramakrishna, Saroj Lal, Ankur Lal, Aparna Bansal, Arjun Bansal, Akhil Kumar, Nilima Kumar, Payal Lal, Anshul Kumar, Anurag Kumar, Vinod Dhawan, Sashi Nair, Vidura (Press Institute of India), Hosathu, a (Kannada Monthly) Issues and concerns (English Monthly) J. Shriyan, S.Sivadas, H.N. Verma, The Hindu Wikipedia and Google.

Dedication

To my friend

Yash Paul Narula

who planted in my head the idea of writing this book by his casual observation that if I were to publish an autobiography he would buy its first copy. With one assured buyer of his eminence I thought the project was worth pursuing.

Contents

1

Introduction

Why are we indifferent to sufferings of others?

Recently I received a sheaf of papers from an organization called "People for Ethical Treatment of Animals". They are conducting a national animal rights poll. But I wish to ask them the question "What about Human Rights?" Are human beings treated any better? Before we worry about animal rights we have to see whether the treatment meted out to human beings by other human beings is in any way better than how they treat animals? The central question that this book asks is why are we so indifferent to the sufferings of others? The question that comes as a corollary to this is that are we in any way the cause of their suffering and, if so, what can we do it remove it? Why is it that despite the plentitude of resources placed in the hands of homo sapiens by their own advances in science, at least eighty percent of the seven billion human beings on this planet are without clean food and water? According Time Magazine of January 20, 2014, in India alone 800 million people are underfed (and this may be an under-estimate). Have we, the educated and progressive intellectuals, ever experienced real hunger for several days? Have we watched our children starving and famished as a poor man watches his children starve, some times to slow death? We are over joyed when a member of our family brings us a gift. A toy given to a child is remembered by him throughout his life. Does a poor man also not want to bestow such tokens of his love upon his near and dear ones? Does he not want to see the smile on his child's face when he brings him a birthday toy? Why is it that we never think of such things?

A global survey of people declared "slaves" in 162 countries has revealed that half of the 30 million slaves found world wide live and work in India. This is not surprising because the Black Money deposited in Swiss banks by Indians equals the combined total of similar funds kept there by citizens of the rest of the world. Extremes of both wealth and poverty are part of India's long cherished tradition. There was a time not long ago when in rural India where more than 95% Indians lived all members of schedule castes and tribals were treated as virtual slaves and untouchable. In some areas of South India they had to make some kind of sound when walking on a road so that upper caste Hindu passing that way could keep away from them. Such people constitute about 40% of India's population. Thanks to Gandhi, Ambedkar and other great social reformers this evil receded to the background and all public institutions were open to every body. But slavery is returning to this country, this time in a different guise. This book is intended to show the how and why of this process.

The Times of India of November 7, 2013 carries three stories on its front page, two relating to torture of a number of house maids by the wife of a Member of Parliament and the third declaring that India has the sixth largest reservoir of billionaires, 103 in all, in the World. In my opinion the three reports have an invisible link which several UN agencies and the World Press have been crying about. That link is the fast increasing chasm between the rich and poor castes in the country. Behind the billionaires is the ever growing number of tens of millions of millionaires who spend many times more than their declared incomes in building for themselves ivory tower of luxury and grandeur which surpass those enjoyed by the elite in far wealthier Western countries. Our newly built air conditioned shopping malls are over flowing with customers, packed flights, both domestic and international, are running with the frequency of local buses, millions of properties are being bought at five to ten times their declared value, weddings are celebrated with top film stars in attendance, five star hotels and hospitals are full to capacity, all the best foreign universities have students from India in large numbers and so on.

This book is a confession that people of my class are actively engaged in doing all this. The question that it asks and answers is that where does this money come from except through compulsive corruption which no government can check? In the mid-Eighties when he was the Prime Minister of India Rajiv Gandhi declared that only 15% of the development funds reached the actual beneficiaries. The rest of it was consumed by the middle men. The situation has only worsened in the last 30 years. On the other side of the divide to which almost eighty percent of India's population belongs there continues to be total darkness, a true picture of Nineteenth century India when the lower castes were treated as slaves. Even today workers are routinely beaten or dismissed if they demand higher wages or what. Nobel Laureate Amartya Sen calls their minimum "entitlement".

How this unprecedented phenomenon poses the greatest danger to Indian democracy and unity is described in this book. It suggests a non-violent movement of the kind Martin Luther King launched in America against this growing menace. The year 2013 marks the 50th anniversary of king's famous Long March to Washington and 150th Anniversary of Abraham Lincoln's Gettysburg address, the symbol of the American Civil War.

In this picture of gloom there is only one great event in human history that gives me the hope that the solution to this horrendous disease of "indifference" to the sufferings of other people also lies in the human heart. That event is the American Civil War when Abraham Lincoln fought for four years (1861-1865) and sacrificed 6,00,000 lives of an army of mostly White soldiers to liberate the nearly four million Black slaves in America. He and lots of Americans of that period felt that it was wrong for human beings to keep other human beings in chains. It gives me hope that given the right leadership and frame of mind man can himself find a solution to all his problems Examples of such altruism practiced on a national scale are extremely rare, if not totally non-existent, in human history.

We should also not forget the role of technology in improving the living conditions of the poor. Though, thanks to the greed of the rich, Mahatma Gandhi's "poorest of the poor (he called him "daridranarayan') in India is still as poor and deprived as he was ten thousand years ago, advances in information technology have given or will give the man on the street enough powers to expose the misdeeds of the upper classes in every field. Already this is happening in Europe and America on a large scale prompting the Economist, London, to bring out a cover story titled "curious case of fall in crime", when everybody expected mafias to dominate all fields of activity in the Western world. The miracle has been wrought by two developments. One is the digitization of all cash transactions and the other the freedom to spread information 'anonymously' through new networks that no government agency can monitor or control.

This book deals with all such issues and appeals to its readers not to miss any opportunity to protest against any action of the authorities or upper classes that seems to be oppression of the poor.

I congratulate Arvind Kejriwal for boldly rising in protest against police inaction in cases of assault on poor helpless women and risking his Chief Ministership of Delhi on January 20, 2014, taking huge crowds with him. Such protests should be often repeated.

Finally, Indian intellectuals have to discuss and decide whether to build a consumer society for the pleasure of ten percent rich people or a society modeled on Western enlightened democracies in which all its citizens are consumers and live in harmony with each other under a government, (as Abraham Lincoln said in his historic Gettysburg speech) "of the people, for the people and by the people" and not as at present under a government (as the world press is saying about India) "of the rich for the rich and by the rich."

According to The Hindu about 1,00,000 poor children are kidnapped every year in India. On January 27, 2014, The Week, a leading Indian weekly, did a cover story which said that 38% of the stolen children are forced into the Sex Trade and 23% forced into domestic servitude". I am also aware that a large number of them are maimed and made to work as beggars as is brought out beautifully in the Oscar winning movie 'slumdog millionaire'. When will my country wake up? Do we really need another Lincoln, Martin Luther King or Gandhi to stir our conscience to its depths?

2

My Religion: Back To Gettysburg

The American civil war is the only armed conflict in the entire history and mythology of the human race that was fought for over four years over the rights of other "helpless" people, and not over the rights and possessions of the combatants. Right from the epic wars of Troy and the Mahabharata war of India down to the French, Russian and Chinese revolutions, among so many others, those who fought for change of regime were fighting for their own rights, privileges and possessions or merely to satisfy the egos of their masters.

I feel sentimental about Lincoln and the war he launched because I am an Indian. In my country extremes of bondage and inequality are sanctified by religion. There is a whole community of untouchables whose plight even in the 21st century is worse than that of the Black slaves of America in Lincoln's day. Unlike the people of America then who rose in revolt against slavery and made tremendous sacrifices to wipe out this pugnacious institution from their country, the noveau riche Indian middle class thrives on these distinctions and would let the poor starve to death, for all they care.

As an Indian I consider the American Civil War as the most glorious moment in the history of the entire human race and not just America. Dalits and tribals constitute about 40% of India's population of 1.2 billion. Most of them suffer the indignities, humiliations, privations and starvation that slaves suffered in America before the Civil War. In India even Christians and Muslims observe caste distinctions.

In such a scenario for a sensitive old man like me the American Civil War is the Pole Star to help humanity find its way through the dark Ocean of misery, destitution and callousness. To me it is the Noah's Ark that will preserve the values of the human race from extinction in the deluge of materialism that has enveloped the world. It is a shining example of the height man can attain on the moral plane— the Mt. Everest of our spiritual ascent. It is the only live illustration known to man of the teaching of the Hindu bible—the Gita. The war was the starting point of movements for racial equality throughout the world.

I believe that every school going child anywhere in the world should be told and retold the marvelous story of the American Civil War and its numerous battles to uphold values that have since been submerged in the deluge of selfishness. He or she should be told what it means to die so that others can live in dignity and peace. I believe that the sacrifices the American people made during the four-year long war to abolish slavery from their land have absolutely no parallel in the entire history and mythology of the world. It taught us a lesson that we have forgotten to our own peril. Our children should also be told that abolition of slavery was the sole cause of the civil war. The southern states of America would not have seceded had they been allowed to keep 'slaves' within the union.

The war was like Crucifixion of Christ followed by His Resurrection. The old America had died and a new nation was born. Loss of life was colossal, far heavier than in any other war in American history. A large number of the over a million soldiers and civilians who lost their lives must have died due to the sheer hardships of life during the war. Those were hard days. Life was harsh. There were no trains, trucks, jeeps and mechanized vehicles. Fighting was done on horse back or on foot. The armies had to march through vast tracts of forests, mountains and prairies carrying with them all their supplies of food, medicines, ammunition and horse driven carriages. Large rivers had to be forded or crossed by boat with all the animals and goods. The soldiers carried a lot of baggage and fire arms on their shoulders. Guns were heavy. Cannons had to be pulled by horses or pushed by soldiers on uneven, roadless, tracks. Life in the camps was a constant fight with nature. Often whole battalions had to live in the open in severe winter. Compared with those days the life of today's soldiers, particularly of the Americans and European armies, can be described as being just "trigger happy". Casualties on both sides were heavy. Some 6,00,000 to 8,00,000 soldiers and 3,00,000 to 5,00,000 civilians died. Together they made up three percent of the population of the nation of 35 million people. According to one estimate 10% of all Whites between the ages of 18 and 42 in the North and 30% in the South died in the four-year war. The magnitude of the sacrifice the people of America made to mark the most glorious chapter in their history and earn the freedom of the nearly four million slaves they owned, cannot be gauged unless we measure it against America 's losses in World War II and more recently in the 12 year long wars in Iraq and Afghanistan. In World War II America lost 4,05,000 members of its armed forces who constituted 0.3% of its population while in the wars in Iraq and Afghanistan a total of 6735 US military men died, (4,474 in Iraq and 2,261 in Afghanistan) making 0.002% of the population estimated at 310 million now. (Iraqi and Afghan casualties would be many times more).

Civilian life was made equally difficult by the conflict. Almost every family had its bread earners in the army. About 70% of the population was on the side of the Unionists and 30% in the camp of the secessionists. As always happens in times of war normal life was completely disrupted during the long years of the conflict.

The people of America bore all these hardships cheerfully because they felt that they were fighting a holy war. Towering above them all was the inspiring and ever smiling face of Abraham Lincoln who repeatedly exhorted them that they had been chosen by God to abolish the evil of slavery for ever from the Earth. They were being driven by the Will of God. The best tribute they could pay to the men who had laid down their lives in this holy war was to finish the task they had begun. Time and again Lincoln said that what they had accomplished was an act of God. No human power could have done it. He claimed no credit for it.

The battle of Gettysburg in late 1863 has become a landmark symbol of the American Civil War. It was when the tide turned decisively in favour of the Unionist army and it was also a battle in which Lincoln 's forces suffered very large casualties. Though brief his Gettysburg Address has gone down in history as a great moment in the war. It was a speech to remember the soldiers who had died fighting in the war. In it he said:

"Four score and seven years ago our fathers brought forth on this continent, a new nation, conceived in Liberty, and dedicated to the proposition that all men are created equal."

He also described what would be the best tribute that they could offer to the dead. "It is rather for us to be here dedicated to the great task remaining before us—that from these honored dead we take increased devotion to that cause for which they gave the last full measure of devotion—that we here highly resolve that these dead shall not have died in vain—that this nation, under God, shall have a new birth of freedom—and that government of the people, by the people, for the people, shall not perish from the earth."

I worship Lincoln for what he did and not what he was physically. I worship the spirit that guided him. It was the same spirit that guided Jesus Christ to offer himself for crucifixion. It was the same spirit that guided Arjun to vanquish his enemies in the Mahabharata war, or breathed in Gandhi the power to hold a whole nation in his sway and fight a non-violent struggle for freedom from the British Empire. I worship the spirit that guided Martin Luther King to carry forward the torch of freedom for all peoples of the world ignited by Lincoln. I worship the spirit that inspired such a large number of soldiers to sacrifice their lives so that slavery was abolished from the world. Most of those killed were Whites and formed a sizeable proportion of people of European stock living in the new continent. I am ashamed to say that I can not remember a single example of an upper caste Hindu laying down his life to abolish untouchability from India which still exists in various forms. Lincoln himself said repeatedly that a divine spirit was guiding him and others who died in the anti-slavery war in America which lasted from January 1861 to April 1865.

Lincoln said once that we did not need the Bible to tell us that man is "desperately selfish." He made this statement during times when so many Americans came forward to join his war on slavery. Today, in this worldwide Deluge of materialism in which the sole motto of human life is to "earn and burn", man is not just 'desperately selfish' but selfishness incarnate. In such times my friends ask me "why do you worry about the poor? Poverty and hunger have always been there and always will be. Now at the age of 85 it is time for you to retire and meditate on God." It is difficult for me to explain to them that meditation on poverty itself is meditation on God.

There is an intimate personal reason for my interest in the poor of India. In 1967 a close relative aged 42 died of a heart attack leaving behind his wife and three children. It made a dramatic impact on the bereaved family. The widow shifted to the house of her parents with her children in a mofussil town. The event haunted me. A year later, while on a tour of America sponsored by the US State Department I had a nervous break down caused partly by my irrational fear of flying but mainly due to a bad stomach which made traveling a hazardous proposition. I had to cut short the tour half-way when I was in Harvard where my brother-in-law, Ashok Agrawala, was finishing his Ph.D. Ashok drove me back to Washington. My host in the State Department, an elderly man, asked me if I would like to travel with a companion. I declined his offer and rushed back home as I thought I was going to die soon.

The thought of what would happen to my family after I was gone tormented me. How would my wife support herself and our three children, the youngest of whom was only a few months old and eldest five years away from his high school graduation. My wife is a science graduate and could have earned a pittance in a private school while living with her or my parents. Thoughts of my own family in poverty which lasted a long time forged a deep personal link between me and the poor classes. I prayed hard to God to grant me just five more years of life so that I could see my elder son a matriculate. With the generous cooperation of my employers, The Statesman, the crisis passed and 45 years later I am still alive and active. My children and grand children have done extremely well in life beyond my wildest dreams for them. But this prosperity has not dimmed my affinity to the poor classes. On Diwali nights when we hold formal prayers before images of Lakshmi (goddess of wealth who illuminates the world with her dazzling splendour) I do not forget to pray to her to also visit the homes of the poor and bring them the light of happiness and prosperity.

People like Jesus, Lincoln, Gandhi, Martin Luther King and Mother Teresa are not to be seen as individual human beings. They were spirits in the truest sense. They were incarnations of that power that lives in all of us but is not as visible in all of us as it is in those great souls. I worship that power in them and not their physical individual selves, as I worship its Presence in myself.

By normal standards of his time Lincoln was not a religious man. He did not belong to any church or denomination. But he had strong and indomitable faith in God. He repeatedly maintained that the War against slavery was God's handiwork. No human agency could have accomplished it. I worship that spirit that drove Lincoln and most Americans of his day to achieve this greatest of all human endeavours in human history. It was to thank God for the victory in the war against slavery that Lincoln ordered that the last Thursday of November would be observed as Thanks Giving Day. Even today it is observed as a solemn occasion.

In our holy scripture, The Gita, Lord Kirshna, God incarnate, tells Arjuna, his disciple, in the midst of the Mahabharata war:

> "I come, and go, and come. When Righteousness Declines, O Bharata! when Wickedness Is strong, I rise, from age to age, and take Visible shape, and move as man with men, Scouring the good, thrusting the evil back, And setting Virtue on her seat again.
>
> Who knows the truth touching knows the truth touching my births on earth on earth
>
> And my divine work, when he quits the flesh Puts on its load no more, falls no more down To earthly birth: to Me he comes, dear Prince!"
>
> —Lord Krishna to Arjun in the Bhagwat Gita

I see Lincoln as an avatar or incarnation of Arjuna of the Indian epic Mahabharata. He took birth on Earth to rid it of the evil of slavery under the guidance of Lord Jesus Christ even as Arjuna, guided by God in the incarnation of Lord Krishna, wiped out the evil forces of the tyrant, Duryodhana, and established the rule of Dharma (righteousness) in the world.

But Arjuna is a myth while Lincoln is a reality. Arjuna fought to reclaim a kingdom that belonged to him and his brothers which his cousin Duryodhana had usurped by fraudulent means. Lincoln, on the other hand, had no kingdom to gain. He was a servant of the people and did their bidding. Besides, the most important difference between Linconln and Arjuna was that Krishna was exhorting Arjuna to do his "Caste" duty as a member of the "Kshatriya" (warrior) caste, which was actually based on "Varna" or colour of the skin. Lincoln, on the other hand was working for a casteless (which means colourless) society. Caste has stuck like an albatross round the neck of all Indians and it is as strong in the 21st century as it has been through the ages. If a lower caste boy marries an upper caste girl the couple are lynched in public and no one bats an eye. Caste is part and parcel of our religion.

More than Lincoln I admire the Whites of America of those times. No hardship was too great for them to endure to abolish the completely dehumanizing practice of slavery from their midst, even as caste is in India. To understand Lincoln fully we have to understand the times in which he was living and the kind of life that prevailed in the world.

In India it is still like old times. Though intellectually some few among us have taken great strides, socially, morally and ethically Indians are a stultified people. We emulate the West in life style, industry, entertainment and defence but remain morally backward. Any movement for relative equality or reduction of growing inequality is dubbed "terrorist" and crushed. Our social structure remains fossilized along caste lines: To understand this juxtaposition of modern living and backward thinking we have to go deeper into the social history of our great land.

Experts in the new sciences of neuro-plasticity and epigenetics and social scientists could reap rich rewards if they engaged in a serious comparative study of the minds of present day Indians and Nineteenth

Century dare devil Americans who fought furiously over the issue of slavery. Why can Indians never rise in a non-violent movement against our caste system the way Americans did under. Martin Luther King in 1963 against racial discrimination towards Black people? Centuries of imperialist rule by invaders from West Asia and Europe, some of whom indulged in mass slaughter and plunder have dulled our sensibilities into silence. We have lost the capacity to protest. Silence in the face of oppression is the highest mark of respectability in today's India as it has been during past centuries.

The process through which this kind of mass psychology has evolved can be briefly described here. Life has always been cheap in India. Nearly the entire population of the world lived in villages and hamlets. Anybody could kill any body and get away with it. Village chieftains and elders had the power to kill any one who disobeyed them or the rules made by them. Women were treated as chattel in large parts of the world. A man could have any number of wives who were used as labourers, besides serving the sexual appetites of their husbands. Wife beating by husbands in a drunken state was all too common. Our fore-fathers were not barbarians. They observed all rules and etiquettes of social behaviour. But when aroused their anger knew no bounds. Life was strictly hierarchical. The person next above you in rank in the family or society could administer to you any corporal punishment he liked. Torture to extract a confession was common and still is. So was denying food and water to a person, or making a student or disciple of a guru in an ashram stand in chilled water all night in winter. There were no schools and illiterates ruled the illiterate. Though each community was ruled by its religious laws, these could be freely violated by ad hoc decisions of one's immediate superiors. Most wars were fought on the whims and fancies of monarchs. At times a king got fascinated by the beauty of the queen of another king and started a war to capture her kingdom and kill her husband. The wars of Troy over Helen and Alexendria over Cleopatra were launched solely by their mad lovers who happened to be kings. Our epic, Ramayana, is another example of this phenomenon. Rama invaded Lanka to reclaim his wife Sita from the demon king Ravana who had abducted her in a forest. Thousands were killed on both sides.

Then there were wars of conquest. Every king wanted to enlarge his territory and become the emperor of a large kingdom. Alexandar the Great, Chengiss Khan, Timur Lane, the Czars of Russia, Napolean of France and the British Empire are some examples of wars undertaken merely with the ambition to take over other people's territory. Our Mahabharata war, the story of the second great epic of Indian mythology was fought between first cousins over control of the empire of what was then known as Bharata or India. Rulers of different parts of the empire joined one side or the other in this great war in which countless thousands are believed to have been killed on both sides.

There was no concept of "Human Rights" at all. Justice was administered on the whims of Rajas or local chieftains. The country was ruled by a hereditary hierarchy of Rajas, maharajas and Samrats. Each territory had to have a raja whose chief duty was to garrison a small army in his fort. The soldiers often went out on night sorties to rob nearby villages and bring back a booty most of which was given to the raja (local king) who, in turn, paid a tribute to the Maharaja who commanded a larger army and was supposed to be the real ruler. But above the Maharaja there was usually a "samrat", or emperor to whom every Maharaja paid a tribute and contributed soldiers in fighting major wars. Conducting wars of defence or offence was a full time occupation of kings. For maintaining discipline in the army and constantly training it in the arts of warfare there were generals and hierarchy of officers under them: At times they went on a looting spree of robbery, rape and plunder into the territory of another raja or Maharaja with or without the consent of their superiors. The rajas tolerated such temporary intrusions and replied in kind by sending their men to other parts of the neighbour's territory which were less guarded. The people suffered in silence. The clan in which they lived was their only defence. Colonies of people, small or big, who could come out as one man to repel a gang of robbers were relatively safe from such attacks. Lives were short. Few people lived beyond the age of fifty. Within this period they became great grand fathers due to the universal custom of child marriages.

By and large a similar situation prevails today in the Indian countryside. The place of rajas has been taken over by the local satraps of whatever political party happens to be in power. The scene in urban areas is no better. On the surface everything seems normal. But in reality the lower castes are distributed in professions earmarked for them by society. It is taken for granted that all manual labour, including that which requires semi-technical skills, is normally assigned to the lower castes who have to work for twelve hours on a pittance, with no rights to complain and claim their rightful dues. They live in ghettos, slums and chawls controlled by toughs of the colony where the house owners keep changing tenants for higher rents every year. With their salaries eaten up by housing and transport they support their families with whatever their wives can earn by doing manual jobs in upper caste homes. For the lowest caste women even such jobs are hard to find because they are still treated as "untouchables". In the villages things are worse and they do not get even subsistence wages for the work they do for the upper castes. The rigid rule against inter-caste marriages prevents upward social mobility and ensures that they remain permanently backward. In village or city, the dalits and tribals are kicked about like animals in India.

So pervasive is the caste factor that even Jawaharlal Nehru, the maker of modern India and the greatest democrat India has seen, was proud of his Brahmin ancestry and carried the prefix of Pandit with his name. Even today old timers remember him as Panditji. Rahul Gandhi, his great-grandson, the heir apparent to Prime Ministership if his party wins the Parliamentary elections due in 2014, has thrown up his hands in despair on the issue of dalits and tribal people. He said recently that they would have to acquire the "velocity of (planet) Mars" to take off. But where is the fuel and the machine to acquire that velocity? Rahul's mother, Sonia Gandhi who is an Italian and President of her party has been ruling the country by proxy for nine years through Prime Minister Manmohan Singh.

The maltreatment of the lower castes, dalits and tribals has never been an issue in India. Caste inequality is an accepted part of Indian culture. Commercialisation of education has made quality teaching beyond the reach of the lower castes. In fact even a cursory tour of the countryside in India will show that education for all or health care for all exists only on paper. The gap between the lower and upper castes is rapidly widening and no politician or sociologist looks at this phenomenon as a caste issue.

The European Parliament (EP) has recognised caste-based discrimination as a human rights violation and adopted another resolution in October 2013 condemning it and urging European Union institutions to address it. The EP consists of 28 member-countries of the EU.

Acknowledging that caste-affected communities are still subjected to 'untouchability practices' in India, Nepal, Pakistan, Bangladesh and Sri Lanka, the October 10 resolution stressed the need to combat discrimination based on work and descent, which occurs also in Yemen, Mauritania, Nigeria, Senegal and Somalia.

In December 2012 the EP passed a similar resolution, expressing alarm at the persistence of human rights violations against Dalits in India. The latest resolution recognised the presence of caste-based discrimination globally and pointed out various forms of caste-related violence against Dalits, especially women.

The EP reiterated serious concern over violence against Dalit women and other women from similarly affected communities in societies with caste systems, who often do not report it for fear of threat to their personal safety or of social exclusion. It pointed out the multiple and intersecting forms of discrimination based on caste, gender and religion, affecting Dalit women and women from minority communities, leading to forced conversions, abductions, forced prostitution, and sexual abuse by dominant castes.

Caste discrimination continues to be widespread and persistent, affecting an estimated 260 million people despite the governments of some affected countries taking steps to provide constitutional and legislative protection, the EP said.

It noted that caste-based discrimination occurred in diaspora communities, untouchability practices took on modern forms and the affected communities faced restricted political participation and serious discrimination in the labour market.

"In a few countries, such as India, mandatory affirmative action has to some extent contributed to the inclusion of Dalits in the public sector, but the lack of protective non-discrimination measures in the labour market and the private sector adds to exclusion and growing inequalities," it said.

The International Labour Organisation estimates that an overwhelming majority of bonded labour victims in South Asia are from the Scheduled Castes and the Scheduled Tribes, and that forced and bonded labour is particularly widespread in the agriculture, mining and garment production sectors, which supply products to a number of multinational and European companies.

The deplorable condition of the dalits and tribals makes me wish and pray for a Lincoln being born in India. They are tossed about like fish in a tank, waiting to be baited by fishermen. Their lands and forests are routinely taken away from them in the name of projects that are started to benefit the rich. They wander about the country homeless and half-starved like stateless people. Fortunately, as described in later chapters of this book modern science and technology has placed tools in the hands of the comman man to fight the menace of caste (class) deprivation in India. A 21ˢᵗ century Lincoln will use them in full and will not have to use the Nineteenth Century weapons of an armed conflict. But there is no Lincoln in sight to save them from this life of misery and degradation. This is why I treat Lincoln's brief Gettysburg Address, reproduced below, as my only Bible. To me it is the essence of all the best scriptures of all religions of the world. Above all it teaches us that in life nothing worthwhile is gained without making huge sacrifices.

The Gettysburg Address: "Four score and seven years ago our fathers brought forth on this continent, a new nation, conceived in Liberty, and dedicated to the proposition that all men are created equal.

"Now we are engaged in a great civil war, testing whether that nation, or any nation so conceived and so dedicated, can long endure. We are met on a great battle-field of that war. We have come to dedicate a portion of that field, as a final resting place for those who here gave their lives that that nation might live. It is altogether fitting and proper that we should do this.

"But, in a larger sense, we can not dedicate—we can not consecrate—we can not hallow—this ground. The brave men, living and dead, who struggled here, have consecrated it, far above our poor power to add or detract. The world will little note, nor long remember what we say here, but it can never forget what they did here. It is for us the living, rather, to be dedicated here to the unfinished work which they who fought here have thus far so nobly advanced. It is rather for us to be here dedicated to the great task remaining before us—that from these honored dead we take increased devotion to that cause for which they gave the last full measure of devotion—that we here highly resolve that these dead shall not have died in vain—that this nation, under God, shall have a new birth of freedom—and that government of the people, by the people, for the people, shall not perish from the earth."

3

Dance of Democracy

Treating my own corrupt life as an illustration this book is essentially a comparison between Indian and Western democracies. A democracy is rule of the people, by the people and for the people. I have, therefore, tried to compare the peoples of some Western democracies with the people of India to prove my thesis that if the "Aam Admi" (common man) like me is corrupt, how can you expect the 'government of the people' of India to be honest?

I was pleasantly surprised to find that my 21 year old grandson Anurag, born and brought up in America and now a student of Penn State University, has been for three years taking part in Thon, which New York Times described as the largest student run charity in the world.

President Pranab Mukherjee said recently that it was "unacceptable" that no Indian university has featured among the top 200 universities globally in the recent international rankings and that the only way forward was for the country's universities to study and inculcate the 'best practices' of foreign universities. Inculcating good practices of foreign universities should also include learning to be better citizens. Recently, I was thrilled on reading in the *New York Times* a report on how college students in America volunteer to serve their country and the world. It said: "Thon is the world's largest student-run charity, which is like a dance a-thon, pep rally, rock concert and tent revival all in one. For 41 years, the students at Penn State—a university known more for its troubles than its triumphs in recent years—have raised tens of millions for pediatric cancer research and family care. They have raised so much—more than $101 million—that they have even financed a wing at Penn State Hershey Children's Hospital. (On Feb 23, 2014 THON declared the year's collection as $13.34 million taking the total to $114 million). They are not really dancing the whole time. The rules are that they must stay awake for 46 hours and stay on their feet. It is a test of endurance. Of course it is uncomfortable and sometimes painful, but when they start to buckle and hallucinate, they remind themselves that if children can go through cancer therapy, they can tough it out. The fact is, Thon probably has more to do with Penn State students than football does. They are not looking to make someone an all-star; they are doing charitable work. And it wasn't just one student, it was thousands doing that. Please note the last sentence of the New York Times report "And it wasn't just one student, it was thousands doing that".

Anurag told me that the enthusiasm of the surging crowd gathered on the dance floor and in the galleries was simply infectious. Young men and women, some not so young, of numerous nationalities and colours danced together and mingled with each other for full two days and nights. Whites, Blacks, Brown, Yellow and people of mixed races were all there. Abraham Lincoln, were be alive, would have loved the sight. This was what he had fought for in the American Civil War.

By American standards of citizenship what my grandson was doing was nothing special. Thousands were dancing in the 48-hour Thon Dance Marathon and thousands of others were generously contributing money to it to make it a success. If a small middle class community can stage a feat like that it augurs great things for the future of America. The real meaning of democracy is not just the right to vote once every five years, but the duty to collectively share the burdens of the poor in a society.

It is my personal conviction that this kind of activity is both democracy and true Christianity in action, for, charity and service are the two uppermost means of attaining heaven in Christian beliefs. I am reminded of Bertrand Russel's book Conquest of Happiness which I read in my University days in the Nineteen Forties. It said "the real pleasure of making money lies in giving it to others and making them happy" (not the precise quote).

State College where Penn State University is located is a small town of about 1,60,000 people. It is largely an educational community which is never credited with much money. If a small town of middle class people in America can contribute to a single charity 12.4 million dollars in a year one must commend the large heartness of the American people. I came to know of it accidentally when I inquired about Anurag from his parents. When I sent to him an email commending his participation in such a noble cause, he merely wrote back, "it was pure fun. I enjoyed every minute of it."

In high school Anurag volunteered as an Emergency medical technician with a local ambulance service. He also did volunteer work in a local hospital in State College. As a student of Penn State University he went to a small island in Panama in March 2011 and another island in March 2012 to teach owners of small businesses how to keep their accounts and also how to manage personal finances.

Anurag's elder brother Anshul went to a remote village in Kenya a few years ago to give health education to its people. While in Kenya he fell and injured his back. But despite this he carried on for the fortnight duration of his project with about a dozen other boys and girls from Cornell University where he was studying. While in high School he volunteered and acted as an emergency medical technician with a local ambulance service in State College.

Anurag and Anshul went on these charitable expeditions as members of 'brigades' of about a dozen boys and girls that are organized by almost all universities of America. Anurag was leader of one of the brigades which went to islands in Panama. Besides the Global Brigades several other organizations arrange development projects in poor countries for university students. These projects which may last from ten days to a month are often out of reach by phone except during emergencies. Their declared motto is "No news is good news." The most striking feature of these brigades is that they are self-financed. The universities bear a fraction of the cost. The volunteers have to collect funds for their mission from the public which is very cooperative. Their parents also contribute generously. So do student clubs.

A number of Anshul's friends came to India on such projects. One of them Angela Hsu, an American girl of Taiwanese origin, who played with him when they were children and happened to be in the same batch with him at Cornel, stayed with us in Delhi for a few days and became so friendly with us that she came again only to meet us on her way to Taiwan where she was going to meet her grand parents. She had taken a break from her studies after graduation from Cornel and, among other things, she worked on an Israeli farm for two months.

Anshul is also associated with a large organization spread across 200 university campuses in America which wants Americans and American companies to stop buying products of industries in poor countries which deny proper wages to their workers and treat them as bonded slaves called "Students against sweatshops" (SASS) it is the most inspiring example of "campus activism" in America, as Liza Featherstone, author of an illuminating book on SASS, describes it. While exhorting Indian students to outclass Americans in studies, our President, Pranab Mukherji, should also make it compulsory for them to vigorously engage in student activism to reform our fossilized society.

My nephew's son Kashev, whose mother is an American, is another example that comes to mind. He achieved the distinction of becoming an "Eagle Scout" which won him accolades from the high and mighly in America. The Congressman (MP) from his district was gracious enough to have the US flag flown from the Capitol Building in Washington in his honor, and sent that flag to him. Several important people in America wrote letters of congratulations to him.

A Boy Scout who is working to be an "Eagle Scouts" has to do a community service project. He has to come up with a proposal, working with the Scout Master, and present it to the Troop Committee for approval. He has to plan out his project, work out the costs, and present the whole plan for approval. He is out of scouting by his 18th b'day. So, this service project is an attempt by the Scouting organization to train teenagers to work with adults to plan things out, and then stand in front of a committee of supportive adults and defend their proposals. They also have to present a plan to do fund-raising to cover the costs of their project. Kashev talked to the folks at the county convalescent center, and got agreement to build a vertical garden for its wheelchair bound residents with funds raised from the public.

Four of my six grand children live in America. My 21-year old grand daughter Aparna, now a student of fourth year of graduation at Brown University in America, has been working to bring out the Brown Daily Herald, an "independent" campus news paper run by the students. It raises its own funds from advertisers and is free to criticize the university administration. Starting as a feature writer in her first year, Aparna is now one of its senior editors and a member of its board of directors. Though she does not intend to take up journalism as a career she is doing this job as voluntary act of service to the community, which means staying awake in the paper's office till four O'clock in the morning, two nights a week, besides pursuing her studies.

I was enthused by the discovery of this trait in the new generation in America since it reminded me of my own days at school and college before Independence in 1947 when some of us did small acts of service for the poor. In those days teachers and parents encouraged such habits. In today's times of one-upmanship and each one for himself or herself, teaching this quality of sharing our bread with others who are more hungry than us seems to have disappeared from the Indian education system.

The boys and girls I have mentioned here are not shirkers or laggards who are running away from their studies. Academically, they are among the cream of American youth. Anshul completed his four-year graduation course in three years at Cornell and is now in his third year of research for a Ph.D. in Sociology at Harvard University. Anurag has been admitted to the coveted combined Honours course in graduation and Commerce. After graduating from Cornel Angela Hsu was admitted to the prestigious London School of Economics for her post graduate degree. Kashev is a student of Electrical Engineering at the University of Illinois. Aparna is one of the brightest students in her class and won awards including a letter from the President of the University for excellence in English. They are doing "volunteering" as an act of duty which every citizen of a civilized democracy must do as part of his education. They wear the cloak of scholars lightly like a loosely worn shirt and never make too much fuss about it.

Fund raising holds the key to this unique phenomenon of volunteering in Western democracies. Besides paying their taxes in full to the government, citizens consider it their duty to donate liberally to good causes. This applies not merely to projects for helping the poor but also to small ventures by individuals in the fields of knowledge and research. Wikipedia, the people's online encyclopedia, is an amazing example of making knowledge freely available to all, largely with donations from the public. Members of the public also participate free of charge in the creation of Wikipedia. It may be one of the largest volunteer ventures in the world.

Wikipedia is a collaboratively edited, multilingual, free Internet encyclopedia supported by the non-profit Wikimedia Foundation. Wikipedia's 26 million articles in 286 languages, including over 4.2 million in the English Wikipedia, are written collaboratively by volunteers around the world. Almost all of its articles can be edited by anyone with access to the site. It has become the largest and most popular general reference work on the Internet, ranking sixth globally among all websites on Alexa and having an estimated 365 million readers worldwide. Wikipedia was launched on January 15, 2001, by Jimmy Wales and Larry Sanger.

Just think of the millions of people around the world who are being helped by Wikipedia. In my view Wikepdedia is volunteerism at its best. It is a boon for the poor and so handy for any researcher or writer looking for instant information on any subject.

I came to know of the true nature of Wikepedia as a non-profit trust through my nineteen year old grand daughter, Payal who lived in Delhi till June 2013 and is now a University student in Singapore. I was taken aback when she told me that she would donate to Wikepedia a substantial part of her income from a unique internet based bsiness that she and one of her classmates had conceived, designed and launched in their spare time while preparing to enter college. It was through her and her younger brother Anmol that I became aware that enterprising Indian youth are doing extra-ordinary things with the internet and it is but proper that we should also contribute our share to such marvelous non-profit ventures that have sprung up throughout the world and transformed our lives.

Seti@home is another example of volunteering. With three million users it is the largest network of volunteers who are giving their time to download extra terrestrial messages in the search for other intelligences in the universe.

Fund raising is difficult in India because, speaking from my own experience, whenever a person seeking funds comes to us we think of him or her as a thief come to steal our money. Public trust in the so called NGOs (non-governmental organizations) has disappeared. Though called "non-governmental" they derive most of their funds from the government or some foreign agency. There have been cases of agents and officials of International aid organizations embezzling huge amounts with the connivance of Indian NGOs. In the West at the citizens' level every thing runs on trust.

Honesty like speaking the truth is a habit of the mass mind. It can not be individualized. If Indians as a 'people' are habitually dishonest, willy-milly they will have a government that suits them, notwithstanding the cries for justice of a small minority of activists. In my view India is truly a democracy because it has a government that faithfully represents the character of the "people" of India. I believe that the story of my own life of 85 years is a typical example of the way an average middle class Indian lives.

The most outstanding act of volunteerism known to me was performed around the year 1940 by Col. Thomas Francis O'Donnell, M.C., an Irishman in Meerut, some seventy kilometers from Delhi in U.P. He was the Principal of the famous Meerut College from 1924 to 1942. Movies were then the only entertainment available to young people. One evening a local cinema hall was screening the premiere of a long awaited movie and a large number of students of Meerut College flocked to see it. Suddenly, while they were in the movie hall communal riots between Hindus and Muslim, then an annual ritual in urban India throughout the country, broke out. A mob of several hundred people belonging to one community gathered around the cinema hall. The owner ordered all exit doors to be closed so that the rioters could not enter the hall. They threatened to burn down the theatre hall unless the viewers came out to face them. Except for clamping curfew on the affected city police usually kept away from rioting mobs. In those days it had only lathis (sticks) as weapons and no fire arms or tear gas. The British ruled the country with a small police presence in the cities and virtually no policemen in the countryside. In the event of a riot people of each community had to organize their own defence.

The news somehow reached the Principal who was perhaps preparing for his dinner. It took him an instant to take his revolver, pick up his car from the garage in the Principal's bungalow, and rush to the cinema hall alone. On reaching the theatre he parked his car in front of the slogan shouting mob, came out revolver in hand, and faced the mob single-handed. This was an eventuality the rioters had not expected. Pointing his revolver at them the Colonel ordered them not to move. Then he asked the owner to open the gates and let the viewers come out. They came out hesitantly in a single file and ran briskly away, there being no transport in the curfew bound city to take them home. Some took up their bicycles from the cycle stand. Within a matter of minutes everything was quiet. The mob turned in another direction into the lanes of the city. The Principal drove back to his bungalow.

I count this as the rarest act of courage shown by an educationist to save the lives of his pupils at the cost of his own life. He didn't think of the consequences of his action before proceeding to the scene. He merely did his duty ("Duty, thou stern daughter of the thought of God"—Wordsworth). He was fully aware of the risk he was taking. The frenzied mob could have attacked him too and killed him. The police could never have found the culprits. Col O'Donnell was a great educationist and after retirement from Meerut College worked for sixteen years as Principal of Colonel Brown Cambridge School in Dehradun.

Contrast this act of sheer heroism by a foreigner to save his native pupils with the murder some years ago of a professor in a north Indian state by the hoodlums of the youth wing of a leading political party in the presence of hundreds of people. His son has been running from pillar to post seeking justice but all that the authorities have done is to erase the evidence of the gruesome crime which is a blot upon the entire educational system in India. The Vice-chancellor of the concerned university should have been the first to stake his job, and if necessary, his life, to seek justice and get the perpetrators of this horrible murder punished. Official and public indifference to such acts is the biggest inducement to corruption in India.

Yet another form of volunteering is spreading fast. Young people all over the world, like my grandchildren Payal and Anmol are burning midnight oil to explore new areas of knowledge and in turn creating new ideas, designs and gadgets that could slowly change the way we think and act. What Issac Newton said four centuries ago still holds good. We are merely "children playing pebbles on the sea shore of knowledge." The more we search the more we realize our limitations. Internet has turned up networks of a variety of disciplines from cooking, to spirituality to politics to space science and so on. In terms of the "ultimate" forms of civilized living we are still passing through the "dark ages" of history, dominated by wars and demonic greed and lust that could destroy whatever gains we have made so far. Payal showed me "Coursera", a collaborative efforts of seventy universities, mostly located in America and Europe, teaching 374 courses online, free of charge, to nearly four million students. She also showed me Venture Lab run by Stanford University which gives free online courses in creativity in different fields.

A separate chapter is devoted in this book to celebrate the legacy of Aaron Swartz, the 26 year old genius who sacrificed his life in the cause of making knowledge freely available to all mankind. Julian Asange of Wikileaks fame is another example of volunteerism. So is Edward Snowden, the man who risked his life to divulge America's biggest and best kept secret, that it was engaged in piling up and processing billions of telephone calls, emails and mobile messages of millions of people around the world. He has proved that information is power and it should be freely available to every citizen of the world. He has also shown that ultimately the governments of the world will not be able to keep anything secret.

This chapter will not be complete if I do not relate here my own little contribution to volunteerism along with that of my partner in the project, the late Dr. M.N. Deshpande, a neighbour and retired Director General of the Archeological survey of India. One day about ten years ago while visiting him I found among the books lying about his shelves a tattered book titled spiritualism in Gandhi and other

Hindi Saints. Around the same time Mr. S. Sivadas, his family friend who lives in our small colony and was then Deputy News Editor of The Hindu, which, before the 50th death anniversary of the Mahatma, had brought us a collection of reports of the daily prayer meetings of Gandhi during the last 200 days of his life which he had painstakingly cut out from 200 papers from old files of The Hindu kept in his room. We had been reading most of them but wanted to preserve them with us. Later the Hindu published them in book form. I borrowed and brought Ranade's book to my house. It was a collection of three lectures delivered in 1947 by Dr. R.D. Ranade, a saint-philosopher in his own right, and former vice-chancellor of Allhabad University, at Ahmedabad under the auspices of Gujarat Vidya Sabha. Being an avid reader of Gandhian literature since childhood when my family used to regulary buy Mahatma's weekly, The Harijan, I at once saw in these lectures a priceless treasure which I thought should be preserved for posterity.

The late Dr. Ranade happened to be Dr. Deshpande's guru. Every year the "humble devotee" that Deshpande was used to visit the small ashram his guru had set up in Nimbal in southern Maharashtra to offer prayers at the saint's Samadhi. I do not believe in gurus at all but this was a different case. Ranade was not a guru in the commonly accepted sense of the word. Like J.Krishnamurty he was a teacher first which shows transparently in his lectures. Nor was Deshpande an ordinary disciple. We got busy to publish those lectures in the form of a proper book. It took us over four years of united struggle to do so. It took us two stressful years of sustained effort of sending repeated letters and asking our most important contacts in Ahmedabad to visit its offices to get the permission of Gujarat Vidya Bhawan and Dr. Ranade's descedants to publish the book.

Simultaneously through my part-time computer operator I sent over a thousand letters to all the owners of Gandhian websites in the world to ask them whether they would buy the book if we published it. We got only twelve replies, two of them from Mahatma Gandhi's grand children, Arun Gandhi who was a professor of Gandhian studies in the USA and the other from Ela Gandhi who lives in South Africa. Arun Gandhi helped us a lot, tried to find a publisher in America and gave the book its new title "Spiritual Awakening in Gandhi and other

Indian Saints." He accepted our request to write a foreword for the book and his son Tushar Gandhi, who heads a Gandhian organization in Bombay, did a marvelous cover design. On hearing Arun Gandhi's name the Sarva Sewa Sangh of Varanasi which publishes only Gandhian literature agreed to publish the book provided we paid the cost of printing. We both agreed and shared the cost equally. Everyday for more than a month Dr. Deshpande would come to my house to edit the book and give a blurb on every page of it. He introduced me to several good books by different saints. His wife, Madhu, was his constant companion and equally enlightened. She lent me a book written by her father, a doctor who used to cycle down to different villages to treat poor people free of charge. The line of the book which I remember says that we must always keep in touch with "the Source". She died in 2007. Dr. Deshpande followed her within about a year at the age of 88.

I found that social service was a tradition in the family. Their grand daughter Meeta, after her post-graduation in the Tata Institute of Social Sciences in Bombay spent three years in a remote village in far off Karnataka treating the sick with herbal medicines, which was later to become a subject of her research at Jawahar Lal Nehru University (JNU) in Delhi. Her two cousins, daughters of an air Vice-Marshal, spent long periods in far flung villages of Rajasthan.

I must also not forget the quiet work that Professor Vipin Tripathi of IIT, Delhi, is doing amongst intellectuals of India and America to highlight the plight of the poorer sections of Muslims in India through his Sadbhav Mission.Commenting upon the media highlighting issues like placing restrictions on people like M.F. Hussain, Salman Rushdie and Kamal Hasan Nobel Laureate Amartya Sen had said in an interview he gave in Kolkata to Sharmila Tagore that the real issue was the step motherly treatment that poor Muslims received. Dr Tripathi's mission handles such matters by holding workshops and teaching programmer in India and America.I have realized that such work by secular forces amongst NRIs is more important than amongst people here. In the matter of religion NRIs try to be more loyal than the King and contribute generously to saffron groups in India.

If I was a woman writer I would have perhaps started this chapter with the contribution of Western democracies to the emancipation of women who constitute half of mankind. Western capitalist companies compete with each other not only in making more money but also in improving the quality of life of their employees. And the welfare rules they frame are applicable to all their workers and not just to officers and managers. The feminist movement of the last century has brought about what is decidedly the greatest revolution in human history. The corporate sector in Western democracies is constantly experimenting with new modalities of work to suit the demands of the family life of their workers. They are conscious that with women constituting more than half of the work force their duty to bring up their children should not be neglected. They are acutely aware that today's children are tomorrow's citizens and workers.

Additionally, the Christian law enforced rigorously in the West against polygamy has released women from the fate of being life-long slaves of men or being thrown out of the house by them.

The Economist of London wrote on Dec 30, 2009: If the empowerment of women was one of the great changes of the past 50 years, dealing with its social consequences will be one of the great challenges of the next 50. Women now make up half of American workers. They run some of the world's best companies, such as PepsiCo, Archer Daniels Midland and W.L. Gore. They earn almost 60% of university degrees in America and Europe. Today women make up the majority of professional workers in many countries (51% in the United States, for example).

Home-working is increasingly fashionable. More than 90% of companies in Germany and Sweden allow flexible working. A growing number of firms are learning to divide the working week in new ways—judging staff on annual rather than weekly hours, allowing them to work nine days a fortnight, letting them come in early or late and allowing husbands and wives to share jobs. Almost half of Sun Microsystems's employees work at home or from nearby satellite offices. Raytheon, a maker of missile systems, allows workers every other Friday off to take care of family business, if they make up the hours on other days.

The capitalists in Western democracies do not mind setting apart a portion of their resources to making such investments in the nation's future. This kind of attitude is unthinkable in a country populated by selfish people like me who always preach socialism out of habit and think only of filling our pockets by extorting from the poor worker the maximum labour against negligible payment and making the prices of his every day needs beyond his reach. We forget that he too has a family that breeds India's future citizens.

According to UN Statistics the place of women in Indian democracy in terms of "gender equality" is among the lowest in the world. They are always at the receiving end in the family and work place and on the streets. As a traditionalist octogenarian I also feel that a woman's place is in the home. Working from the house my wife earns a lot of money from the share market and I earn nothing at all but my writ runs in the house. It has always been so in the fifty-seven years of our married life and her submissive nature ensures harmony and peace in the house. Husbands of my generation seldom danced to the tune of their wives, howsoever fond they might be of them. Ours were days when a man's place in his own house was secure. He alone mattered. The other members of the family were his slaves. In many middle class houses only the male members of the family were supposed to drink milk. The practice of preference to males in the family in serving nutritious food still prevails in most parts of India.

Every improvement in the social order has a negative offshoot. Women's emancipation has had a deleterious effect on the age old institution of marriage which has so for been the sheet anchor of any civilized society. According to Eric Klinenberg, author of "Going Solo: The extraordinary Rise and Surprising Appeal of Living Alone", millions of young people are joining the ranks of 'singletons' who prefer to live alone. Klinenberg, who is a professor of sociology at New York University, says that networking with other people through social media like Facebook and other such forums fills the gap created by loneliness in the lives of these people. The social consequences of this trend on future generations of homo sapiens are wholly unpredictable. All around me I see family ties breaking up amongst young and middle aged couples. Children of school age, by and large, have to fend for themselves. The emotional ties that bind them to mother, father, brothers and sisters are being loosened or removed altogether. We have to wait and see and watch this developing phenomenon before reaching any conclusion.

Environmentalists who have been crying hoarse against the creeping phenomenon of climate change are an unending stream of volunteers who have been trying for more than half-a-century to change our ways of life. The Club of Rome that produced the concept of Limits to Growth and a Blueprint for Survival, E.F. Schumacher's book 'small is beautiful, the much maligned "hippy" phenomenon of The Sixties and Seventies and a host of other movements are efforts to wean man away from the suicidal path of destroying life on the planet by over exploiting its resources as the dinosaurs of the Paleolithic era appear to have done.

During the Renaissance period Russeau, the philosopher said, "man was born free but everywhere he is in chains." He should also have given the cause of this enslavement of man. The truth is that man was born poor and he wants to be rich. Our historians paint a false picture of ancient and medieval India as a land of milk and honey. The truth is that the whole of humanity has lived through extreme poverty throughout history.

In the last three centuries Europe managed to improve its standards and colonise parts of the world through a knowledge revolution of its own in which the discovery of new sources of energy was the principal instrument of change.

Our great epic, the Ramayana is testimony to the fact that in ancient times most people lived in forests on the produce of the jungle. Even today in large parts of the country people live in hamlets away from any village. In Africa there is a big government sponsored movement towards "villagisation" of such people so that basic facilities could be made available to them. A case of "darkness at noon" is Saudi Arabia. It is supposed to be among the richest countries in the world. Yet in it millions live in dire poverty.

Any rational analysis of the situation would lead you to the conclusion that you cannot make all the seven billion people on earth rich. The number may even rise to nine billion. Given the present economic and political systems which allow every one to grab as much as he can, it is almost impossible to give the majority of people even clean food and water, leave alone other basic needs like education, health, public transport and above all a two-room dwelling. At the same time it is impossible to introduce any form of "socialism" among a people whose sole objective in life is to pander to their own and their families' whims and fancies. "Me and mine" is their motto in life. The only rational solution of this impasse is to place an upper limit on individual acquisition and consumption.

All around me I can perceive a sea of humanity whose only ambition in life is to make money for its own sake, not because they need it. If a group of economists would care to make a list of 'scams' that have surfaced in independent India in the last sixty years or so, it would show that most of the people involved in those scandals are abominably rich. They have no dearth of money. They can buy villas abroad, travel in private planes and spend a hundred crores on a wedding, openly. And yet they want more. The question is can we allow such things to happen and yet call the world a "global village"? Can you ever have peace in a village where some people are enjoying all the luxuries you can imagine, while the majority is starving, without food and water and living on the verge of suicide? Ninety percent of the population of the world, or over six billion people have to be kept tied in chains so that they don't rise in revolt against the ten percent rich.

Again, what is the use of being rich in a poor world if your wealth only brings you immense misery in the shape of a life of eternal conflict? In India the obsession for wealth is aggravated by an equally obsessive attachment to one's progeny. Every Indian wants to secure the future of ten generations of his children, grandchildren, great grand children and so on, that will follow him. Everyone wants to establish a dynasty. No sacrifice is too great to make our sons and daughters happy and prosperous. Look at the way we squander money in the marriage of each child. Powerful politicians throw caution to the winds and spend hundreds of crores of public money on the wedding of a son or daughter. The family consisting of the spouse and children is an Indian's whole world. Be he a saint or sinner, all rules of law and social obligations are put aside for the sake of the family. The Indian is so completely family centred that he is loathe to part with a penny of his income or a tithe of his labour for society. This kind of over indulgence in a single aspect of life can only be called a disease of the mind which makes it impossible for an Indian citizen to think rationally about the rights of other people and share his good fortune with other less fortunate citizens. These qualities are essential to the functioning of a vibrant democracy which the people of West seem to have in abundance.

Sooner or later man is going to realize this central point about material wealth and turn to other avenues of seeking real peace and happiness. Perhaps the knowledge revolution will accomplish that miracle and turn men's mind to things other than this mad pursuit of money. There is hope in the new science of neuroplasticity which determines the mind-brain connection and shows how the mind can change the circuitry of the hundred billion neurous in the brain. Let us take the example of man's fascination for money. We do it out of habit and also due to the "We" factor in the mind, which means that everyone else around us is doing it too. Suppose the mind of the "We" gets fed up one day with this money making routine. Will it not then search for other sources of happiness?

Once we recognize that the obsession for money is a disease of the mind of the "We", or of the individual mind influenced by the "We" factor (which then becomes the cause of the disease) it should be obvious that its cure also lies in the mind. According to the science of homeopathy (which has kept me alive and active all these years) all diseases flow from the 'centre'. The centre of this disease is the mind of man. Once scientists discover that all this havoc plaguing human history through all these wars and conflicts and mass slaughters and genocides, driving whole races of man to extinction, is caused by a turbulence in the mind of homo sapiens, a remedy for this disease will perhaps be found. Science has yet to go deeper into the hidden recesses of the mind where its presiding deity the spirit, or the soul of man, resides. It is emblazoned with many other energies which ensure lasting peace and happiness. A separate chapter is devoted in this book to how man can overcome poverty and its consequences by exploring his internal hidden sources of different kinds of energy within himself.

The current knowledge revolution will never be complete until it links man to the original "source" of life itself.

In my childhood days our teachers were fond of repeating the couplet "West is West and East is East; The twain shall never meet". Those were days when it took six weeks by ship to travel to America and three weeks to reach London, our Mecca. Telephonic contacts were a rarity. The new wave of globalization trigerred by the advent of air travel and information technology has changed everything. Today people describe the world as a 'global village' or 'global university'. It would be more appropriate perhaps to call it a 'global market place'. I am saying so because now the real worth of a human being is determined not in terms of what he does in his own little locality but his value in U.S. dollars. Whether he is a businessman, professional or intellectual what determines his status in his chosen line is his rank in the international market. Today dollar is the king.

The West remains where it was in the last two centuries, dominating the rest of the world. It is the East (now called the South) which has to catch up with the West (now called the North). This has led to a social upheaval in the entire developing world. It is no longer enough to be Lord in your own manor. To be some body you must be recognized abroad. Whether it is a branded product of everyday use, a medicine, garment or, cosmetic, or a work of art, a movie or a book, to be a success at home it must first have the stamp of approval from a Western authority on the subject. A book which sells only a few thousand copies in the local market is not worth reading any more. Nor is a movie not nominated for the Oscar worth seeing. Once a product has gained such approval, dollars automatically rain upon it.

The real objective thus becomes dollars, not the true quality of a product. Your true worth socially lies in money and in no other quality of head and heart. How you got the money does not matter. In India the fastest vehicle to get 'there' is speculation in property and shares. And that is what every body who is anybody in India today is doing, ruthlessly and shamelessly. Whatever his profession, he is a fool if he is not operating on the sides in property and shares. Because that is where real money is. And money is what you want. Money makes the mare go. You will find most of our scientists' intellectuals, teachers, bureaucrats and other professionals doing just that. Media magnets who run chains of newspapers and TV channels make most of their money on the properties they own and acquire. This is globalization in Indian terminology. It was never so before. Land, urban or rural, had practically no value and nobody knew anything about the share market. Today land values have gone up a million times in about half-a-century and worth of shares of some companies has shot up a thousand times.

Combined with globalization, this phenomenon has led people to evaluate their value in the international market in terms of the money they can splurge abroad. It is not easy to get rich quick by going on the straight path. When you are climbing up a hill the safe and metalled path is along a gradual and winding slope around the mountain. But in our haste to reach the top we skip the metalled road and take short cuts to the peak of the hill. This is what is happening all over the country today. Everybody is eager to get there anyhow. If it means squeezing the poor, turning them into criminals, appeasing the police, keeping corrupt authority always on your right side and engaging in and encouraging lawlessness, so be it.

Mr. Arvind Kejriwal, Chairman of the "Aam Admi Party", whom Time magazine has named among the 100 most influential people in the World, thinks that the character of the whole country will be transformed by the mere appointment of a Lok Ayukt, a statutory authority with powers to punish even the Prime Minister for act of corruption.

Mr. Kejriwal, you must be dreaming. You must have heard the aphorism 'Yatha raja Tatha praja' (As is the King so are his subjects). This rule applied to monarchies. In a democracy the reverse principle is true: 'People get the government they deserve'. What is the use of having an honest Prime Minister if he is surrounded by hordes of criminals, thieves and rogues as his supporters. You cannot point a finger at the personal conduct of Charan Singh, Morarji Desai, Atal Behari Vajapayee and even the present incumbent Prime Minister Manomohan Singh who is himself credited with saying "it is said that my government is the most corrupt of all". Mr. Kejriwal is barking up the wrong tree. If he really means what he says, that is, to eradicate corruption from the country the leader of the "Aam Admi party' should tackle the 'aam admi' first.

Indians are not lagging behind in individual acts of voluntary action. Chief among those path breakers that comes to mind is Bindeshwari Pathak, the owner, director and founder of Sulabh International. Acting alone he has brought about a revolution in the lives of the lowliest class and caste in India—the scavengers. Starting from scratch in 1973 as a man who worked as tea boy at his uncle's tea stall to finance his education and later drudged for years in the pursuit of his passion to propagate a toilet system he had designed to liberate scavengers from manually lifting human excreta, he is today running a social service organization with a lurn over of hundreds of crores, all built by his own effort. He has built lakhs of toilets and relieved the drudgery of millions of scavengers. I regard him as the incarnation of Dr. B.R. Ambedkar, because he has actualized what Ambedkar only dreamed of. He has also achieved Gandhi's ideal of serving the poorest of the poor. The Mahatma always said that Daridranarayan was his God. Pathak is serving him and him alone. So impressed was the Supreme Court by his efforts that it asked him officially to do something to relive the distress of widows of Vrindavan. Besides money, he gave them dignity, which has been his formula in uplifting the seavangers. He has taken teams of scavenger women to UN forums at his own expense. On his own initiative he later started a centre for the widows of Varansi.

There is no dearth of examples of this kind of volunteerism in India. I have given several such instances of ordinary people devoting their entire lives and money to social causes. But alas! All these efforts of individuals have no impact on the direction of the doom India is heading towards.

While advising Indian universities to inculcate the systems of the best universities in the world Mr. Pranab Mukherji should also advise them to inculcate this habit of voluntary labour for social causes to make Indian students better citizens.

India is the largest democracy in the world but it is a democracy of 'slaves—slaves to the dollar. It is not the same thing as the democracy of the 'masters' who own the dollar. Democracy in the West guarantees the Fundamental Rights to life, freedom of speech, freedom to practice and preach the religion of your choice, the Right to Work and so many other rights that are totally absent in practice in Indian democracy. The whole concept of Fundamental Rights is fundamentally alien to our culture of "slavery" to the "master" who is the sole repository of all our rights.

New technology will also bring about automated management practices and reduce cut throat competition as well as the scope for creation of monopolies and cartels. Though not like India where the highest incomes can be tens of thousands times more than the lowest, there is a wide gap in the incomes of the two groups in the West too. In America barring the 10% penniless people at the bottom, the ratio between the lowest and highest levels is 1:35. But what is most astonishing is the wealth gap in America. At present one percent of the country's population owns thirty-five per cent of the wealth of the world's richest nation. Another four percent own twenty-seven percent more making a total of 62% of wealth being owned by a mere five percent of the population. Fifty percent Americans own no wealth at all. Their total share of America's wealth is less than half percent. According to one study 40% Americans own only 0.2% of the country's wealth though there are no such sharp disparities between the monthly incomes of the poorest and richest groups. Sooner or later, people will realize the futility of owing so much wealth in the new environment of openness. Already people like Warren Buffet and Bill Gates are shedding large slices of their wealth to charity. Bertrand Russel has said in his book conquest of Happiness which I read fifty years ago that the real pleasure of earning wealth lay in giving it to others and bringing joy in their lives.

The 50% Americans who own no wealth at all are not really miserable on that account. If they were they would have long ago abandoned their system of government. They believe in the philosophy of "earn and burn". This is how their money keeps circulating and their economy keeps moving. They do not believe in hoarding money like the Indian Middle Class. Strict enforcement of a minimum wages act, in place in all civilized countries, ensures that every one has enough purchasing power to meet his family's basic needs. Besides, unlike us, even the common people there don't mind contributing their mite to good causes.

One great difference between the West and India is that all the wealth of the rich is out in the open and it is in circulation all the time. It is used to meet the common needs of all citizens of the country. It is not hoarded in secret vaults in safe havens or invested in property as black money which happens in India without a word of protest by leaders of all political parties including communists.

4

Our Changing World

A Knowledge Revolution Is Sweeping across the Globe

Norman Borlaug is a name that does not ring a bell in the minds of most people in India today. My countrymen will be shocked by my 'blasphemy' if I say that the real "liberator" of India was not Gandhi but Borlaug, the American Nobel Laureate, and his dedicated team of researchers. But for the high yielding varieties of wheat and rice discovered by them millions of us would have died a slow death. Borlaug is reputed to be the father of the Green Revolution which made it possible for most Indians to survive. He is officially credited with "saving a billion lives".

Attacking environmental lobbyists who expressed preference for 'organic food' instead of the high yielding hybrid varieties which needed chemical fertilizers and more water he said: "if they (the lobbyists) lived just one month amid the misery of the developing world as I have for fifty years they'd be crying out for tractors and fertilizer and irrigation canals and be outraged that fashionable elitists back home were trying to deny them these things"

Speaking for myself as a journalist who has extensively reported on agricultural developments in India, I feel that unless we develop safer alternatives to chemical farming we have no choice but to follow the path shown by Borlaug. M.S. Swaminathan the most respected agricultural scientist in India and former Deputy Chairman of the Planning Commission, told me in an interview about 30 years ago that theoretically speaking India had the potential to produce 4500 million tons of food and fodder. Our scientists have to come up with even better solutions than Borlaug's to save future generations from starving.

Borlaug also advocated taking more grain from existing farmlands so that deforestation could be avoided.

Just try to visualize what life would be like if the green revolution had not happened. At the time of Independence in 1947 India was producing roughly about 50 million tons of foodgrains for a population of nearly 380 million people. By 1960 foodgrain output was wavering between seventy and eighty million tons for about 540 million people and India's optimum grain capacity was 125 million tons. Today, thanks to the green revolution, India is producing 280 million tons of foodgrains for a population of 1.2 billion people. If half the population is still going hungry while food stocks are exported or rot in open godowns, it is the fault of our greedy middle class and the government which diverts the nation's resources to making life more and more comfortable and luxurious for the elite while ignoring the basic needs of the people. Even the Supreme Court's appeal that food stocks going waste in government godowns be distributed among the poor and hungry has fallen on deaf ears.

Food first was Gandhi's slogan. In a lengthy controversy with poet Tagore who preferred variety to Gandhi's mad devotion to the Charkha, (spinning wheel) The Mahatma said a bird whose music Tagore enjoyed could not soar into the sky and sing for the poet's delight without food. Gandhi wanted every one to have a job in a cottage industry so that he could survive and feed himself with dignity. Describing the nation's condition Gandhi said in his magazine Young India of June 29,1921 that India was "naked and starving. He quoted a piece from the Bible:

"I was naked and you clothed me not

I was hungry and you gave me not to eat."

I toured numerous states of India on behalf of The Statesman to cover the food crisis of 1962-1966, before the advent of the green revolution. Wherever I went I could see half-starved people. American wheat supplied to India under the famous PL 480 programme through ration shops was the mainstay of the urban population while the villages fended for themselves. Rice was not available in the market except at a very high price. People in the South were boiling PL480 wheat, as they boil rice, because they had no means to grind wheat into flour, Half the food needs of Kerala were met by the banana-like Tapioca fruit, staple diet of a large section of Malayalees.

Amongst the most memorable scenes I witnessed happened during a night visit to a village in Yeotmal District of Maharashtra in December 1965. It was a hamlet of a few stone huts atop a shallow gorge about 100 feet deep. I was being taken in a jeep from Nagpur to Adilabad in Andhra for a drive through the worst famine stricken parts of Maharashtra by a rustic looking district planning officer who appeared to be every inch a farmer himself, when my attention was drawn by the sound of music in the wilderness and I asked my guide to stop for a look at the scene.

With light from the headlights of the jeep we could see men, women and children trudging up and down a narrow hill track in the gorge. They were carrying water in their small pots and pans to water their cooperative vegetable farm near their houses from the narrow strip of water they called a stream. It was their only lifeline against hunger and thirst. They sang a folk tune as they walked. Perhaps it helped them to stick together in the dark. We were led to a small and empty panchayat *ghar* by a lantern and treated to tea by the villagers.

We were not far from our destination, the village of Chief Minister V.P. Naik, who had told me only a few hours earlier in Nagpur "Hang me if I fail. I shall make Maharashtra self-sufficient in foodgrains within two years." With such hardy and determined people at his back which chief minister could fail? The line quoted above was a banner headline over my story published a week later on an inside page in the Calcutta and Delhi editions of the *Statesman*.

My guide was a typical IAS officer of the Nehru era when districts were manned by officials who were low paid but high in morale. They were still in command and local politicians had not started interfering in their work to make money and share the loot with them. Even a B.D.O. (block development officer) was the king of the area under his control and took pride in the development work being done in his block. When in 1961 I visited what was the first community development project in the country in the Chambal ravines in Etawah district of U.P., the name of D.P. Singh, who was the sub-divisional-magistrate when the project was started some years earlier, was already a legend. It was said that he used to carry bags of seeds to be planted in the ravines in his own car and some times carry them on his back from the car to the field where the seed was to be planted. I visited him fourteen years later in the Pant Nagar Agricultural University where he was the Vice-Chancellor. Later he became the chairman of the National Agricultural Commission. I can relate many such stories of dedicated officers.

The following year I happened to arrive at a large farm in Tanjore district barely an hour after police had to fire at a riotous mob of farm laborers, a migratory tribe of landless workers from the southern tip of India along the Tamil Nadu-Kerala border, demanding higher wages. All round me was a sea of green. Tanjore was declared the IADP (Intensive Agricultural Development Project) district in Tamil Nadu, and was known as the granary of the state. The government was clearly on the side of the rich farmers and dismissed the agitation as a communist inspired revolt. The story is the same all over India. At harvest time large numbers of workers from poor regions of the country travel to the richer areas to earn some money that would carry them through the rest of the year. Landless workers from Bihar meet the same fate in Punjab where their life is no better than that of construction workers who come to Delhi from Rajasthan, Orissa and other backward areas. Many of them lost their arms while working on mechanized thrashers. No compensation was paid to them. They are hired by rich labour contractors and treated as Black slaves were treated till 150 years ago in America before Abraham Lincoln abolished slavery in that country. I regard Lincoln as the greatest man ever born.

During the food crisis a Member of the Planning Commission told me that they proposed to ban the serving of rice in Delhi's restaurants. My story on it got a front page banner headline. South Indians in Delhi panicked and the story was immediately denied by the Food Ministry.

Even in the North most people were half fed. Traditionally, for ages they had been accustomed to eating a single meal of coarse grains like jowar or bajra in 24 hours. Hunger has always stalked the country though this fact has been cleverly kept under wraps for centuries by our rulers, aided by their supine middle class cronies.

In the monsoon season of 1966, I happened to be the first newsman to break to a shocked nation the news that America was immediately stopping the supply of PL 480 (Public Law 480) wheat to India. It was a law passed by US Congress under which the wheat was given free to India and the government of India could spend the money it got from the sale of the wheat on various development projects in consultation with American authorities. My story about the ending of PL 480 wheat supplies was immediately denied by the Indian Ministry of Food and Agriculture but confirmed to a large crowd of reporters by Orville Freeman, the then US Agriculture Secretary, who arrived in Delhi the same day, much to the consternation of C. Subramaniam, India's Food Minister who had gone to the airport to receive Freeman. A source in the American embassy had tipped me off about it the previous day. (As a reward for my scoop I got a special assignment from Washington Post the very next day. Its Delhi correspondent, Warren Una, who had come only a few months earlier sought me out at Freeman's Press Conference and offered me the part-time job of assisting him in news gathering).

It was in this environment of utter gloom and despondency that Norman Borlaug brought a smile on the faces of the Indian people with his green revolution and liberated them from the scourage of hunger. Thus an American scientist had stepped in to more than fill the food gap created by the U.S. Government's abrupt decision to withdraw its PL 480 food aid to India. It was a triumph of science over sentiment.

If the last half of the 20th century was the age of the green revolution (which would have liberated every Indian from the menace of hunger, had not our greedy elite and middle class grabbed all the nation's resources for their own use) the 21st century has ushered the information technology revolution which, one hopes, will liberate the country from its rampant corruption at all levels of society. IT (Information Technology) is a multi-face giant with X'ray eyes that can drive driverless cars on public roads, peer inside your brain, scan every document, watch every transaction, hear every telephone talk, record every movement and instantly track a false step of a criminal by putting together and analyzing all available information on his dubious activities, in a split second. Sooner or later paper currency is going to be obsolete. All financial transactions will have to be in the digital mode. Scandanavian countries have taken the lead in going digital in the matter of buying and selling all goods and services.

Driverless cars are now a reality. Google has already run its prototypes of driverless cars for 3,00,000 miles on public roads. By the end of 2013 such cars will be running on public roads in Britain, which has planned an investment of 28 billion pounds in its roads to reduce congestion. America and Europe have planned similar investments to automate their transport system and make it safer. With such marvelous achievements made by information technology, it should be the easiest thing for this science to trace illegal payments or non-payment of dues and put an end to the corruption that is rampant in India today.

I have been intimately associated with information technology since its inception in a nascent state in India. My Harvard educated brother-in-law, Ashok Agrawala and his colleague Satish Tripathi who were working as Assistant Professors in the department of Computer Science in the University of Maryland in America came for a long stay in their summer vacation in 1977 and taught me how with the use of "key words" and a new technique called "pattern recognition" one could retrieve and analyse at a fast speed any amount of information and data. Later I interviewed the Managing Director of O & M (Organisation and Methods), one of the few consultancy firms then operating in India. He told me that they had processed on their computer voluminous data of a large pharmaceutical firm producing scores of medicines and selling them through hundreds of outlets throughout the country. Their analysis had revealed that half the profits of that company came from the sale of only one of its products. "Only the computer can perform such miracles", he told me.

The first time I came face to face with a computer was when I visited the headquarters of Amul Dairy in Anand in Gujarat. V. Kurien, the founder and managing director of the giant cooperative enterprise was a great visionary. He had equipped his vast milk collection system as well as production units for various milk products with the latest machinery. The computer occupied the greater part of a large fully air conditioned and dust proof room, perhaps, 20 feet square. Spools of information tapes were stacked in shelves along the walls. Later the same year I happened to see a many times larger computer system at the Tata Institute of Fundamental Research (TIFR) at Bombay. Dr. Narasimham, the director himself took me around the place. It consisted of a seemingly endless row of rooms along a corridor, each containing stacks of electronic processing devices. Also in 1980 my elder son, Akhil Kumar, joined the computer multi-national firm, Tata-Burroughs after doing his B-Tech from IIT, Delhi and MBA from IIM Ahmedabad. Today he is a Professor of MIS (Management Information System) in a university in America.

The computer became a household word for us and I started dreaming of a computerized library for newspapers so that information needed by staff writers and sub-editors could be accessed instantly. In 1982 I made out a plan for creating such a library in The Statesman based on three or four eight-bit portable Osborne computers which had come out in America only a year earlier. To my great surprise the Managing Director of The Statesman, to whom I gave the plan, approved it immediately. I was made the head of the project, in addition to my duties of Assistant Editor, which meant writing two editorials a week. An air conditioned room, about 12 feet long and seven wide was built inside the huge library hall for four operators and their computers. No one, not even the MD, could enter it with shoes on. Within a year 16-bit computers had come out in the market and we decided to buy a bigger computer since the Osborne units were not able to cope with the large volume of information that had to be stored. Several large companies were jumping into the new emerging market. Bharat Ram, the famous industrialist, personally telephoned Irani to recommend his adopted brand. Ultimately, I found that I had bitten more than I could chew and the project was given up. But I revived it in my post—retirement job of editing a ruling party weekly and even managed to produce a book attacking the Opposition combine by using a software designed jointly by me and Monica Chaddha, the software sales executive of CDM, the company that had supplied us the computers.

In 1991, my younger son Ankur, who did his B.Tech from IIT Delhi in 1990, started his own software export company which has grown since and now has clients world wide. I edited for his firm an electronic magazine, Telcomine, for three years the year from 2000 to 2003 containing information about the latest developments in Telecommunications Technology. It was circulated all over the world to about 1500 potential clients. Once we interviewed by teleconferencing the chief executive of the team that produced Blue Tooth. Telcomine had to close down because the two non-engineer girls Seema Dhawan and Pragya Singh, who were collecting the data for it from internet got married and migrated to America with their husbands. None of the engineers in the company were interested in this 'boring' task. They had joined the firm to learn software development and not to bring out a magazine, they said.

My 35-year long close association with information technology has taught me two things. One, that the two software tools of search by 'keywords' and "pattern recognition" continue to be among the main pillars of information technology. But at the same time the hardware has acquired fantastic speeds and runs perhaps a million times faster than it did 40 years ago. The transistor count per integrated circuit has gone up from 2300 in 1971 to 2,600,000,000 in 2011. Under Moore's Law the processing speed of computers doubles every two years. You can imagine what it will be like ten to twenty years hence.

As a result a new function has been added to information technology, that of "access". Till 20 years ago the science was confined to storing, analyzing and communicating data or information. Now new software tools have been developed to "access" with lightning speed data or conversations digitally stored anywhere on an information "cloud" like internet. The dimensions of this development are far reaching, both good and bad. It has accelerated progress in every field and marks the beginning of a new era of openness in human civilization on earth. I find that my grand children know more about the latest developments in information technology than their fathers, who are recognized experts in this field. In any event, they seem to know ten times more about any subject than I did at their age because they are connected to the internet constantly and can 'access' any piece of knowledge which I could not.

The process of storing knowledge on internet has been accelerated by millions of "volunteers" in Western countries who are contributing valuable data to encyclopedias like Wikipedia. Nick D'Aloisio has officially earned his seat at the cool kids' table. In March 2013, the 17-year-old London high school student sold his news-aggregator app Summly to tech giant Yahoo for a reported $30 million in cash and stock. While he's finishing up his diploma, he'll also start work at Yahoo's London office. Meanwhile, Yahoo plans to enhance its own mobile apps with the technology developed for Summly, which uses an algorithm to automatically produce easily digestible summaries of news stories. At the same time young experimenters are inventing new software tools to ferret out digitally stored secret data.

India's contribution in this area is marginal, if not negative. Most of us, including me, are in the habit of buying pirated software. How could this industry have grown with such leaps and bounds if people in the West also had gotten into the habit of using pirated software? That is a question we never ask ourselves.

For more than a century now Indian newspapers in English and all other languages have been suppressing news in the guise of self-censorship to maintain what they call a "respectable" image of themselves but in reality not to disturb the established order of society and not to annoy rich and powerful people who give them huge concessions in their other enterprises as the price of their silence. They will no longer be able to do so because the truth will reveal itself any way. Tools are now available to "access" every bit of data or telephone conversation and spread it fast through the social media. This is just the beginning of the IT revolution. It will keep growing at mind boggling speed and never end in the foreseeable future.

This book paints a depressing picture of present times in India. After all it is an autobiography of a corrupt Indian. But even a corrupt person has the same conscience that a saint has. My conscience tells me that all this will change. I have no doubt in my mind that the whole of humanity has a bright future. It may take a few decades, or even a century to materialize but any one with eyes can see it coming.

Its key elements are transparency, equality and rule of law. Information Technology is fast approaching the state where it will be impossible to stop any one from accessing any piece of information. In other words it will be impossible for any one to cheat without being caught. Cash transactions are already becoming 'primitive' and outdated in Western countries, specially the Nordic nations, and it is only a matter of time when this scourge which is a hotbed of corruption disappears from the entire world. Every transaction involving money will be instantly recorded in dozens of places. A secret note sent by the American embassy in Delhi to the US State department makes the "cynical" observation that in India corruption grows in direct proportion to the number of laws passed to curb it because it means "more people to bribe". Advances in information technology alone can check this menace, not new laws passed by Parliament.

Knowledge, even class room lectures by the highest authorities on various subjects, will be freely available to every one. The Western world has already taken several steps in that direction. In short, there will be no premium on knowledge. You cannot claim more salary because you are more learned than me. A form of calculation called the Gini index has estimated that one of the reasons for growing inequality in the last few decades is the premium placed on certain vocations like legal, medical, financial and consultancy services. Universalization of knowledge of these subjects will restore an equilibrium between various vocations and no one will be able to claim functional superiority over others.

There is no doubt that Western technology coupled with the advent of democracy and the concepts of human rights evolved in Europe and America have made a difference to the quality of life throughout the world. That process is now being accelerated. Newton once said "we are children playing pebbles on the sea shore of knowledge." The time has now come to dive deep into this ocean and bring out its choicest pearls. We have a similar legend in our ancient mythology, called Amrita Manthan. The rate at which science is reaching out to new vistas of knowledge is transforming our whole concept of life. Neuro-science is penetrating the inner recesses of the brain to uncover our thoughts which were hitherto considered private. One would no longer be able to hide his evil intentions or thoughts.

Brave men like Aron Swartz, Julian Asange, Bradley Manning and Edward Snowden have proved that already it is impossible to keep any secrets, official or private. As this technology advances, an all pervading force will be able to unlock the doors of the most securely locked vaults where secrets are kept. You will not need a Right To Information Act to get to the Truth.

Western democracies are fast liberalizing laws so that those snooping for digital information do not get punished for it. The US Congress is considering what, if passed, will be called Aaron's law to reduce the powers of prosecutors in such cases and also sharply reduce the period of sentence when convicted of cyber crimes. China and India which are extremely touchy about these matters because they have so much to hide from public view will have to gradually fall in line or will be defeated in their evil designs by advancing technology. A person sitting in another country could unlock all the secrets of his own nation. At the risk of his life. Edward Snowden has proved two things. One that the 'cloud' called internet can and eventually will map out every detail of your day to day life from birth to death. And two, you will not be able to hide anything from the searching eyes of cybernetic observers and the law. In short we are fast heading towards an age of TOTAL TRANSPARENCY. How the human brain will react to this change cannot be predicted. The mind of man is mysterious phenomenon. It has developed over the ages through secret thoughts which no one could fathom.

Instruments are being developed that can detect the thoughts the brain is thinking by the use of electrodes. Through such instruments we can read the mind of a person and view his thoughts as they arise in the brain.

Writing in Time Magazine of July 8, 2013 Fareed Zakaria says "We are living with the consequences of two powerful, interrelated trends. The first is digital life. Your life today has a digital signature. Where you eat, shop and travel; whom you call, e-mail and text; every website, café and museum you visit even once is all stored in the great digital cloud.

The second is Big Data. Americans were probably most shocked by the revelation that the U.S. government is collecting massive quantities of their digital signatures—billions of phone calls and e-mails and Internet searches.

The NSA program Prism aims to identify suspicious patterns to allow the government to prevent terrorism (i.e., to act before an attack takes place).

The Economist of July 20, 2013 has a cover story with the title "Curious case of the fall in crime". It shows how crime has fallen steeply in all the rich Western countries despite the rising gap between the incomes of the rich and poor and a sharp increase in unemployment. The secret of this phenomenon is the massive use of the tools of information technology by not just the police but the whole society. Crime has become unprofitable.

Private software companies in America and Europe have developed tools that can predict where and when a crime can take place and by whom by processing various patterns of behaviour of criminals, likely situations and locations, as well as a combination of all these factors coupled with the psychology of the criminal.

According to the figures released by the Crime Statistics Bureau of the Government of India there has been a steady increase of various serious crimes, specially those committed against women and children. Considering India's record of all round corruption only use of the latest tools of information technology to check crime can control this menace.

Several years ago I read a book "End of Science" by John Horgan, an eminent scientist. He thought Science had reached the end of its tether, its twilight years, and there were no more basic or fundamental discoveries to be made by scientific research. All that I can say in my own twilight years is that the real fun of science has only now begun. Until now we were Newton's children playing pebbles on the seashore of knowledge. It is only now that we have entered the ocean to dive deep into it and bring out its choicest pearls so that all mankind can live in an environment of health, happiness and peace.

After the information technology revolution I am hoping that the next major revolution will be a big leap in medical science, specially neuro science. Arjun, my eldest grandson, who is a neuro-scientist in one of the biggest labs in the field in America, tells me that a 1.3 billion dollar project has been approved to make a super-computer that would be an exact replica of the human brain. So far neuro-scientists have not been very successful even in simulating brains of animals.

America is spending 2.8 trillion dollars a year on health care, which is 20% of that country's GDP and 60% higher than India's total GDP of 1.873 trillion dollars and still all Americans are not covered by it. Considering that Americans constitute only five percent of the population of the world what are we to do about the health care of the remaining 95% of humanity? Surely a cheaper substitute has to be found to end the reign of anti-biotics which has lasted for more than half a century. I am hoping that our neuro-scientists will discover that self-curative power within the brain which was known to the ancients but has been lost during the wars of attrition that mankind has engaged in all the time. Arjun tells me that a handheld health scanner is being developed that would give you an instant health check. We need gadgets like the mobile phone in the field of health care so that every one can keep a constant check on his own health. His company, Qualcomm, has offered a ten million dollar award, called X Prize jointly with the X Prize Foundation to any team of scientists who develop such a gadget. According to the sponsors this will make 23rd century science fiction a reality in the 21st century.

May be the day is not far when a combination of information technology and medical science can put that power in your mobile phone. Already this small 'toy' can do wonders unnumbered for you. It can show you a full length movie, keep all your accounts, act as your credit card and enable you to have a video-talk with any one around the globe. Through it you can access the secrets of your rivals provided you load it with the necessary software.

Technologies are also fast developing that will automatically reduce waste of energy and thus save the earth from the spectre of climate change looming before it. If, for instance, you can walk through the streets of New York, attend a seminar in Moscow, or actually participate in a film festival in Cannes sitting at home. These visions look like a mere dream today. But the day is not far when they will turn to reality.

In this environment it will hardly be necessary to arm the law enforcement agencies with extra-ordinary powers. When everything is out in the open and the people are educated, law and order will come as a natural corollary.

While visions of real three dimensional experience of far away places may be distant dreams the immediate objective of mankind should be to augment its depleting fresh water resources. Many imaginative ideas have been tried including ferrying of icebergs from the Artic zone to a tropical desert. But the more likely source would be desalination of the water of the sea. Like solar and wind energy research, there has been some progress in this field in the desert area of Qatar where farming with desalinated water has already begun. Seeding of clouds is another alternative which offers scope for the supply of fresh water in large quantities.

A silent revolution in education is sweeping across India too. Schools and colleges, specially professional institutes, are springing up in every corner of India at an astonishing rate. Newspapers, magazine and TV channels are overflowing with their fancy ads, each promising the moon to the new entrants. At the international level the world's best known universities are competing with each other in starting new facilities all over Asia In my own small home town, Gangoh in District Saharanpur in U.P., Shobhit Kumar, who happens to be a nephew of mine, has started the Shobhit University, along with an institution of the same name in Meerut city to train MBAs and engineers. Our family has a century old tradition of starting educational institutions. He had even started a medical college in Gangoh but it could not take off because no doctor would go to a small town to teach medicine. Only 25 years ago Shobhit was just a computer operator. With some capital borrowed from his father he started a computer school and from there, step by step, climbed to the top of his trade. My father's elder brother Babu Maharaj Singh, a leading lawyer of Saharanpur started the Maharaj Singh Degree College about fifty years ago. Since then it has been growing from strength to strength.

Even more heart warming is the story of a gentleman farmer, Pawan Kumar, who owned an orchard adjacent to mine on the outskirts of Gangoh. A rich man had created a trust of only Rs.5,00,000 for a starting a degree college named after him and made Pawan Kumar the main trustee. Since it was to be a regular non-profit institution the going was tough for my friend who used to pay neighbourby visits to my orchard with his plans whenever I was holidaying there. This horticulturist persisted for twenty years to clear all hurdles and succeeded in establishing what is now acknowledged as one of the best degree Colleges affiliated to the Chaudhury Charan Singh University in Western U.P. Such examples abound, not merely in Gangoh but all over the country. A close relative who lives in Dehradun and keeps visiting Delhi from time to time informs me that private educational institutions, some of them fakes, have virtually taken over the capital city of the new state of Uttarakhand.

According to one estimate on an all India basis these institutions are together turning out professionals and graduates who are twice the number of available jobs. My own fear is that the proportion of unemployed professional graduates may be even higher, because they are prepared to join a job at any cost, even on the salary of a peon or clerk. It is a great tragedy because their parents have paid a hefty fees ranging from half a million to two million rupees to the private institutes to educate them. But my hope is that these unemployed graduate professionals will be the harbingers of the next revolution towards equality, transparency and the rule of law. Some of them will apply their minds and bodies seriously to the task of reforming the country and giving it a new personality. As teaching in schools and colleges shifts more and more to computers, children of the poor have been thrown out of the periphery of good education. Some day they will become conscious of their rights as human beings and demand justice. There is already a movement in Europe for not denying any child or teenager an opportunity on the grounds of his or her parents' vocation. These things will take time but they will come to India too.

An egalitarian society of tomorrow will not use terms like socialism or capitalism to describe itself. It will be a society that is 'aware' of itself with its members marching together towards higher things than mere possessions. The famous philosopher, Emanuel Kant, once said: "The mere contemplation of beauty gives us joy apart from the vulgar desire for its possession and use." Tomorrow's society will be so absorbed in the sheer beauty and joy of living in tune with the pulse of the universe that it will have no time for fighting over mere possessions. The day is not far, may be a century or two hence, when all this will come true.

The inquisitiveness of people of the West is amazing. They seem to be stopping at nothing and are always going beyond vistas they have already achieved in various fields. While examining the outer world with a microscopic eye, a very large number of people in Europe and America are turning their attention to what lies within their souls. Like the ancient mystics of the East they are beginning to ask themselves the ultimate question "Who Am I".

5

'Are You Being Served?'

In the early Nineteen Eighties I watched a BBC serial "Are You Being Served?" It was shown by government owned Door Darshan whose black and white single channel then heralded the dawn of the television era in India. The serial which ran for several weeks was about a department store in London. Its most interesting aspect that reminded me of the novels of Charles Dickens and P.G. Wodehouse was the strict order of precedence in the placement of the staff. An apprentice started with the ladies' under garments department as the number two salesman at a counter. In course of time, when some one at the top retired from the service of the company with due honours, the apprentice moved up the ladder and graduated to the hats and ties department. Each department had a person called the "floor walker" whose job it was to direct a customer to a "free" counter and sort out any other problems that the intending buyer might encounter to make sure that he or she did not leave the store without something under the arm. It was he who occasionally asked a customer the question "are you being served?" In course of years our apprentice of yesteryears moved to the shoes department and then quickly graduated to stalls selling costlier items and, if he was lucky, some day became the chief sales manager.

Ruminating over this serial now I find that my career in journalism had not been dissimilar to that of the typical salesman in the serial. It was his job to deal with strangers and keep his customers happy. So was mine. I was essentially a glorified salesman for my newspaper. Like any other reporter when I first joined The Statesman which I served for thirty-one years, I was assigned the beat of crime and courts, in those days the easiest job for a 'field man'. All that I had to do was to go to the Press room in Tees Hazari courts at about 3 p.m. About a dozen reporters of all newspapers used to gather there. An old man, whom we informally called our "news editor" and who represented a news agency would brief us about the main stories of the day. We called it a pool because the "news editor" would assign to each of us the court and the case we were to cover the next morning and bring the story to the Press room to be shared by all. A lawyer whose case was covered in the newspapers would gladly send us a bottle of whiskey which we would share at a common rendezvous, usually the home of one of us. There was nothing wrong in this small gift from a lawyer since we were covering only the important cases, we felt. A reporter who broke the pool or objected to the whiskey bottle would be debarred from the pool, which meant he would miss the main court stories of the day and get pulled up by the real news editor of his own newspaper. The same pool system applied to crime reporting. We went to a briefing conducted by a Superintendent of Police and any one who did his own story and did not share it with others would be debarred from the pool. Only stories suggested to a reporter by the editor or news editor of his paper were exempted from this rule.

From crime and courts one moved to the city corporation which was a mine field of both information and favours. The chairman of the Standing Committee, the executive arm of the municipality, was also chairman of the city's largest firm of builders and developers. Being close to him could get a person a plot of land in the right spot and at a concessional price. He had made it his mission to make his plots available to all journalists who applied for them including those not covering the corporation. From the corporation a reporter was promoted to do features and had the choice of obliging any one he liked with a feature. In practice he was his own master. News editors were always competing with other papers in features and it was the easiest thing for a clever reporter like me to sell a feature idea to his news editor. There was no state assembly in Delhi then. The city was a centrally administered Union territory headed by a chief commissioner. In my days as city reporter Bhagwan Sahay an ICS officer and an old "Allahabadi" like me was the chief commissioner and the now famous

Jag Mohan, ex-Governor and central Minister, was his personal secretary who had joined the IAS a few year earlier. Then a genial young man it was his job to keep the reporters happy. All that the Union territory could offer to an accredited reporter was a free bus pass to travel on buses run by the Delhi Transport Corporation.

After I had done the crime and courts beat for over two years P.W.J. Crosland, the news editor who was an Englishman, decided to put a junior reporter on my beat and created for me a new designation of chief crime reporter. This meant I was no longer bound by the diktats of the 'pool' and could do my own stories. As an insignia of my new office I was allotted a telephone at my residence. I got it instantly under the Press quota, though common citizens including shop keepers, had to wait for years for their turn to get a telephone. Those who needed a phone urgently had to pay heavy bribes and also a special charge to get a phone under a "special category".

My news editor liked out of the way stories. Once I pursued a story on a case a diner had filed against the most prominent restaurant in Connaught Place for serving him bad chicken. It became known in The Statesman as the "chicken case". Every hearing of the case was covered by me. I also did a story on the theft of bottles of Scotch/Whiskey from the houses of our resident editor, A.E. Charlton also an Englishman, and a Canadian diplomat who was his neighbour. Later I did a series of thirty articles on "crime in Delhi" with the help of two junior reporters. This gave me a lot of contacts in the police since the series was concentrated on the modus operandi of criminals and the areas from where they operated. I took care not to offend the Delhi Police, nor did my paper want to portray the police in a bad light. Once a senior editor of a rival English newspaper approached me to intercede on his behalf with the chief of Delhi Police in a case in which he had been needlessly dragged. The chief of a news agency also sought my help in another case involving the Delhi administration. I gladly obliged. It was a favour for which he always remained grateful. Both these jobs were of a routine nature and, in any civilized country, should have needed no recommendation. But India being India only money or influence can move a file from one table to another. A Mayor of Delhi once said in a meeting of the Delhi municipal council half a century ago that a high court judge had told him that even he had to pay the architect of the municipality his "fee" to get the design of the house he was building cleared.

Local railway affairs were another beat that I handled. In those days the word "The Statesman" was open sesame to any office in Delhi. The British owned paper was the staple news fare of all top politicians and bureaucrats in the national capital, including ministers and secretaries to the government of India. The chief PRO (public relations officer) of the Northern Railway which controlled all train traffic in Delhi, quickly became my friend. Within a few months our roles were reversed. I found myself acting as the PRO of the editorial department of The Statesman for getting instant railway reservations to any destination. The Chief PRO was a very senior officer in the railway hierarchy and all bookings and reservations in Delhi came under his charge. Normally train bookings had to be made months in advance. Colleagues in our editorial department who belonged to distant places in South India often came to me to get their rail reservations done. These days I find that most journalists travel by air. Train reservations are still as difficult to obtain as they were fifty years ago. Once I asked the PRO whether he could arrange a special coach for the marriage party of a close relative to travel from Meerut to Lucknow, a distance of 300 miles, within 24 hours. He tried hard but failed and said, "if only you had given me a day more Mr. Lal I would certainly have arranged it."

I could do a whole article on the powers of a Statesman reporter in Delhi of those days. Getting a friend's son or daughter admitted to any school of his choice was child's play for me.

After thus spending five years as a staff reporter I was promoted to the Bureau which then consisted of five special correspondents who covered the Government of India and the national political parties. While giving me this news Crosland said, "of course, you will have to buy some clothes." Of all the newspapers in Delhi The Statesman was very particular that its special correspondents dressed impeccably and looked every inch like "burra sahbs" whom they had to meet everyday in their offices and at cocktail parties which in those days in Delhi were plentiful. Coming from a semi-rural background I had never been particular about the clothes I wore. For that reason alone I had never expected to be promoted to the bureau and had, in fact, nearly accepted the job of staff Correspondent of The Hindustan Times at Jaipur. There was one hitch which saved me from taking a false step which would have changed the entire course of my life and that of my three children. S. Mulgaokar, the editor, refused to waive the six-month probation clause applicable to all new entrants to that organization. Mulgaokar had the reputation of being a temperamental employer and I did not want to take any chances with him. So I gave up the idea and within a few months, in November 1962 when there was a vacancy in the bureau, got a promotion in my own paper. Among the numerous benefits of my new job was a government flat at a nominal monthly rent with the facility of unlimited maintenance services.

My new assignment opened vast vistas of power and influence I had not dreamt of. My chief, Krishan Bhatia, was a stickler for protocol and considered it beneath his dignity to go to daily foreign office briefings by a mere joint secretary of the External Affairs Ministry at Hyderabad House. Instead he sent me, his understudy, to these briefings. Those were the days when China had invaded India and all the big wigs in journalism were flocking to Hyderabad House to get the latest news from the front. I got to know all of them rather early in my career. I continued covering Hyderabad House for several years. In 1964 Bhatia moved to Hindustan Times as its editor and Inder Malhotra, then a dashing young man, younger to me by two years, took over. He continued the practice of using me as his aide in the foreign office. Among the joint secretaries who briefed us was K.R. Narayanan, who later became the President of India. I came to know him closely when he returned from his post as our ambassador in China in 1978 and was staying in a small two-room apartment in Curzon Road (now Kasturba Gandhi Marg) with his daughter. He was then living in rooms meant for officers in transit. Being a member of the Hyderabad House circuit meant receiving invitations to cocktail parties thrown by various embassies who kept lists of all journalists covering the foreign office. This gave me an opportunity to meet Indian VIPs and foreign diplomats and use them as sources of information when required. I remember standing in the corridors of the Prime Minister's office in South Block for hours during the Swaran Singh—Bhutto talks on Kashmir and similar other important events.

But this was only part of my job. My main duty as the junior most special correspondent of The Statesman was to 'cover' various 'miscellaneous' ministries like Food and Agriculture, Education, Health, Science and Technology, Housing and a few others. I also covered the Rajya Sabha when it was in session and occasionally the Lok Sabha when our Parliamentary Correspondent was away.

Covering ministries meant daily visits after 5 p.m. to the Press Information Bureau. It was a pigeon hole of a building on Parliament Street next to All India Radio. Information Officers of each ministry sat there in small rooms on one side of an L-shaped carpeted corridor and handed out to us Press notes which were usually single page print outs that were rarely important enough to be reported in the main English newspapers published from the capital. But sometimes they contained major announcements which made it necessary for a special correspondent to visit the PIB every day. Generally, we tried to get our stories from interviews with joint-secretaries or secretaries of ministries allotted to us. Ministers often preferred to meet us at their homes. For brief inquiries a special correspondent could walk into the house of a minister any time of the day till 10 at night and telephone his personal secretary even at a later hour. Similarly secretaries and joint secretaries could be met without appointment for urgent inquiries or contacted on phone after office hours. Even Pandit Nehru was available for replying to queries if a special correspondent caught him coming out of his office or a function or public meeting somewhere. So were other Prime Ministers. A week before his death I managed to have a word alone with Nehru when he landed at Palam airport on his return from Dehradun where he had gone for a holiday.

But there was a price attached to these contacts with top Ministers and bureaucrats. You must not have the reputation of writing nasty things against the government, more particularly against your contacts in the ministry you covered. Otherwise you could be bullied and insulted in public. I had this experience on many occasions. A minister who later become a Deputy Prime Minister was so incensed with me personally that he rebuked me at a Press Conference with the words "you always ask mischievous questions" when I asked him a most innocuous question. It seems he was only waiting for me to open my mouth. I have had such experiences with several ministers and chief ministers though some other members of their clan even did me the honour of visiting me at my house with their wives.

To cut a long story short at this point, you will perhaps ask me where is the parallel between my career and that of the apprentice salesman of a department store in London in the BBC serial "Are you being served". The parallel is obvious if you place the VIPs we meet in the position of our main customers at a department store called a large newspaper. After sixty-five years in the profession I have realized that a big newspaper is a facility "of the rich, by the rich and for the rich". Poor people's problems are dealt in it the way the rich people want them to be dealt. They don't want their newspaper to play the role of a storm trooper for the poor classes. Admission to cocktail circuits, private drink parties, ministers' houses and top bureaucrats' offices is generally reserved for journalists who are favourable or at worst mild in their criticism of the government. The reverse is also true. In course of time, hobnobbing with the rich and powerful, the minds of senior journalists become fully conditioned to think like their powerful contacts. They say "Power corrupts. Absolute power corrupts absolutely". But proximity to power has an even more intoxicating effect since it is power without responsibility. All that you have to do is to toe a certain line laid down by your 'contact' and blessings in kind will rain upon you. When I was the bureau chief in The Statesman during the Janata regime 1977-1980, CR Irani, the Managing Director, asked me to explain why the stories of our special correspondents portrayed the ruling party pursuing different philosophies. I told him one of our special correspondents was aligned to the RSS, and perhaps had been its member in his youth, another was more or less committed to Charan Singh's Bharatiya Lok Dal and a third was a socialist of the Madhu Limaye School. (Incidentally, I regarded Limaye as one of the most honest politicians I have ever met). But in practice all these politicians pleaded the cause of the rich and powerful.

We journalists were merely pawns in the game. The real harvest of the power of the Press was reaped by proprietors and editors of newspapers. While a mere special correspondent may be satisfied with a plot of land, a flat, a junket, money for a daughter's wedding or floating a cooperative housing society for journalists and pseudo journalists, the proprietors demanded (and still do) large lands ostensibly for establishing a branch of their newspapers but actually to build a commercial complex to be resold or hired out at huge profits. They also demand licenses and "aid" for starting factories to manufacture consumer products which have nothing whatever to do with news. An editor once asked me "how can you get news if you do not circulate?" Not being fond of drinks I later began to avoid cocktail parties. I did not give a direct reply to my editor but merely said "I prefer to meet my contacts on a one-to-one basis." Like it or not, the newspaper is an institution that helps to forge a bond among those endowed with power and money. Their opinions, activities, statements and photographs are the mainstay of a newspaper.

You will never find any Indian newspaper ever doing a campaign or even a story or article about black money pouring into the building sector, both commercial and residential, and vitiating the entire economy. Nor will you find stories about people dying of starvation, disease and infected water. All such issues are left to the ever vigilant foreign press to handle. You will never find stories or articles about more than 90% of workers not receiving even half the minimum wage fixed by the government. A realistic discussion of the problems of housing, land, water, wages and food is virtually banned.

The owners and staff of newspapers in the states behave like lords of the manor so long as they can keep the state government of the day happy. I remember the case of an enterprising journalist who was given a large property virtually free by the state government to start a Hindi daily. The paper thrived and grew in circulation and influence. In course of time it opened branches in other major cities of the state. The owner tried the same 'trick' in a neighbouring state and was welcomed by its chief minister with open arms. In a few years, after the newspaper had established itself, the owner started cultivating other politicians who were rivals of the chief minister. When the news reached the C.M. he became furious and saw to it that the paper was shut down within a year. District newspapers and correspondents live entirely on the mercy of the Deputy Commissioner of the district and local MPs, politicians and goons. They can make enemies of them at their own peril. On the other hand, whether in a district or the national capital, so long as you avoid real critical issues facing the nation, the red carpet is rolled out for you. You can ask for the Moon and you will get it. In short, the profession of the entire media world at all levels in India can be reduced to one phrase "influence peddling".

In course of time, like the apprentice salesman in the department store in London shown in the BBC serial "Are you being served" I too climbed the hierarchical ladder step by step and reached near the top of my profession. In the process I imbibed the 'culture' and traditions of my company, the foremost among which was to keep our "customers" happy and satisfied with the editor playing the role of 'the walker' in the serial and asking members of the elite classes whether they had any complaints with the paper. Starting as a member of the working class I gradually joined the ranks of the elite of the country. I still remember the night in the winter of 1953 when Ravi Shankar Shukla Chief Minister of what was then the State of Madhya Pradesh, came out in the portico of his official bungalow in Nagpur to see me off after an interview. He was a stalwart of the freedom movement. I picked up my bicycle parked near where we were standing and rode back to my newspaper Nagpur Times, three miles away. I had a one-room house in a chawl and used to sleep on the floor. I took my breakfast of pakodas and tea at the subsidized office canteen and had my meals in dhabas (cheap eateries). Most journalists then were only slightly better off. I remember a scraggy looking middle aged free lancer who used to do a daily column of satire for the edit page and got paid five rupees per piece. Like teachers, journalists were a class apart—respected but low paid. Today we are eminent members of the elite with no link with the lower classes and their problems.

By contrast the bungalow I lived in 20 years later in Lucknow as the special correspondent of The Statesman had been occupied by Nehru's sister, Vijaya Lakshmi Pandit, when she was the health minister of UP in the ministry headed by Pandit Gobind Ballabh Pant during 1937-39. It was a high ceilinged corner mansion spread over a one—acre plot facing the Lucknow zoo. It had three large lawns in one of which some peacocks had made their home. The lawn was covered with trees and situated on elevated ground. There were nine servant quarters and two garages. Its kitchen itself was the size of a modern flat with a huge chimney. Every bedroom had a fireplace with a mantle piece. So had the drawing room which was large enough for a conference hall where you could place forty folding chairs. Every bathroom had a built in full sized porcelein tub. The house had two large studies, verandahs on all sides and a gallery opening into all rooms. Obviously built in the late Nineteenth or early Twentieth Century for a British advisor to the Governor its tree lined drive way alone was about two hundred feet long. Its maintenance must be costing the government a large sum of money. As far as I know The Statesman paid nothing or a nominal rent for this huge property which one of my predecessors must have wangled by currying favour with the chief minister after Independence.

Likewise, when earlier I was posted in Chandigarh I inherited a huge bungalow meant for secretaries to the state government. Evidently the special correspondent posted in the State when Chandigarh was built had "managed" it with the government of the day. The states were only too willing to extend such largesse to the Press. The Chief Ministers saw to it that "troublesome" correspondents were hounded out of their states. I can relate many such examples. For all practical purposes we were all glorified public relations officers of the governments we wrote about. This was how our proprietors and editors wanted us to behave, like the successful salesman of the BBC serial! The nexus between the "respectable" newspapers and the political high-caste establishment of the country is not new. It has always been there. Even non-journalists posing as journalists can extract a lot of favours from politicians. I knew a sales inspector of The Statesman who was closer to the Chief Minister of a State I was covering than I was as the paper's special correspondent.

Intelligence agencies of the Government had begun arm-twisting journalists after Indira Gandhi declared Emergency in India following her disqualification to hold office by the Allahabad High Court. I was in Lucknow then. Contacts with Americans and the US embassy were the first target. An Indian information officer of the American embassy whom I had known from my Delhi days quickly alighted from his auto-rickshaw one evening, hid himself in the bushes near the peacocks in my bungalow, and took a zig zag route through the lawn to meet me. He was evidently being followed. When a counselor of the US Embassy, an American, visited Lucknow and came to my house for breakfast, the deputy chief of central intelligence for U.P. called on me within an hour of the diplomat's departure to inquire in detail about what transpired during our meeting. His chief also called on me socially with his wife. For a deputy superintendent of police of the intelligence bureau my house became a regular beat which he would visit every week to discuss U.P. politics. The message was loud and clear: keep off foreign diplomats. Already, in Delhi one of my former editors, Kuldip Nayar, had been arrested and put in jail for protesting against the imposition of censorship after the declaration of Emergency. After the Emergency was lifted and the Janata Party came to power all the restrictions on the media, except censorship, were kept in place and in fact tightened. By then I had been shifted to Delhi as the Bureau Chief. Today the situation is worse. The government has armed itself with draconian powers ostensibly to fight threats from terrorists and Maoists but, in fact, to throttle whatever little remains of the freedom of the Press. In the so-called "sensitive" areas which extend to nearly 40% of India's territory one can be jailed for even possessing literature that is unpleasing to the authorities. There is no question of opening one's mouth against the atrocious acts of oppression and extortion being committed by the security forces of the government against poor and innocent citizens. Today the surrender of the media to the powers that be is complete.

I salute the people and Press of Brazil for protesting loudly against their government's extravagance in preparations for the 2014 football World Cup. Contrast this with the tame submission by our leaders and the media to the wanton waste the Indian government indulged in on staging the Commonwealth Games when money was squandered like water. This, in a country where millions die quietly every year of starvation, malnutrition and disease, unattended and uncared. I have yet to see a countrywide demonstration in India against the non-payment of the minimum wage fixed by the government to crores of people by greedy employers who horde the unpaid amount as black money. Nor will you ever find an article on these subjects in the national newspapers.

My two articles on land prices in Delhi shooting up a hundred thousand times in sixty years and on the Minimum Wages Act being a non-starter were rejected by all national newspapers. At the same time I wrote to them suggesting that if my articles were below their standard they should do their own stories about them which they never did. The reasons are obvious.

A comparative study of the newspapers of today and those of 30-50 years ago will reveal several interesting facts about modern journalism. I would like to compliment Mr Samir Jain and Mr Vineet Jain, the two brothers who own *The Times of India,* the world's largest circulated English daily, for frankly admitting they had dismantled the wall between the editorial and advertisement departments since their main business was not News, but Advertising. They said this to Ken Auletta, media critic for the *New Yorker* magazine: "We are not in the newspaper business. We are in the advertising business." After interviewing other editors and newspaper owners, Auletta says in his article Why Indian Newspapers are Thriving? that the pattern set by *The Times of India* of accepting paid news was being followed by other newspapers in India. He quotes Krishna Prasad, editor-in-chief of *Outlook* Magazine, as saying, "those who deny this fact are simply lying". This then is the first major change between the newspapers of 50 years ago and today.

Another big wall, that between the proprietors and the editor had been broken down under dramatic circumstances by The Statesman about 45 years ago. But it was not the same thing as today's blatant commercialization of the entire newspaper industry. It was essentially an ideological war which gradually led to the virtual extinction of the institution of the Editor as an independent entity in practically all newspapers in India. It not only involves complete surrender of the powers of the editor to the proprietors but also imposes severe restrictions on the freedom of all journalists working or a national daily to report whatever they find worth reporting within the bounds of "respectability" as this word is defined above. The freedom of the journalist to write whatever he pleased was further eliminated by the virtual abolition of the Working Journalists' Act in all newspapers and its replacement by the three-year contract system. In my time my job in The Statesman was as secure as that of an IAS officer in the government. Today's journalist is entirely at the mercy of his bosses.

In 1967, Andrew Yule and Company, British owners of *The Statesman,* decided to hand over the newspaper to a consortium of Indian companies headed by the Tatas who took 13 per cent shares in the new firm. Under the terms of the transfer were created a Board of Directors, headed by N.A. Palkhiwala and a Board of Trustees, chaired by M.C. Setalvad. The trustees were to guard the editorial independence of the paper. Both men were leading jurists of international repute. C.R Irani was appointed the managing director and Pran Chopra the editor.

Within less than a year, the Government of India under Indira Gandhi dismissed the Communist Ministry in West Bengal. Chopra wrote an editorial attacking Indira Gandhi's decision as an encroachment on the federal rights of the states. Irani thought otherwise. He also perhaps thought that on such crucial issues, the MD should also be consulted. The matter went to the trustees who upheld the editor. This provoked the board of directors to abolish and dismiss the board of trustees and remove the editor. The drastic action of the directors sent shock waves throughout *The Statesman* and the media in general.

The Statesman developments attracted the attention of the world Press. Besides being a full-time special correspondent of the paper, I was also correspondent of *The Times,* London. Its Delhi Bureau chief being away, its foreign news editor asked me to file a detailed story on the episode and keep a close watch on it. However, Chopra advised me in my own interest to stay away from the story to avoid possible victimisation by the new management if I wrote any thing against it. My reporter's instinct revolted against Chopra's advice and I went ahead and phoned up Setalvad. He came running to the phone when he was told by his assistant that the caller was from The Times, London. However, he cooled off when he heard an Indian's voice at the other end of the line. "I am not here to be cross-examined like this", he said brashly when I asked him the first question sent to me by the Foreign News Editor of The Times and banged the receiver in my face.

Not to be put down I solved the dilemma by walking into the office of Reuters in Delhi and told its chief, an Englishman, that *The Times* wanted the story. He was only too glad to oblige. I gave him the list of questions I had received from London. He grilled Setalvad for a full twenty minutes. I advised the foreign news editor to take the report from Reuters instead. So much for our great champions of civil liberties and human rights! All my great respect for Setalvad vanished that night. To be fair to this man, however, I must add that almost all our leaders, including Gandhi and Nehru, suffered from this weakness for the White skin.

The epilogue to the whole drama came when in June 1975 Indira Gandhi declared the Emergency and imposed censorship on the press. Irani was a brave man. He took a bold stand against it. The owners of *The Statesman* who included big names such as the Tatas and Mafatlals developed cold feet and dissociated themselves from the paper by proxy sales of their shares to senior members of the staff. Had the trustees remained in place they would have acted as a buffer between the government and the owners and the latter would not have had to wash their hands off from the prestigious daily.

Nobel Laureate Amritya Sen recently said in a dialogue with Sharmila Tagore, Chairperson of the film censor board of India, that the Indian Press avoided covering "real issues" facing the public and cited the example of the plight of Muslims of West Bengal while taking up frivolous Islamic causes. Frivolity, thy name is Indian Journalism!

Today reporters write pure advertisements in the form of news stories. Journalistic ethics apart, who will then write hard news? A quick look at any newspaper today will show that it is packed with photo features narrating the activities of celebrities who have probably paid for it. This makes an Indian newspaper an exact parallel of the department store in the BBC serial "Are you Being Served?"

I can recall unpleasant encounters with several editors for reporting facts which I saw actually happening but which offended a powerful politician or bureaucrat, for the simple reason that it is not the policy of big newspapers to be harshly critical of those in positions of power, including the almighty police. All of them are treated as "customers" are treated in a department store.

The aphorism "power corrupts" is widely known. But what is little known is the fact that proximity to power also corrupts. It is like passive smoking. If you are habitually in a room with one or more smokers you are breathing the same polluted air as your companions. If your husband or wife is a chain smoker you can feel his or her presence in the room from a mere whiff of smoke flowing in your direction. When it is not there you miss it. Constant proximity to those holding high positions has the same effect. It makes you as power drunk as them and therefore equally corrupt, if not more so since unlike them what you enjoy is power without responsibility. And also unlike them you do not admit even to yourself that you are corrupt. Your conscience is crystal clear about it. This issue has belatedly raised its ugly head before me in the wake of Anna Hazare's India Against Corruption movement and Arvind Kejriwal's Aam Admi party to eradicate corruption at top levels from the country. I started wondering whether the common man like me is corrupt too. Turning the same searchlight on myself which I have so far directed at our top politicians and bureaucrats I discovered that I may be one of the most corrupt individuals in India, and that too without knowing it. Here are some examples of what I mean:

Around the year 1960 when I was the chief crime reporter of The Statesman six bottles of Scotch Whiskey got stolen by burglars from the house of A.E. Charlton, an Englishman and Resident Editor of my paper, who lived in Tughlak Road. Promptly Charlton went to the Tughlak Road police station to register his complaint. The sub-inspector in duty gave him a sheet of paper and asked him to write down his complaint. A day later the same thing happened in a neighbouring house of a foreign diplomat, possibly Canadian. P.W.J. Crosland, my news editor, asked me to investigate and do a story. Every drop of Scotch Whiskey was in those days worth its weight in gold since its import had been totally banned. Only foreigners, diplomats and the few big hotels then operating could be given a license for importing a fixed quantity of it. Accordingly, after the day's round of my beat in an office car I drove to the Tughlak Road police station. The Station House Officer (SHO) happened to be present in his office. I told him I had come to investigate the Whiskey thefts.

He looked surprised and said "What Whiskey thefts."

I then narrated to him the whole story as Crosland had told me. He called sub-inspector Balbir Singh (name changed) who happened to be the person to whom Charlton had given his complaint in writing.

"It was a mirror matter so I threw it away", said Balbir Singh.

"What about the complaint of the Canadian diplomat?" I asked.

"That too", replied Balbir Singh.

Realizing the seriousness of the issue in which an Editor was involved the SHO assured me that the police would do all that lay in its power to track down the culprits.

As I was coming out of the SHO's room and moving towards my car parked in the spacious compound of the police station a jeep drove in. The man who alighted from it was none other than the Chief of Delhi Police whom I knew very well since I used to meet him twice a week in his office in Kashmiri Gate. After exchange of pleasantries he asked me the purpose of my visit. His brows knit as I told him my story. By then, hearing of the Chief's visit, the SHO had rushed out of his room to meet him.

With a flushed face the Chief walked to the SHO's room, picked up the phone and dialed the number of the Superintendent of Police of South Delhi district.

"Come here at once", he shouted addressing the officer by his surname. Within minutes the SP arrived.

All the while Balbir Singh had been standing in a corner like a statue.

"Suspend him", the Chief ordered pointing his finger at Balbir Singh. Revoking suspension is a long drawn out process. I was keeping track of the case. As far as I can recall it took Balbir Singh nearly two years to be restored to his post with a black mark on his service record.

On coming back to the office I reported what had transpired in the Tuglak Road police station to Crosland who telephoned Charlton about it.

Charlton later phoned me to say that we should forget the whole event and not write a report on theft of whiskey bottles by what we suspected was a gang of Scotch Whiskey thieves operating in elite areas of the city.

"It is a small matter afterall", he said and added "they (the police) have been so nice to us. So let us forget it."

The chief of the Delhi Police had served his purpose. He now had one national newspaper, in his pocket, and that too a paper which Nehru and all his ministers and top officials read then. The Statesman was their first choice.

Taking the hint, I too became careful while reporting crime not to be too harsh on the police in my reports.

This is just one instance of how ministers and top officials corrupted our minds by showing us small favours. They made us feel that we had all the powers that they enjoyed.

I learnt early in life that "governance" in India is the fine art of distributing favours and "nothing else". Whether it be government, a private company, a political party, university, NGO, a social service society or any other institution, on assuming the tiniest tithe of power in it, every Indian considers it his birthright to serve only himself and his favourites and ignore the rest as far as it lies in his power to ignore them. Their letters and petitions remain unanswered and unacknowledged, a habit peculiar to this country.

Back in 1960 I happened to be the general secretary of the Delhi Press Reporters' Association with a membership of barely about 20 reporters. I sent a resolution that we had passed against certain anomalies in reporters' emoluments to all seven or eight Editors in Delhi. The only reply I got was from A.E. Charlton, Resident Editor of The Statesman and an Englishman. Since I was working in the same paper the reply could have been easily given to me in the office. Instead, it was delivered to me at my house, five kilometers away by a Statesman peon who bicycled all the way to New Rajinder Nagar to give it to me. It was a two line note acknowledging my letter and to say that he had 'noted' its contents. The other editors, all Indians, simply ignored my letter.

Lest the example of A.E. Charlton being the only editor to respond to my letter gives the impression that British private companies took the narrow and straight path of straightforwardness in their dealings, I must submit that the Statesman thrived on its aristocracy—its Grade I and Grade II executives who stood apart, an island unto themselves, mostly Britishers. They silently practiced a caste system between them. For instance, a man from Ireland could never rise to the top. A Scotsman? May be, but doubtful.

The Statesman was the only paper that in the thick of World War II severely criticized the British Government for not doing anything to save lakhs of people from dying on the streets in the infamous Bengal famine of 1943. But normally there was complete bonhomie between the top brass of The Statesman and the ruling elite of the day. The practice continued for two decades after Independence till the ownership and management of the paper passed into Indian hands and wings of the editorial department were severely clipped with the sacking of its first Indian Editor so that it could never fly high again. It was essentially a war between two factions of the aristocracy of the day in which the vital interests of the common man had no play, a war between feudalism and modern day capitalism. In both favourites were favoured and others ignored. Somehow despite my anti-capitalist views I managed to stay in the former category by keeping my mouth shut. If this is not corruption I would like to know what is?

I am writing this book because my case portrays the true state of the Indian intelligentsia. It is a silent and often approving spectator of a real life tragedy happening before its eyes. As I write these lines I have lying before me a newspaper with a front page story of how an accident victim died on the highway near Jaipur because hundreds of cars and other vehicles passed by him, saw him lying in a pool of blood and drove away. This happened only yesterday. TV footage of this event is even more horrifying and reflective of our social attitudes. The incident did not shock me at all because this is precisely what all of us have been doing all the time. Millions of people have been dying of hunger and thirst all over the country every year on the highway of life because of the crimes against humanity perpetrated by different sections of the ruling elite while we, the intelligentsia, have been making merry all the time because we are also share holders in the general loot. All the time violence on the streets and in homes is increasing, striking fear in the hearts of crores of people. Lakhs of children from poor families are being kidnapped every year and maimed and forced into prostitution, begging and other illegal trades. Also lakhs of women are routinely raped. A fascism of goondas, politicians, bureaucrats and convenient intellectuals rules the country and, in fact, most of the "developing" nations of Asia, Africa and Latin America, right down to the level of the village or cluster of villages. At every level mafias form very quickly and invariably these gangs include policemen as their active members.

In India all these crimes can be stopped if the police wants to stop them. They know each criminal by name and the place where he lives.

I can assert with confidence that if the police really girds up it's loins to attack child litters with the same vigor which it shows in dealing with terrorists it could not only reduce this crime but totally stamp it out even without DNA samples of the children and their families.

On an average poor children are kidnapped from the streets of Delhi every day. It is like 13 terrorist bombs being blasted in the homes of the affected families.

In the year 1961 a teen aged South African girl had been lured away to India by two persons. Her father wrote to editors of Indian newspapers to help in finding the girl. My Editor asked me if I could help. I drove down to the small office of the then Delhi police chief in Kashmere Gate, gave him a few points about the profile of the girl and told him my chief editor was personally interested in this case.

"The police called the police officer concerned who called back within five minutes to give the address of the flat in Lajpat Nagar where this girl was staying. I drove to the flat which was located above a shop. I stood under the staircase and heard people talking and laughing in the room upstairs. As luck would have it, within about 10 minutes the girl came down with two young men, one of whom was an Indian. I walked into the shop to avoid suspicion and had a good look at the girl to confirm that I had found my quarry. My editor was dazed by the speed with which the police had done the job.

"Those were relaxed times when even Pandit Nehru, the Prime Minister, drove about the city with a single escort car and without disturbing the traffic. Today, with our gun toting police looking for a terrorist under every bed and doing verification of every tenant and every domestic servant in the city, they are better equipped to find out, if they want to, the hideouts of these gangs of child litters who have ruined the lives of countless children in this country."

Before writing to a few top editors the father of the girl in South Africa must have exhausted official sources like the Foreign Ministry and Interpol. When he got no response from them he wrote the papers. Evidently his other requests were simply ignored by the police because flesh trade is a lucrative source of income for it.

Indifference to everything that happens around him, I think, is the biggest quality of a slave. Every year over 3,00,000 children in India die within 24 hours of their birth, reports South Asia post quoting a study by a Child Rights Organisation. But nobody cares.

6

Our sex-obsessed Media While Ominous Clouds gather over it

Both in display and content the coverage of the alleged misdemeanour of Tarun Tejpal with a junior female colleague in a hotel lift in Goa by our newspapers and TV channels far exceeded their reportage of the devastating cloudburst over the holy Himalayan city of Kedarnath which killed at least 5000 people, left lakhs of pilgrims standed in bitter cold and hill residents homeless. Some people called it a Himalayan Tsunami. Media gave similar treatment to the cases against Asa Ram Bapu, the holy man, for allegedly raping a young female inmate of his ashram and Narendra Modi snooping on a girl through his police.

Media coverage for several days all over the country of two Karnataka Ministers watching pornographic films on their mobiles inside the state assembly led to their resignation without which the furore in newspapers and TV news would not have died down.

A TV Channel even pried into the privacy of a veteran dignitary, holding a rank the equivalent of a Union Minister, in his bedroom at midnight and secretly took pictures of him carousing with three women. Within days of these being repeatedly shown on TV Channels and reported in newspapers the VIP had to resign. His whole career of over sixty years in politics was ruined at the fag end of his life.

By contrast in America, whose life style our elite emulate, similar charges against Bill Clinton by a White House staffer did not prevent him from completing his term as President of the United States and also win a second term by a comfortable margin. In India too there are regional differences in such matters. I am fairly positive that if the case of Karnataka Ministers watching pornographic films in the Assembly had occurred in Punjab with a different political party in power, it would have been simply laughed off by the members of the House as well as the public. The ministers would not have resigned over such a small matter.

Not for nothing did the Nobel Laureate Amartya Sen tell Sharmila Tagore in a recent interview in Kolkata that Indian media shied away from tackling "real issues" and indulged in sheer sensationalism.

Dealing with similar issues the Economist, London, said as early as December 30, 2009 that "if the empowerment of women was one of the great changes of the past 50 years, dealing with its social consequences will be one of the great challenges of the next 50." Women now make up half of American workers. They run some of the world's best companies, such as PepsiCo, Archer Daniels Midland and W.L. Gore. They earn almost 60% of university degrees in America and Europe.

At the same time according to the US department of justice:

Every two minutes, somewhere in America, someone is sexually assaulted. One out of every five American women has been the victims of an attempted or completed rape in their lifetime.

Many professional women reject motherhood entirely; in Switzerland 40% of them are childless. Others delay child-bearing as long as they can. Poor parents are the hardest hit. Work leaves them no time to spend with children.

In India much the same process is happening and women are going through similar experiences. U.N. Studies suggest that rape is even more prevalent in Asia than in the West.

Media is clearly doing a disservice to women's causes by over playing this issue. Already people in high positions are avoiding taking female "interns."

We should also draw a line between sexual harassment and rape. At present in its anxiety to serve the cause of working women the media appears to be lumping together the two entirely separate issues. This may be because, unlike my time when a woman in a newspaper was a novelty and there was no TV, today's media is virtually flooded with women. I call this phenomenon "feminization" of the whole profession of journalism. In cases of sexual harassment there is always the other side of the story. It may be that a complaint is made on this head only when a cosy relationship turns sour. There are various nuances to sexual harassment and it cannot be put in the same category of sexual crimes as rape.

It must be admitted that in all public affairs concerning the business community, people's problems, NGOs and corruption our media enjoys all the freedoms granted to it in Western democracies. The politicians and bureaucrats whom it accuses of corruption have left it free to abuse them as much as it likes. In fact in this respect it is more free than its counterparts in the West because when it chooses to it looses all sense of balance and runs after the same story day in and day out as if nothing else is happening in this wide world. Whether it is Anna Hazare's movement against corruption or anti-gang rape campaign the entire media goes full blast after it till it has beaten the story to pulp. The politicians must have heaved a sigh of relief when the gang rape story broke out and their alleged misdeeds were all but forgotten.

The irony of the situation is that the media owners have imposed a regime of self-censorship to suit their commercial interests and build their own business empires. This is evident from the long interviews that media owners and editors like the Jain brothers who own the Times of India group gave to Ken Aulette of New Yorker magazine of America. The ramifications of this dangerous development have been discussed in this book.

Self-censorship by the media in respect of any activity that might harm the business interests of the media moguls is another hurdle to achieving the objective of complete transparency in public affairs.

For instance, as discussed later in this book, you will never find a line in any national newspaper on certain issues which are destroying the economy and social structure of the country. Land prices in Delhi have shot up 1,00,000 to 3,00,000 times (and even many times more) in the last 60 years and house rents a thousand times. But today owners of newspapers are landlords first and publishing news comes a distant second or third in their priorities. Besides, property developers are their bigger advertises. Also, you will never find a story about non-enforcement of laws, specially the minimum wages act, because they and their middle class readers are all themselves the culprits as poor pay masters. The self-imposed dos and don'ts of the media are far too numerous to be listed here. I, as a senior member of the profession, have knocked on almost every newspaper door to get such issues highlighted and have met with zero success.

The Indian tycoons who own the media are declaring from house tops that their columns and channels are open to the highest bidders. The fig leaf of so called editorial independence has at last been removed. The implications of this cataclysmic dismantling of the Fourth Estate, one of the two last remaining bastions of democracy in India (the other being the judiciary) have to be studied seriously by those who have India's interest at heart. Almost every one in the profession from proprietor to the cub reporter seems to have made influence peddling his main business. Professional integrity is being sacrificed in the pursuit of contact building. I now recall that throughout my career, despite all my pretensions of going straight, I too have been victim of this disease like everyone else.

Thanks to new advances in information technology the next few generations are going to see a game of hide and seek being played by the authorities and the public over matters which each of them wants to keep secret from the other. Tools are fast developing that will make it impossible for any individual to hide his actions. Theoretically speaking, there will be no private space for him. Likewise any individual will make use of the same or other tools to watch the actions of the rulers. Even your thoughts will not be safe from prying eyes. Neuro-scientists and information technologists are teaming up to develop software that can read your thoughts as they occur inside your mind. Some time ago the American government developed a network which hackers could not locate or tamper with. Criminals and drug peddlers are now using it in their world-wide network called the "deep web". Their will always be brave people like Aaron Swartz who gave up his life at the age of twenty-six to make knowledge freely accessible to all. Edward Snowden, Julian Asange, Bradley Manning are other examples of such bravery. All censorship laws can fail before information campaigns launched from abroad. The Arab spring, a revolution in dictatorial Arab countries, was entirely the result of sustained campaigns launched by what is called "the social media." I receive at least a dozen emails every day from various social groups asking me to sign a petition involving the rights of the oppressed and persecuted people in India and the world. Besides my relatives and friends abroad send me by email copies of articles appearing in American and British newspapers and magazines about the scandalous state of affairs in India. This facility is available to subscribers of all dailies and periodicals today.

It is our good fortune that the entire globe is divided into power conglomerations each of whom will always strive for supremacy over the whole world. While this imbroglio between the big powers lasts technological advances will place enough scientific resources in the hands of the common man to unite with other like minded people and defeat the designs of the government to impose a totalitarian regime.

Already the illiterate tribals of Eastern India have developed a network that operates through cell phones. Criminals apart from the "deep web" which criminals are using all over the globe large departments have been created by governments in every country to pry over secrets of their rivals as well as friends. A secret eye implanted on a person can watch every move of the people he meets.

But, for India such activities by individuals or groups are still a dream. For the present the government is trying its utmost to bully and brow beat all those who dare to criticize its policies or the actions of individual autocrats who are accustomed to thriving behind the smoke screen of false publicity.

We should never forget that in America, which we hold as an example of true democracy in all matters, there is something called the First Amendment to the US Constitution which guarantees unlimited freedom to every citizen to speak out his mind freely. Other Western democracies have similar laws. Recently the Supreme Court of America went to the extent of granting the right to privacy in a public place to a criminal whom the New York police had arrested on the basis of CCTV footage on an open road.

But there is a catch here. Eternal vigilance is the price of liberty. All Western democracies, including America, have an intellectual elite which is very zealous in guarding their freedom of expression and shout in unison against the slightest inroads that those in authority seek to make into the constitutional rights of the people. The Right of Freedom of Speech is one of the most important fundamental rights in our Constitution. It must never he diluted. But those who can and should protect it—the members of India's intellectual community—have with few honourable exceptions adopted a staid and status quoist attitude towards the whole related issue of the right to protest. Even in the recent case of the assault on the rights of Expression of The Hindu and Zee TV in Andhra it remains a silent spectator. Our intellectuals are good at making flamboyant appearances in TV debates but most of them shy away from direct action. These comments appear to be a harsh censure of this leading lights of the media and the academic world, but unless they wake up to this dangerous trend of intolerance of the slightest criticism, the nation will be heading towards totalitarianism. Fortunately we still have amongst us stalwarts like Kuldip Nayar—the only Editor who has courted jail to uphold the freedom of the Press—N. Ram and B.G. Verghese who can guide the media community in defending the freedom of the Press. Justice Markandey Katju, Chairman of the Press Council of India and a supporter of the widest media freedom of the right kind can be an asset in such deliberations.

Unfortunately for us, the wings of the fraternity of journalists have been clipped by the virtual disappearance of the Working Journalists Act and its replacement by the contract system under which a journalist can be hired and fired every three years. My job in The Statesman where I served for 31 years was as secure as that of an IAS officer. Today the higher the position a journalist holds in his newspaper or TV channel, the more he is at the mercy of the proprietor who has his own private business interests to pursue on the strength of his media empire. Likewise, members of the academic community are too easily lured by universities for a year or two, attend seminars, to get involved in the mundane and seemingly pedestrian level task of shouting slogans in defence of the Right to Freedom of speech.

The arrest of two TV journalists for their coverage of the visit of the Director General of Andhra police to a godman in the summer of 2013 raises many questions relating to the freedom of expression guaranteed—not only to journalists but to every citizen of India—under the Constitution. An almost identical report of the incident appeared in The Hindu. The state police has slapped a criminal case against the Resident Editor of the newspaper. The Editors Guild of India has described the action of the police a "gross abuse of power over a personal grievance." The Police complaint also alleged that the reports of the visit had tarnished the image of the godman whose family filed a separate complaint about the media coverage.

The Supreme Court and High Courts have upheld the right of the media to criticize "in the public interest" the conduct of government functionaries, which is not becoming of them however high the rank they hold.

The facts of the case are clear. If these factual reports have damaged the image of the DGP and also perhaps that of the holy man he visited, the blame lies with them. But still if they feel aggrieved the laws of the land provide ample opportunity to seek redress for such grievances, in the law of defamation of any individual, not just the police or officers and ministers of the government. There are no two defamation laws, one for ordinary citizens and the other for the dignitaries who happen to be in power who feel that they have the right to arrest any one defaming them.

I can cite a court case which has a direct bearing on the recent developments in Hyderabad. Vacating the interim stay granted by her on the publication of a monthly "pamphlet" called "Devils' Trumpet", Dr. Neera Bharihoke, Additional District Judge cited two important judgements of the Delhi High Court involving noted celebrities and corporates. Vacating the stay it had granted on the "publishing, circulating or selling" the autobiography of Khushwant Singh in a case filed by Maneka Gandhi on the plea that the book damaged her reputation, a bench of the Delhi High Court observed that "the reason (for dismissing the case) is because the interest of the public in knowing the plaintiff in maintaining his (her) reputation."

The other judgement of the Delhi High Court cited by Dr. Bharihoke is even more specific and elaborate. It pertains to a case filed by Mother Dairy Foods and Processing Ltd against Zee Telefilms Ltd. The judgement said:

Hon'ble High Court of Delhi in the matter of Mother Dairy Foods & Processing Ltd. Vs. Zee Telefilms Ltd., AIR 2005 Delhi 195, observed by referring to decision titled Fraser Vs. Evans & Ors. (1969) All E.R.8 as 'The court will not restrain the publication of an article, even though it is defamatory when the defendant says that he intends to justify it or to make fair comment on a matter of public interest.'

The Court also observed "these are some things which are of such public concern that the newspapers, the press and indeed everyone is entitled to make know the truth and to make fair comment on it. This is an integral part of the the right of free speech and expression. It must not be whittled away." Hon'ble High Court of Delhi held that the settled legal position is that where truth, justification and fair comment are pleaded, there is to be no prior restraint on publication unless the court can find it to be a case of malafides.

This is perhaps why the DGP chose the route of direct action to terrorize the media and shut its mouth for all time. Even if the charge that the TV pictures were morphed is true, the channel was merely lampooning the DGP for his misdemeanour. In fact the Chief Minister should have pulled up the police officer for staging such a bizarre exhibition of his powers. The TV Channel or the newspaper did not even remotely suggest that the DGP had committed a cognizable offence.

This is not the first case of its kind. The authorities seem to be applying to the media, including authors, the laws meant for terrorists.

A year ago a TV journalist was arrested and prosecuted in Gawhati for photographing the molestation of a girl by twelve men. Had he not taken the pictures of the event all twelve culprits would have gone unpunished. It was alleged by the police that the journalist instigated the gang to molest the girl. It defies common sense to believe that anyone would commit such a crime knowing that a TV camera shot of his deed when screened on the channel would certainly land him in jail.

On August 29, 2013 the author of a Kannada novel was arrested as his book is alleged to have hurt the religious sentiments of Hindus. Again, in U.P. recently a Dalit writer Kanwal Bharti was arrested for portraying the real plight of dalits and for certain remarks he made on Facebook on the demolition of a madarsa in Rampur district of U.P.

A number of arrests have been made of people making what the authorities consider to be objectionable remarks on Facebook or Twitter. In short, you exercise the freedom of expression guaranteed to you under the Constitution at your own risk. Any moment you can be arrested like a suspected terrorist if your observation does not suit the personal copy book of the officer examining it. These are merely a few examples of what is happening in India today. But these are enough to strike terror in hearts of all Indians to watch their words or be prepared to go to jail any moment. These examples from metropolitan cities are enough to show how public opinion and the media are "managed" in the rest of the country.

The big question that these developments gave rise to is: "Are we heading towards a police state?" I have spent nearly sixty-five years in the profession and I have never heard of a journalist or author being arrested for what he wrote in a newspaper or a book. The only exception is that of Kuldip Nayar who was arrested and kept in jail for several months for heading a group of journalists opposing censorship of the Press when Mrs. Gandhi imposed the Emergency in 1975. But even his arrest was not due to anything he had written. Are we going back to that situation now? Is there a state of Emergency in the country today which justifies the giving of such draconian powers to the police and magistracy? We call ourselves a democracy but in all matters behave as if we are living a dictatorship.

This is not all. We are attacking the Andhra police because we are protected by the laws of the land in capital cities. But what about the goons of political parties operating openly in the rest of the country and furtively in the metropolises? Even in Delhi and other major cities there are gangs who collect the weekly "hafta" from every shop keeper or vendor in their "beat". Lower ranks of different departments like labour, health, sales tax and police operate in much the same way. It is claimed that the money finds its way to the higher ranks as well. They are all mixed up with the "Dadas" of the area who run their own little fiefdoms without regard to the law.

Clearly, there is a case for our media to revise its beat system and put the protection of fundamental rights, not only of the media but of all citizens, on top of the list of beats. Organisations, both governmental and private, engaged in this exercise should be contacted regularly and their activities publicized. Violations of Rights should be widely reported in the national as well as regional media. The present insular tendency of each media house speaking up only when it is attached will not do if the nation is to be saved from the onslaught of growing intolerance and authoritarianism. Likewise media should regularly give "action taken" reports in departments known for their laxity in enforcing the laws. The labour department can be asked for what action it takes against those who do not pay the prescribed wages to their employees. It should report every case of prosecution of an employer for violating this law. Similarly, the health department is supposed to act against a variety of abuses by suppliers of food, milk and water. "Action taken" reports should be obtained from them as well. Sales Tax is another source of public revenue which nobody pays and nobody demands either. If the media got "action taken" reports from the concerned departments, they will wake up and give up their laissez faire attitude.

7

Protest or Perish

The slow death
of Gandhian Austerity

When, about a year ago, Sabita, an Indian woman died in Ireland because doctors refused to abort her fetus as it is an illegal act under Irish law, there were street protests in Europe and America and ultimately the Irish government had to amend the law to permit abortion in such cases. The incident caused no ripples here in the media or public by way of dissent.

Lakhs of children of the poor are kidnapped every year and we hear nothing about it from the Press or public where as there is an instant popular outcry throughout. Europe and America against such offences going unpunished in any corner of the whole region. The shooting of an unarmed Black teenager by a White youth in America and the latter's acquittal by the jury has sent shock waves in the whole of America and Europe which are being expressed loudly by the media and through street protests by people of all races. The US President has himself condemned the judgement of the jury. In India such things are simply hushed up by every body. I was going to give this book the title "Protest or Perish" but desisted because it would have obscured other more important issues covered in it.

The same sentiments were echoed to me by Ram Manohar Lohia, the late socialist leader, nearly two decades later in 1967. Parliamentary democracy by itself would never succeed in changing our social structure unless it was supplemented by the citizens taking to the streets and forcing the Government's hands to bring about the desired changes in the law. I headlined the story of my interview with him for the Statesman Lohia advocates "Socialism of the Streets". He was mighty pleased by the phrase I had coined and repeated it on many occasions.

Lohia's warning of the failings of Parliamentary democracy is more valid today than it was when he uttered it to me forty-five years ago. Today, about a dozen Parliaments later, a penniless pauper like Lohia has no place in our Lok Sabha. The passage of time has transformed the class composition of the House. True, then also a sprinkling of erstwhile Maharajas and Maharanis adorned the House but the bulk of the rest of the members, elected half a century ago in 1962, were sons of the soil. They included some of my own contemporaries at the Allahabad University who occasionally gave me a surprise by their presence in the Central Hall of Parliament which I used to frequent as a special correspondent of The Statesman. Today, barring a handful of leftists, one has to be a multi-crorepati to be an M.P. Most of them practice a diabolic dichotomy, directly or indirectly supporting laws that make the rich richer inside the House, while espousing pro-poor policies in their public speeches and statements. I could feel this downfall in ethical standards of our leaders as time went by, from 1950 to 1990. Chief Ministers like Ravi Shankar Shukla, V.P. Naik, Sucheta Kriplani and Pratap Singh Kairon and Central Ministers like Lal Bahadur Shastri, S.K. Patil Ram Subhag Singh and Biju Patnaik whom I interviewed always meant what they said. I still remember the remark. V.P. Naik, then Chief Minister of Maharashtra, made to me during a two-hour interview in Nagpur in the winter of 1965, a famine year, "Hang me if I fail. I shall make Maharashtra self-sufficient in food within two years". His observation was a banner headline in The Statesman and Naik lived upto his promise.

As I was then on a countrywide tour to assess the extent of the famine, I spent the same night in Chief Minister V.P. Naiks village in Yeofmal district as a guest of his brother who looked after the family property. The total austerity of the place reminded me of Gandhiji's ashram at Sevagram which I had visited twice, in 1944 and 1952.

The only sign of a Chief Minister's pomp I came across during the month-long tour was in Karnataka. Coming from Bangalore I had stopped by to take a look at Mysore's famous Vrindavan Gardens.

As I got into the car to proceed to Mysore we were stopped at the bridge over the river Cauvery and told we could not proceed further till the motorcade of the Chief Minister, Mr. S. Nijalingappa who was expected any moment, had passed. We had to cool our heels for over half-an-hour for the dignitary's cavalcade to precede us on the road. By contrast, in Delhi Jawaharlal Nehru, the Prime Minister, traveled virtually unescorted with only one car traveling ahead of him to clear the way and without interfering with the traffic. An officer of the level of Superintendent of Police traveled with him and usually drove his car. Press reporters would collect around him as soon as he arrived at the venue of a function where he was to speak. A police officer accompanying him jokingly said to us once "you are his security guards". On one such occasion my picture appeared on the front pages of newspapers along with two or three reporters standing behind Nehru.

As Chief Minister of Punjab, Pratap Singh Kairon used to stay in a friend's small house in Hanuman Lane in Connaught Place when he came to Delhi. Likewise Sucheta Kriplani as Chief Minister of U.P. stayed with her husband, the famous Acharya Kripalani, in their modest house on Aurobindo Marg. Ram Subhag Singh, Union Agriculture Minister, sat in his banyan (vest) and Kachha (underwear) milking his cow with his own hands in the back lawn of his bunglow in Lutyen's New Delhi when I called on him on a holiday. He offered me a glass of raw unboiled milk which he was drinking. I had to decline. "It is very good for health", he said.

In 1980 Bhairon Singh Shekhawat, then Chief Minister of Rajasthan, took me to the cattle shed in his bungalow to show me Rajasthan's high yielding cow of which he was very proud. Bhim Sen Sachar, then Chief Minister of Punjab himself took me on a round of some flooded villages near Jullunder in his jeep in 1955 when I was working for The Tribune. The famous Sardar Swaran Singh was a lawyer living in a small bungalow in Jullunder when I met him in 1951 for the publisher of a Who's Who directory. He winced when, as per the instructions of my employer, I told him at the end of the interview that "Of course, Sir you won't mind making a small contribution of Rs.250 (equal to today's Rs.10,000) towards the cost of the directory". He quietly paid. (The publisher was of the view that once a "clever" interviewer had made his victim look like a real hero through his questions he would be only too happy to pay for the service we were rendering to him. I never disappointed my boss in the "cleverness" he expected of me). I can reel off a lot of such names to prove my point that Ministers, M.P.S. and MLAs of the early decades of the post-Independence era were ordinary people with roots in the soil of India. Another trait which I cannot forget is the habit of numerous central and State ministers and M.P.s, including prime ministers, to transact official business and meet people squatting on the floor with or without bolsters. Charan Singh, Morarji Desai, Lal Bahadur Shastri, Ravi Shankar Shukla are only some of them. Kamlapati Tripathi, as UP's Chief Minister and later Railway Minister at the Centre, used to sit or lie on a settee with his feet stretched outward for the convenience of his visitors and subordinates who had to kneel and touch them before they sat down. Journalists were the only class perhaps that was exempted from this practice. He was a real Pandit in the true sense of the word. All these dignitaries were humble, down to earth, people and some of them like Nehru (before he became Prime Minister) and Ravi Shankar Shukla (as Chief Minister of M.P.) even came upto the verandah to see off a reporter. Shukla used to take Sant Tukdoji Maharaj, a revered saint of Madhya Pradesh, to sing bhajans (devotional songs) at his election rallies. Today's politicians use Bollywood stars for this supporting role to win elections. Among all these leaders who came to power at the time of independence, Charan Singh is the only one who completely identified himself with the peasants of India. E.F. Schumacher's book Small Is Beautiful was his bible. He stood for a caste-less India. He kept his simple profile intact when he became Prime Minister. He is one of the few old time leaders who did not promote his family member's fortunes. His son, Ajit Singh, joined politics during the last year of his father's life to save his party from extinction. Before that he was a computer engineer in America. I and my wife were stranded in Baraut, charan Singh's constituency, on a winter evening in 1979 when our car broke down on our way to my home town, Gangoh. We approached the nearest wayside petrol station. It had a small one-room office. Its young proprietor offered us a room on the terrace of his modest three-storey house crammed inside a narrow lane. While leaving in the morning after getting my car repaired I offered to pay him for the night's stay. He declined and told me casually "my wife is a grand daughter of Chaudhary Charan Singh, the Prime Minister of India."

I was surprised. The house was so ancient with only two Hessan cots as the sole furniture in the room, and though educated, the man so simply dressed, that it seemed hard to believe that he could be a person of such high connections.

But Charan Singh was a politician of a different mettle. He persistently opposed Nehru's view of farming through Soviet style collective or cooperative farms and paid a heavy price for it. He could take criticism in his stride. When he became Deputy Prime Minister with the Home portfolio after the elections in 1977 I went to see him. As far as I remember he was then convalescing after an illness in a quarter of Ram Manohar Lohia hospital and holding court squatting on a carpet in the verandah surrounded by his coterie of confidents including his wife. As soon as he saw me enter the small courtyard he hailed me and said "M.B. Lal now I know what opinion you have of me. I have seen the secret letter you sent from Lucknow to your editor about me during the Emergency." He said it in good humour and without bitterness which was unlike any central or State Minister I had dealt with.

C.R. Irani, Managing Director of The Statesman was a stanch opponent of the Emergency imposed by Mrs. Gandhi to continue ruling the country after the Allahabad High Court had disqualified her from being a Member of Parliament for six years. In view of strict censorship on the Press, the Statesman correspondents were asked to keep the Editor informed of major developments through personal notes. I had come to know that after he came out of jail in 1976 Charan Singh was negotiating a secret deal with Mrs. Gandhi through a common friend who had sought my advice on how this could be done. I had sent a note to Mr. Irani and the Editor that Charan Singh may prove to be a "turn coat" and was not to be trusted. As usual I had sent this report on the teleprinter little knowing that before reaching the Editor it would first land on the desk of Mrs. Gandhi's censor officers.

Apparently some smart official had considered my report important enough to be forwarded to the intelligence department from where it found its way to Charan Singh's dossier in the Home Ministry. The first thing Chaudhary Sahab must have done on becoming the Home Minister of India would be to summon the file on him maintained by the Ministry.

After reading such a report about himself any other politician in his place would have unceremoniously thrown me out of his house. As I was coming out of the quarter allotted to him by the hospital, Kuldip Nayar, then Editor of the Express, was walking in. Besides being an editor he had been a fellow sufferer with Charan Singh during the Emergency and was perhaps the only senior journalist to be jailed by Mrs. Gandhi. Soon after coming out of jail he wrote a book about his prison experiences which had a good sale. In the crucial, U.P. elections of 1973-74, when he was my boss in The Statesman Nayar's forecast after a hurried trip to parts of U.P. had proved to be more accurate than mine which I had written after a month-long grueling trip of 35 districts. He had concurred with me that Congress would win the elections but he gave Charan Singh's BLD the second place while I had given that slot to the Jana Sangh (now BTP). He was right.

The only dark side of Charan Singh's otherwise clean record was that in his constituency in Chhaprauli village Dalits were not allowed to caste their votes in the elections because of their animosity with the dominant Jat community to which Charan Singh belonged. I visited a polling booth in Chhaprauli during election time. It wore a deserted look. I was told by the timid election officer that all voters had caste their votes in the morning. It was alleged by the opposition parties that Jats of the village had taken control of the booth and voted for the Harijan voters as well. Raj Narain who called himself Charan Singh's Hanuman was an equally simple man. An ardent Lohia follower he always espoused peasant causes.

The new generation of Ministers, M.P.s and M.L.A.s, many of them sons and daughters of the above mentioned old guard, are entirely a different breed. Most of them are mere sound and fury without substance. Real speakers like Bhupesh Gupta, Renu Chakraverty, H.V. Kamath Ram Manohar Lohia, Vasant Sathe, Krishna Menon and a host of others like them are gone. I happened to be in the Press gallery of Lok Sabha when Lohia made his brief and historic intervention which reverberated throughout the country for a long time. "Pandit jee", he said shouting at the top of his voice, "for all your rhetoric and claims of progress the average income of the Indian farmer is still three annas a day. You can have this figure checked by your officials. I shall resign my seat in Parliament, if I am proved wrong". Such self-assurance and such commitment to the interests of the common man is rare to be found among today's leaders.

I am not sure at what point of time national parties started using their Chief Ministers to clandestinely collect funds, ostensibly for fighting elections, by granting illegal favours to industrialists, businessmen, and contractors property developers who build urban colonies. The judgement of Justice Jagmohan Lal of the Allahabad High Court in the case against Indira Gandhi which I attended and covered for The Statesman, suggests that the practice might have started during her regime but I cannot be sure on this point. I am a great admirer of Mrs. Gandhi. She pushed India ahead on the road to freedom by eliminating, as far as she could, the influence of feudal elements within the country and were acting in league with imperialist forces who wanted to impose a new kind a colonialism on India. By abolishing the privy purses of erstwhile princes she completed the process of national integration set in motion by Sardar Vallabhai Patel who forced all princely states to merge with India. He had to send the army into the Nizam's territory to force the accession of the princely state of Hyderabad. Mrs. Gandhi realized that the Maharajas were misusing their residual powers and privileges like privy purses to stage a comeback. Their mischief had to be nipped in the bud. She took courage in both hands and abolished their privy purses. Likewise big private banks were diverting public funds to serve the private ends of speculators and international agencies. She promptly nationalized 14 major banks and thus brought the economy on the right track. But the crowning glory of her reign was the acceleration of the liberation of Bangla Desh which the freedom fighters in that country would have taken a few decades more to accomplish. It was inevitable that such an impetuous ruler would commit Himalayan blunders such as population control through forced sterilization of men and women and sending the army into the Golden Temple in Amritsar, the holiest of holy shrines of the Sikhs. Each time she had to pay a heavy price for her mistakes, in the latter case even lose her life. If she was imperious in her behaviour it was because it was not possible to rule such a large country in any other manner.

During a Press meet in 1971 when she was on a whirlwind election tour of the country I asked her in Chandigarh, "Madam, why have you come to address an election rally here even before you have decided the name of your candidate from this Parliamentary constituency?"

"We ask for votes for the party (meaning herself) not the candidate" she replied.

A few minutes later she repeated my question and her answer at the mass rally of about 1,00,000 people. To her the word "Congress" was a synonym for Indira Gandhi. She won the election with a thumping majority, securing for her party 352 seats in a house of 518(?) That was the period when the Assam Congress Chief, Deo Kant Baruah, had made his famous pronouncement "India is Indira and Indira is India". During the Emergency the same Baruah switched over to the opposition side. Soon after she returned to power she chose V.P. Singh to be Chief Minister of U.P. The young, starry-eyed V.P. Singh had told me then in an interview in U.P. Niwas in Delhi, "I am a servant of Sanjay Gandhi (Indira Gandhi's younger son and the power behind her throne) and will do whatever he orders me to do. Narayan Dutt Tiwari, expressed similar sentiments to me when he succeeded H.N. Bahuguna as Chief Minister of U.P., in Lucknow in 1976.

Mrs. Gandhi ruled the country like an empress. Her word was law. As soon as a Chief Minister became too big for his boots and courted popularity in his state, she called him to Delhi to become a cabinet minister in her Government. This was precisely the fate of Kamlapati Tripathi as Chief Minister of U.P. and Bahuguna, his successor. Bahuguna bided his time for some months and later revolted to join the opposition along with Jagjiwan Ram and other leaders during the Emergency.

The rise of Sanjay Gandhi and his coterie of young politicians and Chief Ministers as an extra-constitutional authority started a chain of events over which she had no control. I had heard Sanjay Gandhi and Maneka whom he had recently married speak at an election meeting in Amethi in February 1977. The gathering was thin. Only about a hundred people had collected to hear them. Their speeches were equally disappointing. Sanjay, his mother's spoilt child, liked to be treated by her party as a demi-god. His faithful advisers had encouraged him to make a small car named Maruti and a site was selected near Gurgaon. It became a subject of controversy. When I posed this issue to my communist friend R.K. Garg, the Supreme Court lawyer, he brushed it aside. "Do you expect Indira Gnadhi's son to make a bicycle?", he quipped. The CPI was then blindly supporting Mrs. Gandhi. Political morality was judged by national and international alliances and not by the principles of ethics. I am not for a moment suggesting that starting of Maruti car factory was the beginning of irregular practices and loss of probity in our political ethos. In the early Fifties Nehru had to ask T.T. Krishnamchari his Finance Minister and his very close friend, K.D. Malviya, the Oil Minister, to step down for their alleged nexus with some big businessmen. Then followed the Kamraj Plan which trigerred the "voluntary" resignations of several Central Ministers and Chief Ministers of States, including stalwarts like Pratap Singh Kairon and Bakshi Gulam Mohammad. Like the case of Sanjay's Maruti, the allegations against these VIPs have never been proved. They are all mere conjectures or suspicions. By the year 1990 secret funding of political parties and politicians became the talk of the town. There was the infamous Bofor's deal and the so-called Harshad Mehta scandal. Around that time I was myself a witness to the General Secretary of a political party issuing orders on phone to his Chief Ministers of his party to give large sums of money to the couriers (all of them party leaders) he was sending to them for a party project. What must have started like a trickle at the dawn of Independence has now become an uncontrollable flood. In 1947 while I was a university student, I was traveling in a car with a Parliamentary Secretary (a junion Minister) to Pandit Gobind Ballabh Pant, U.P.'s Chief Minister, from Allahabad to Lucknow. On the way we stopped by at the house of the District Superintendent of Police, Pratapgarh, who gave us a lavish tea.

Congressmen throwing their weight about had begun the moment India became Independent in 1947 and so had corruption.

Foreign influence to exploit India's wealth to benefit giant multi-national corporations which was kept in check till the Seventies and early Eighties has by now virtually taken over the nation's economy. Its harmful effect on the masses is transparently visible and yet nobody points an accusing finger at the culprits, the Indian politicians and businessman who derive the benefits from them. In the Nineteen Sixties the American Embassy was distributing among journalists through its publicity arm, the USIS, free copies of the book "Brain Washing in Red China". But what China and Russia did then to promote Godless socialism of their respective brands, pales into insignificance before the tsunami hurricane like avalanche of the doctrine of "consumerism based on globalised capitalism" that has swept almost the entire intelligensia of the world, including that of China and Russia, off its feet. Forgotten are Mao, Gandhi and Lenin. Also forgotten are our great writers and poets like Wordsworth, Thoreau, Emerson and Whitman as well as more recent revolutionaries like Tariq Ali and the great Beatles who spawned the so-called Hippie movement throughout the world which spurned glamourous living and all pomp and show, and showed by their own example how to enjoy life like Tennyson's Lotus Caters. Forgotten also are astute warnings by august institutions like the Club of Rome that gave the world the charter called A Blueprint for Survival. Also in the Sixties a plethora of books like E.F. Schumacher's famous "Small Is Beautiful" came out. And finally, we now have the Greenpeace Movement and the long harangues at international governmental and non-governmental conferences on the spectre of climate change looming before us, giving what sounds like a last warning to save the planet from an irreversible catastrophe whose sole cause is the doctrine of "consumerism based on globalised capitalism". In India this process has been accelerated by the emergence of several extra constitutional authorities who were lying dormant or were plainly suppressed during 1947 to 1984 when Nehru, Shashtri and Indira Gandhi held the post of Prime Minister. They made their first appearance during the "Khichri sarkar" of the Janta

Party from 1977 to 1980 which was a loosely knit coalition of several anti-Indira Gandhi parties.

For the first three decades after Independence in1947, with the abolition of Zamindari and the advent of the green revolution, the common man in India came into his own. Villages thrived, labour laws were rigidly enforced and farmers ruled the country. Most of the Central and state ministers and Chief Ministers had a rural background. They were truly 'sons of the soil.' The entire cabinets of Maharashtra and Gujarat were packed with Ministers who ran rural cooperative societies. So were most of the MLAs. In Punjab and Haryana nearly all the ministers were farmers. The picture all over the country was more or less the same. Almost all of them preferred to transact business sitting on the floor. And some like Kamraj, Lal Bahadur Shastri, Charan Singh, and Morarji Desai conducted even Press conferences sitting on carpeted floors lined with large bolsters. They understood the dignity of rural labour in their veins. There was no Maoist movement worth the name then. Many among them were noted trade unionists. If they mad some money on the sidelines, they took care to conceal it from public view so that it did not become a scandal. They sent their children to study in the same schools and colleges where our children went. Even clerks and peons could afford such education for their progeny. The trend towards westernisation of education had begun in a hush manner in the sixties even in the homes of communists but there were no special schools which only the rich could afford. During that period I visited the house of a communist leader with a colleague who hailed from her home state and knew her well. She used to occupy the front benches on the opposition side in Parliament, was a vivacious speaker and with her shrill voice which rang through the Lok Sabha, she reminded me of the late Sarojini Naidu. She gave us tea when suddenly an elderly gentleman, a leading light in the party, arrived unannounced. On hearing from her attendant about the visitor she rushed to the adjoining room where children were playing Western rock music. She asked them to stop it saying "so and so Dada has come (she named the leader). What will he say if he bears this?" Foreign educated was confined to those who got scholarships from the host universities.

Likewise, during the first three decades after Independence there were hardly any private nursing homes or hospitals, accept those run by religions missions which were preferred because they gave excellent service at a low price. When I had a tooth problem and went to the PGI, the famous government college in Chandigarh, Brish Bhan the ex-chief minister of PEPSU, was waiting for his turn in the ante-chamber of the dental surgeon. The superintendent of the union territory government hospital, Dr. Preetam Singh, was widely known for being an excellent surgeon. He used to perform many operations on VIP's in the city.

There were few cars on the roads. Barring exceptional cases only two indigenous makes, Ambassador and Fiat, were permitted to sell cars. Standard motors joined the league later. Most people used public transport for local and long distance travel. Air traffic, both domestic and international, was confined only to the top one percent of the population. Most people traveled by bus and train. All-in-all there was not much difference between the life styles of the man on the street and the rich. Even the poorest man could aspire to join the other class.

During the next three decades everything changed. There arose an ever burgeoning stinking rich middle class from almost nowhere which not only looked down upon the lower "classes" (a word which in essence means "castes") with contempt and arrogance but also created barriers which the other group could never cross. They built for themselves air conditioned shopping centres called malls which the lower castes could not afford to enter, schools which charged for each child fees that was equal to a months pay of an ordinary worker, hospitals and missing homes whose charges for a minor ailment were equal to a year's salary of the common man and pleasure resorts and picnic spots which cost a fortune to enter. Cars priced a hundred times more than the ordinary Ambassador and Fiat that we used to drive mushroomed in their millions on the country's roads. Flats that cost a thousand times more than our old homes in posh newly built multi-storeyed colonies sprang up everywhere as land prices to 1,00,000 times of those that had prevailed about sixty years ago. Weddings and receptions which cost crores of rupees each became the order of the day. Every major city in India got connected by air. The big airports looked like bus stands with a plane taking off or landing every minute. Air conditioned metros came up for the convenience of the middle class. Its fares as well as those of other public transport were placed at levels at which the ordinary worker paid through his nose. The list of luxuries that this new middle class created for itself to outside wealthy citizens of Western countries in interminable. So is its greed for money for which it is prepared to sacrifice every cherished value or principle. I know all this because I am myself a member of this class of parasites whose unearned incomes are a dozen times more than what they earn by dint of hard labour.

The question that the whole world, except the Indian elite, is asking is that where did all this money come from considering that per capita incomes have been rising only about two percent and GDP about six to eight percent per year? The obvious answer is that all this is the result of polices that suck the poor man's blood till he is left with only bones and no flesh. These policies are pursued in the name of so-called 'reforms'. Even the multi-national corporations which are pleading for 'reforms' should realize that they cannot sell more of their products unless we put adequate purchasing power in the hands of the people. That is why Nobel Laureate Amartya Sen has been saying that the masses much get what he calls their minimum "entitlement". China has done this before introducing reforms, India has not, he says. This is why I admire people like Medha Pathak, Arundhati Roy, Rajendra Sachar, Kuldip Nayar, Binayak Sen, N. Ram, P. Sainath and so many others who plead the cause of the poor and injustly persecuted and displaced masses of India whose only fault, frankly speaking, is that they belong to the lower castes who have since times immoral been slaves' of the upper castes.

Simultaneously, irons gates were fixed on all these colonies of the novae riche, and sentries posted on round the clock duty to keep out lower caste people. Some colonies placed further restrictions like finger printing of all blue collar workers who entered them, production of identity cards and submission of two photos.

Instead of being equals that they were during the first three decades after Independence they became objects of charity. Free schools, dispensaries and mid day meals were started to take care of the people whom we have rendered poor because of our zeal for "reforming" the economy.

There can be no better assessment of what foreigners think of us than an un-contradicted confidential report believed to have been sent by the American Embassy in Delhi to the US state department. It is part of the documents leaked by Julian Asange's Wikileaks and published in The Hindu of April 11, 2013. They show how the virus of corruption has seeped into the blood stream of Indian society.

The proof of the U.S. Embassy's secret report to Washington on corruption in India will be visible to you if you only care to drive through any of the lanes and bylanes of our metro cities. You will find them jam-packed with gleaming large limousines (not just ordinary cars) from end to end of the city. Ornate fronts with decorated balconies and a team security guards posted at every gate will greet you amongst other signs of opulence and luxury.

At the same time if you walk through the crowded lane of a slum which must adjoin every habitat of the elite, you will find it wallowing in its own squalour, with no municipal services except a common tap for the whole street, an electric pole which hardly ever gets power supply, stinking drains with half the pot holes removed for ever, people shitting on the roads in the absence of toilets and at the doors of the one-room dilapidated houses not even a bicycle, which used to be the poor man's friend as it was mine till the age of 29 when I joined The Statesman.

The contrast between the elite styles of the elite class and the poor who live like slaves and caged animals is disgusting but most members of our new middle class do not think so. The question is where did all this money that the middle class is squandering come from? The U.S. Embassy's secret note answers that question.

8

To Sewagram

How I was turned back from Gandhi's Ashram in 1944

In the year 1944 when I was in my sixteenth year and a student of the twelfth class in Meerut College at Meerut in Western U.P. I decided to plunge into the freedom movement and go to Gandhiji's Sewagram Ashram near Wardha to offer my services to the nation. I was living in the Muslim hostel in sylvan surroundings, close to the cantonment where large battalions of the Indian army led by British officers lived. Some all White units from England awaiting orders to move to the Eastern Front were also camping in it. For their entertainment there existed in the fashionable wide streeted Bombay Bazar a picture house where they all congregated to see English movies. Being a regular fan of English films I used to see them there. The rich flavour of the pastries and cakes I used to devour from the canteen of the theatre hall during the intervals lingers in my mouth to this day. Most of the films we saw were about the war. I still remember the very touching last scene of a movie in which all five sons of an American railway guard had joined the war. One day when he was standing near his cabin at the tail end of a long goods train, flag in hand, an officer of the American army comes and salutes him and says

"I have bad news for you Mr . . . ."

"Which One?"

"All Five"

"All five!"

Driven by habit and instinct the dazed father of five young American soldiers of whose death he had just been informed, looked at his watch, blew his whistle, waved the green flag, climbed into his cabin which had just jerked as the train moved and standing in its door responded to the salute of the army officer who stood rooted to the ground watching the train till it disappeared from his view.

The movie ended there but I have thought about this haunting scene ever since. This is the ugly face of wars of all kinds. You may call it jehad, crusades, genocide, ethnic cleansing, heroism or by any other name. The end result of all wars is pain for which there is no cure. Like most young Indians of the time I passionately longed to see Subhash Bose marching triumphantly at the head of his Indian National Army to the Red Fort in Delhi and hoisting the national flag to mark India's independence from British rule. We looked forward to the victory of the Axis powers led by Hitler. Subhash Bose's clarion call. "An enemy's enemy is our friend" had rung true in my ears ever since I had heard it from his own lips at a massive public rally in Meerut in the winter of 1939 to attend which I and my father had walked a mile when I was only eleven. Hitler had declared himself to be a pure Aryan, "the most superior race on earth," and adopted our Vedic symbol the 'Swastika' as his national emblem. Here was a man who would restore our Hindu religion to its pristine glory, we thought then. At the same time I was an avid reader of books by Gandhi, Nehru, Lokmanya Tilak, Tagore and other national leaders, besides the Hindustan Times then edited by Mahatma Gandhi's son, Devdas Gandhi. All of them preached a non-violent struggle for freedom.

My mind at that time was a mixture of emotions. In fact, till this day it has always remained like that. Hamlet's "to be or not to be", has always remained the central question of my life.

It was not that we hated the British rulers. If it was so how could merely an estimated hundred thousand Englishmen resident in India have ruled a nation of two hundred million people. The strategists in England quickly realized that besides being habitually corrupt Indians made good "slaves". A friendly master-slave relationship quickly developed between the rulers and the ruled. They invented the institution called Brown Saheb and through it ruled an empire on which it was said that the Sun never set. Not only did they rule India through this mechanism but exported Indians to their other colonies throughout the world with remarkable success. That is how Mahatma Gandhi went to the British ruled country called South Africa. He went there as a Brown Saheb.

They took away labourers from U.P., Bihar and Tamil Nadu, babus from Bengal, traders from Sindh and Gujarat, soldiers from Punjab (which comprised a large chunk of present Pakistani Punjab and Haryana) West U.P. and Nepal and teachers and intellectuals from all over the country. They soon realized that Indians made good "slaves" of the empire so long as Britain recognized them as a race superior to the natives of the colony they governed and gave them a free hand to make money by whatever means. It was Indian soldiers who brought victory to England on all fronts in World Wars-I and II. Indians were loaded with medals, knighthoods and other titles and awards to make them feel distinctive and great. This is all they wanted. In India the system worked beautifully. A cozy partnership was quickly formed between the British imperialist power on the one hand and the rajas, zamindars and taluquedars, and Indian administrators on the other, to rule the country and exploit the poor masses. The pattern continues to this day, with the imperialist powers having gone underground and ruling by proxy.

In this environment of bonhomie between the ruler and the ruled where everything appeared to look normal it was difficult for a sensitive youth like me to choose between Gandhi and Bose. Was Gandhi not playing into the hands of the British rulers was a question many young men like me were asking.

Nehru was one of the greatest scholars India has produced in modern times. Had he not become prime minister he would have been acclaimed as a great historian. His three books, the Autobiography, Glimpses of World History and Discovery of India are among the great classics of Indian literature. I read them all as soon as they were published. He was opposed to the Hitler doctrine and was largely responsible for shaping the pro-British policy of the Congress during World War-II. The Congress had launched the Quit India movement from August 9, 1942 but had not declared its support to Hitler or Subhas Bose. It had continued to believe in non-violence.

The violence that occurred in some places during the movement was because all Congress leaders had been put in jail and there was no one left to control the mobs agitating for freedom. For a while Chitoo Pandey, a local leader, had liberated Ballia, the eastern most district of U.P., in what is known today the Maoist or Naxalite style. Similar incidents were occurring in other parts of the country. But due to the strict censorship in force then none of these events were reported in the papers. We heard of them as they spread by word of mouth. Lal Padmakar Singh, a student of Allahabad University which I joined later was shot dead by the police when the youth of the institution were staging a huge demonstration. To this day his statue stands as a memorial of that ghastly outrage perpetrated by our British rulers upon innocent Indian students, in the quardrangle facing the university's main gate and the students' union hall. Similar battles between the youth and the police were going on all over the country. The whole nation was in turmoil. I remembered that on August 9, 1942, the Quit India day, my classmate in class X, R.K. Garg (later a famous Supreme Court lawyer and a leader of the Communist party) was sitting outside the school gate with a few fellow students trying to persuade us to boycott school. I also remembered the 'prabhat pheri' (morning procession) that I had joined in the winter of 1939 to protest against the dismissal of popular governments in the provinces by the British Government on the declaration of war against Hitler's Germany. About 5000 students belonging to almost all the schools in Meerut marched in formations of four abreast, class-section-wise, through the narrow markets, streets and lanes of the city, singing Gandhi's favourite songs of freedom and devotion. Prabhat pheris were a common way of propagating a movement, ideology or religion. At the break of dawn people in small or large numbers would walk through the streets of a city or village singing devotional songs.

When I was ten my father had given me the three-volume book in Hindi by Pandit Sunder Lal called 'Bharat Mein Angrezi Raj' (British Rule in India) It was a proscribed book whose possession could lend a person in jail. The book describes in detail all the atrocities committed by the English army and its cunning officers since the Seventeenth Century to gain control of the country I had also walked a mile with my father from our house to attend a rally addressed by Subhas Bose in the Parade Grounds beyond the Clock Tower in Meerut. Apart from Jawaharlal Nehru's funeral in Delhi in May 1964, it was the biggest public meeting I have ever seen. An estimated 1,00,000 people had gathered to hear him explain his theory "enemy's enemy is our friend". It was also perhaps the last public speech Subhas Bose delivered in India before he slipped quietly away to Germany by a land route via Kabul and Russia. I was thus inadvertently participating in a great event in the history of India's freedom movement. Though a government servant my father, Jagdish Prasad, was a nationalist at heart. He had also encouraged me to make an album of pictures of the war appearing in the newspaper which is perhaps partly responsible for my taking to journalism as my profession.

Gandhi was the only leader to be released in 1944. Other leaders, including Nehru, remained in jail till the end of the war in the following year. I longed passionately to plunge into this struggle and play my role in the movement for freedom. The only course to realize my ambition at the time seemed to be to seek Bapu's guidance by going to his ashram and offering my services to him. Without revealing my plan to any one, not even my roommate in the hostel, I set off for Wardha. Before going to the Meerut railway station I got my head shaved by a barbar to look a real brahmchari. I had been reading Gandhi's Harijan and other small books that he used to bring out recommending the ascetic's way of life and imagined that a young man with a shaven head would please Bapu. The journey was uneventful but for the unique experience of traveling in a railway guard's cabin for a short distance at Itarsi. The Indian railway network had been distributed by the Government among several British owned companies which worked in tandem with each other under a complex accounting system they alone knew. I took the North Western Railway (NWR) from Meerut to Delhi, Great Peninsular Railway (GPR) from Delhi to Nagpur via Itarsi where I had to change to another train going South. I had to take another GPR train from Nagpur to Wardha. I could have taken a direct GPR train from Delhi to Nagpur but this would have meant a long wait at Delhi railway station which was in a state of perpetual activity due to movement of war supplies and troops needed simultaneously for The Eastern Front and to control the disturbances in trouble spots where the Quit India movement had gained momentum. Japanese troops and the Indian National Army led by Subhas Bose had entered Kohima and Imphal and could open another front on the eastern coast of India which had to be guarded. There was no New Delhi railway station then and the ill equipped Delhi main station had to handle all the heavy traffic. So I chose a train that would involve the least wait at Delhi. By contrast Itarsi, though the hub of all railway traffic passing through central India, was a small village. It had huge platforms and railway yards. The platforms wore a deserted look when my train arrived there around midnight. I was hungry and went to one of the few food stalls mounted on small trolleys parked near the exit gate. There I struck acquaintance with a uniformed railway employee who turned out to be the guard of the train I was to take for my journey to Nagpur. He became interested in me when I told him I was going to the Sewagram Ashram of Gandhiji to seek his guidance. Mere mention of Mahatma Gandhi's name seemed to be "open sesame" that could open any door to a stranger. He plied me with several questions about my parentage, education, ancestry and home town. After chatting with him for a while I asked him hesitantly whether I could travel in his cabin for an hour or two. He was taken aback. No one had ever made such a request to him. He glared at me inquiringly. All my belongings—a change of clothes—were contained in a jute hand bag.

"First, I shall have to examine your ticket."

I showed it to him. It was like a hotel bill on a printed and duly filled form of NWR since Meerut station did not have a direct ticket to Wardha in its stock. "Come with me", he said.

I had a special reason for my curiosity to observe the life of a railway guard at close quarters. Three years earlier in 1941, a relative of mine, husband of a cousin, had been selected to class I service in the East India Railway, one of the highest jobs an Indian could aspire to. It was on the basis of his new position that my uncle had offered him his daughter in marriage. But my uncle was not aware of a snag which lay ahead for the new entrant to the class I railway service. Every officer had to serve for the first one or two years as a guard, starting with a goods train and then slowly graduating to the passenger and mail trains.

British employers were hard task masters in matters of the routine of a job. An I.C.S. officer, Forest conservator or an irrigation engineer must know horse riding to be confirmed in his job. My relative had found the duties of a guard too tough for him. He had passed with a first class first in the M.A. examination in Political Science from the Allahabad University. When he applied for a lectureship in the university he was bluntly told by the Head of the Political Science Department, the appointing authority, "You backed the wrong horse". The term meant the professor's rival in the department whose favorite student he had been. He then sought this job in the railways and got it. But at heart he was a scholar. Working as a guard of a goods train meant keeping irregular hours, being stranded for hours or some times days, in no man's land at some unknown rural railway station. During war time they had added a few more coaches and wagons to the trains which the platforms were too short to accommodate. The result was the guard's cabin was usually parked on hard gravel, far away from all the facilities of the station. To these hardships was added the terror of unwanted intruders like wild animals when the train stood stranded in a forest. An accidental fall from a moving train was for my relative the proverbial last straw on the camel's back. He resigned his post (a decision which he regretted all his life) and looked for other options in business and industry.

My encounter with a railway guard at Itarsi offered me a good opportunity to get a first hand glimpse into a guard's life. The train left at about 2 a.m. After settling down in his cabin when the train had left Itarsi station and its outer signals, I related my relative's story to my host. "College education makes our young men faithless sissies. They have neither faith in God nor in their own prowess. Sitting glued to their books they lose touch with the real world of plough and harrow"

On his small shelf lay a copy of the Ramayana and a small booklet with a picture of Lord Hanuman and the words Hanuman Chalisa printed on it. There were also a few small books of Hindi short stories and novels.

"Whenever I feel lonely and bored I recite the Hanuman Chalisa or read a portion of the Ramayana. In a corner of the hard berth, his only seat which he shared with me, I espied a copy of the latest Illustrated

Weekly. "I am fond of solving crossword puzzles of this magazine", he explained.

"It was my hobby too in my high school days. Now I get no time for it", I said.

"Yes it needs a lot of time and intelligence too", he said

He told me a guard's life was hard but also peaceful. This was perhaps the only profession in the railways which provided no opportunity to make a "little extra money".

"What about railway drivers?"

If they want they can sell the coal they burn by dropping it at a few fixed points where the buyers, mostly owners of brick kilns, pick it up." He said and added "but I have no complaints. The company has given me a quarter in the railway colony at Itarsi. My children go to school in the village. I have a big cow which grazes freely in the nearby fields and gives our family all the milk and ghee and butter we need. When I retire I will go back to my village in Yeotmal district and tend my farm."

This is the only part of my conversation with the railway guard that I remember since I have been narrating it to my friends over and over again. At the next halt of the train, about two hours away, I picked up my bag and moved to the adjoining ordinary compartment where I managed to find space on an upper berth and went to sleep. I woke up about lunch time near Nagpur where I had to take another train to Wardha. I reached Wardha in the evening. A fellow passenger on the train had told me that some provision stores in the main market of Wardha took lodgers. I found a place in one of them. It was a long room with three doors opening on the market. Half of it was a shop selling grain, sugar and other food items. In the other half night boarders could sleep on the floor on a charge of half-a-rupee per night. Sleeping on the hard floor was not a novelty to me. I had only two months earlier slept on a circular dining table in a crowded guest house in Sialkot on my way back from a holiday in Kashmir. In the previous year, while traveling from Saharanpur to Mirzapur I had spent a night on the crowded floor of the small verandah of a dharmshala (a free inn), at Benares (now Varanasi)

Next morning after a light breakfast at a nearby shop selling hot milk, I walked the three or four miles to the Mahatma's Sewagram Ashram in a gay and carefree mood. Sewagram turned out to be a small cluster of huts plastered with mud which shone bright in the light of the Sun. The place wore a deserted look. All around it, as far as the eye could reach, were green fields. Only on one end of the road which had brought me to this idyllic habitat of the greatest Indian ever born, I espied the outline of a village. Not far from the gate, in the middle of the small campus stood a long room, parallel to the road. I peeped into it through a window and saw a youngish person sitting and arranging some files. I walked to the door around the corner of the wall and entered. The young man turned out to be one of the assistant secretaries of Gandhiji.

He looked surprised when I told him the purpose of my visit.

"I appreciate your patriotism but we do not recruit freedom fighters here. You have to do constructive work in your own area. We are doing a lot of work in Meerut. The Khadi Ashram is there. You can approach those people. At the moment Bapu is not giving any fresh call to youth to launch a movement or court arrest. The best course for you will be to go back to your college and complete your studies."

I was crest fallen but persisted. "Bapu also advises us to boycott colleges established by the British."

"Bapu is not against higher education. What he means is we should start our own colleges like Kashi Vidyapeeth. When he gives a call students in the universities should come out and join our movement."

"Can I have a 'darshan' (glimpse) of Bapu?"

"Yes, at the evening prayers, not before."

"Can I speak to him?"

"Of course, after the prayer meeting".

This would have meant walking back to Wardha for my lunch and coming to Sevagram again and then spending another night at Wardha.

There was no one else I could talk to. If there were more people in the ashram they must be busy in their rooms. Nor did I ask if I could meet any one else. Though I had occasion to visit Sewagram with my class as a student of journalism at Hislop College, Nagpur, in January 1953, five years after Gandhi's death, my memories of the place are vague. All I remember is that besides the small table and chair where the young man whose name was Desai sat, there was placed in front of it a long table with newspapers kept on it and a wooden bench on which people could sit and read them. There was an almirah in the small wall behind Desai's back for files and a few books. On the walls of the room an artist had painted a few designs.

Of my second visit to the place nearby nine years later all that I can recall is the mud plastered kitchen. Squatting before it on mattresses we had a simple meal.

After my brief talk with Desai I picked up my bag which I had placed on the bench near me and walked out of the room crest fallen. Before leaving I took a long look at the seemingly empty ashram. Then with leisurely gait I walked four miles to Wardha railway station to retrace my long journey back home.

To say I was dazed at the moment would be a gross understatement of my state of mind. My summary rejection by the Mahatma's assistant had left me floating in an ocean of uncertainty like a rudderless ship which does not know whether it would hit a rock or a beach inhabited by civilized human beings. I did not know where I should go. I was restless. Desai's idea of working at the Khadi weaving factory set up by Gandhiji at Meerut did not appeal to me. This was not a time of doing constructive work. It was when youth should resort to direction action against the British Government. Tormented by these thoughts I walked to Wardha station. My mind is a complete blank about how I returned. All that I remember is that somehow I reached the house of my cousin in Badaun, an out of the way district town. Her husband was posted as a sub-judge there. How and why I went there I cannot make out to this day. The city is connected to Bareilly by a railway line. But Bareilly is not on any route from Nagpur to the North. The only reason I can recall this event is the shocked look on the faces of my hosts when they saw me with a clean shaven head, wearing rustic khadi clothes and carrying a jute hand bag as my only luggage. I was treated like a V.I.P. during the two or three days I spent there, taken to movies and feasted on sweets. Badaun was a small city of narrow lanes and markets. Its only claim to fame was, Shakeel Badauni a lyricist whose film songs we heard every day over the radio.

Who could have imagined that my cousin's husband, who only two years earlier had been handling petty cases as a Munsif would within 25 years rise to the emmince of a judge of the Allahabad High Court and do the family proud? Its officers climbing to the top from the lowest rung of the ladder was the first of the four pillars on which the British administration in India stood, the other three being strict adherence to the order of seniority in promotions, complete security of service with life-long pension after retirement and, fourthly, looking the other way when officers and ordinary employees made "a little extra money" over and above their salaries. The British rulers observed this last rule with their "other employees", as well. The thousands of landlords, rajas and Maharajas were in fact the "most obedient" servants of the British Crown. They paid a fixed revenue or tribute to the royal treasury and did what they pleased with their serfs and subjects to extract and extort from them as much money and grain as they could. This policy, which continues unchanged to this day, endeared the British authorities to the vast army of their Indian employees who served their imperial masters with unflinching loyalty. To the peasantry it made no difference since they had been accustomed to the same free use of their services for centuries under rajas and nawabs most of whom were half-rulers-half-dacoits. Whether in city or village the great majority of Indian people suffer the same fate even today with leaders of almost all political parties and their henchmen and big industrialists playing the role of the landlords and maharajas of olden times and the bureaucracy becoming ten times bigger and more rapacious.

My only regret of the Sewagram trip which has haunted me to this day was that I could not see Gandhi face to face when I was separated from him merely by the mud wall of his hut whose doorstep I had reached.

9

Learning To Cheat

How Bribery took formal shape during British Rule

Bribery was never an issue during British rule. Only I.C.S. officers and High Court judges were regarded as absolutely clean and straight forward in their conduct. Other professions, both official and private, were amenable to influence in cash or kind Junior Employees of leading industrialists like Birlas and Tatas themselves became industrialist in course of time by making money "on the sidelines". Their masters did not object to it so long as their company made profits by the work of their executives and clerks. The clerks of lawyers, compounders of doctors, teachers of private and governmnet schools made extra money over and above their salaries which were very low and not enough to keep body and soul together as a member of the middle or lower middle class. Even peons expected tips to carry a businessman's card to his officer. The higher the officer the move his peon's tip. Clerks and peons of all offices, government or private, had to be tipped to more a file from one table to another. In our small zamindari of dozens of villages the revenue collectors, Jaafar and Nazir, were paid a salary of one rupee a month. Yet they were always immaculately dressed. They were paid handsomely by the tenants for delaying the payments and reporting their "absence" from their homes. All these payments to various functionaries by their clients were considered as "perks" of their jobs, not bribes. No clerk or teacher and official of that level Yet they were always immediatley dressed. could afford to keep his children in a hostel in a school or college by remaining content with his meagre salary.

"Let them earn through any means as long as they do their job properly", was the motto of the government and private employers.

The fact is that during British rule a government officer accepting money for favours rendered in his official capacity was as legal as the unwritten British Constitution, regardless of the stringent punishment provided against it in the written law.

When marrying off a daughter to a government or private employee the parents always enquired openly about the "outside income" of the prospective bridegroom. Historians specialising in British rule in India are aware of how East India Company agents worked their way into the hearts and minds of Moghul kings and other sovereign potentates throughout the country by liberally bribing the courtiers.

This policy proved a boon to the British Government during critical times like the Sepoy Mutiny of 1857 and again during World War II. In the 1840s, my great-grandfather was a supervisor under a British engineer during the construction of the historic dam on the Ganga above Haridwar. Every few months he would trudge about 30 miles through dense jungles carrying on his head a large wicker basket packed with one-rupee coins and concealed in grazing grass to escape being waylaid by robbers.

Those days the monthly salary of a labourer was two rupees. What my ancestor carried was presumably money earned by making fictitious muster rolls. Despite this, he was a favourite of the British engineer. He gave ample proof of his loyalty to the Englishman by concealing him in a secret place during the Mutiny and thus saving his life. As a reward for this service, he was awarded an estate in the form of zamindari rights over scores of villages. The family never looked back. This is just one example to show that the British rulers could not have succeeded in crushing the Mutiny without the active support of their loyal Indian employees.

Again, during World War II all that the Viceroy had to do was to print currency notes in unlimited numbers and leave it to the Indians to spend them on the "War Effort." Prices shot up by eight to 10 times during the six-year war as contractors, goods suppliers, transporters, bureaucrats, engineers, freshly created industrialists, aristocrats, traders, ration shop owners and other supporters of the regime gobbled up the money but at the same time ensured that work for the War was accomplished in full and beyond the expectations of their masters. Indians worked day and night at breakneck speed to build aerodromes, hospitals, whole cantonments, new railway yards and a host of other facilities not only to defeat the Japanese attack on India but also to feed the war machine on the western front.

Partition and the mass genocide that followed it opened the floodgates of corruption on a massive scale. The "war efforts" drill of the British days was revived with redoubled vigour. We were fighting on two fronts now, the war with Pakistan over Kashmir and the campaign to rehabilitate millions of refugees in the shortest possible time. Money flowed like water. An allied field of added attraction was allocation of millions of homes and establishments left vacant by Muslims who had fled to Pakistan. If World War II bred large-scale corruption during the British rule, the aftermath of Partition and the war with Pakistan formalised it. The same administration which had 'delivered' results during the War came in handy for repeating and multiplying its ingenious practices.

Today the same drill is being performed by our government in the name of fighting so-called "terrorism" and "Maoism", which provides "free" funds to a host of functionaries involved in these campaigns.

Immediately after passing my matriculation examination in the coveted first division in my home district in 1943, I had traveled some five hundred kilometers to Kanpur to join the BNSD College, then regarded as the best in the state. Six of its students who had passed the twelfth class had figured in the merit list of sixteen for the whole province in the board exams taken by eight thousand students. How this institution had accomplished the 'miracle' consistently for several years is something I cannot comment upon. The hostel where I stayed for the year was situated in sylvan surroundings. It consisted of two bungalows with a large compound, one of which was occupied by the Warden, Satguru Sharan Awasthi. Being a good debater I attracted the attention of the Warden. He moved me along with another boy, who later joined the IAS (Indian Administrative Service) to a spare room in his bungalow. Awasthi was a well known Hindi writer and also the vice-principal of the college. It was at his house that I made the acquaintance of Makhan Lal Chaturvedi, the famous Hindi writer and poet after whose name the Madhya Pradesh Government has built the Makhan Lal Chaturvedi University at Khandwa, his home town. Chaturvedi, then a frail old man, stayed for about a week at Awasthi's house. He liked young people and I used to sit with him for some time in the evenings. Once I asked him the question uppermost in my mind, "how does one become a good poet?"

"But you are so wooden, how can you ever become a poet?", he quipped.

During my conversations with him he had learnt that I had thoroughly imbibed Gandhi's ideas of brahmcharya (celibacy), fasting, austerity and all that goes with it. Apparently, what he meant was that to be a poet one had to have flesh and blood in his body which meant having a heart with feelings and emotions. To him I looked to be a dry and dusty boy scout. He later took me to the house of our principal, Hira Lal Khanna. The house was a mansion in the old lanes of the city. The drawing room was furnished with a carpeted settee of the size of a double bed and a few reclining chairs. Another classmate of mine, Sushil who was perhaps the son of a family friend of Khanna, was also there. Sushil played on a sitar for about half an hour to the audience which consisted of Chaturvedi, Khanna, Awasthi and me. I am grateful to Makhan Lal Chaturvedi for taking me along to this meeting and showing me that there was more to life than mere books and politics. That, incidentally, was the first and last sitar recital I was to hear for seven years until a co-ed, Shipra Banerji, played her sarod for a few of us during the Wordsworth Centenary celebrations we had organized in the Allahabad University.

Musical instruments like harmonium, tabla and sitar were found in homes of girls. Having no sister, I did not have them in our house.

The year at BNSD College, was useful to me in many ways. How Khanna managed to achieve such outstanding results for his college, getting two to six of his students on the merit list of sixteen for the whole province, year after year, was itself an education. Khanna was unique in many ways. He always wore achkan and churidar pyjama, then the traditional dress of the aristocracy. The college maintained an excellent library and the most competent staff capable of teaching graduate classes. I chanced to meet my class teacher who taught us English, A.R. Srivastava, in Allahabad where he was teaching in a university college. There was absolutely no scope for manipulation of board results by Khanna because the British Authorities kept a strict watch on school education.

Khanna would often invite rare personalities to give us lectures in the main hall. I still remember the talk that an Indian intellectual gave us on his return from Mexico where he discovered the ancient links between Indian and Mayan civilizations.

From Kanpur I moved to Meerut College from where I made an abortive trip to Gandhiji's Ashram in Sewagram and wasted a year of my education. The country was in turmoil.

We had had the Bengal famine of 1943 when millions of people starved to death. It was said that whatever food was there was being diverted to feed the soldiers of the Allied forces on the Western and Eastern war fronts. Subhash Bose's army was knocking at the eastern gates of India to liberate the country from British rule. Youth all over India were excited about it and others like me who were politically minded were eager to make their contribution to the freedom struggle. To save people from dying from hunger in Bengal Gandhiji had given a "miss a meal" call. Many people all over India fasted a full day in a week to save food. Old clothes and utensils were collected in large quantities to be sent to the needy in Bengal. Several sewa samitis of citizens sprang up to undertake the job of sending food and other articles to Bengal. There was no fear of pilferage because it was established deep in everybody's mind that stealing from a charity was a sin that would send the perpetrator straight to hell. The Muslim principle of Zakat, or compulsory charity enshrined in the daily Islamic prayers, was also very popular in Urdu speaking areas like our U.P. and Punjab where Urdu was the official language.

By the 1970s, with modernization, all these beliefs had changed. Ship loads of blankets sent by a reputed International organization for the cyclone victims of Chittagong in Bangla Desh through its Indian representatives were allegedly selling in the streets of Calcutta and Dhaka. Most of the consignments never reached the intended beneficiaries. Rural poverty was spilling into the streets of cities where groups of beggars, some of whom were dressed as sadhus or bards, were a common sight.

But it was not until I joined the Ewing Christian College at Allahabad in 1945 that I understood the true meaning of Gandhi's message that service of the poor was the highest service that one could render to God. I learnt this under the guidance of a middle-aged American missionary, W.S. Gould, who taught English at the college and was an ardent follower of Gandhi. Every Friday at 5 p.m. he would hold in the drawing room of his small thatch roofed bungalow, situated alongside the yamuna river, a Gandhian prayer meeting. It consisted of charkha spinning for about 20 minutes, readings from the Bible, Gita and Quran and a small talk by any of the six or seven participants amongst whom I was one. Spinning one's own cloth was the main pillar of Gandhi's principle of self-reliance and boycott of British goods.

Our practical work consisted of providing critical help to dwellers of the slum near the college. I was assigned the task of visiting a 25-year old young man who was suffering from tuberculosis twice a week and delivering medicines to him. He lived in a small room with his mother who had put his bed in her small verandah so that he could see the movement of people around him. My visits used to cheer both of them. My job was to report the patient's condition to Mr. Gould who, in turn, told everything to the mission's doctor for further directions. I was also among the volunteers who taught the servants in our hostel mess and a few of their children how to read and write in an hour-long class. Each volunteer was assigned three to four students. The class was held in an empty garage on a jute mat in the light of a kerosene lantern.

Though I spent only one year at Ewing College the Principal, Dr. B.B. Malviya, took a liking for me and appointed me the social secretary of the college. My job was to invite important people to give us talks on Saturday evenings in the lecture hall over looking the river. One of the memorable visits I remember was that of the eminent scientist Dr. Meghnath Saha, a Fellow of the Royal Society, who had moved from Allahabad to Calcutta. (Only five Indian scientists held the title of FRS then.) He was extremely humble and polite with me. I and a friend accompanied him to the railway station in a tonga to see him off. When the coolie entered the train and lowered his holdall which was supposed to contain his bedding, it split in the middle under the weight of books it was carrying. The literature instantly poured out over his berth. All that remained inside the bedroll was a thin sheet by way of the professor's bedding. That was the stuff our great scholars were made of in those days. I can relate many such instances of little known facts about great professors of my university days.

Gould knew Jawaharlal Nehru personally. In the winter of 1945 Gould and I bicycled down to Anand Bhawan where Nehru lived when he was not in a British jail from where he had only recently come out. We invited him to give us a talk. He readily agreed. The Principal, Dr. Malviya, did not like the idea but kept quiet. On the appointed evening Nehru came in his Baby Ford car sitting alongside his son-in-law Feroze Gandhi, who was in the driver's seat. Accompanying them in the back seat was Jawaharlal's daughter, Indira, with son Rajiv in her lap. Who knew then that three future Prime Ministers of India were traveling in that small car and honouring us with a visit? We were not allowed to use the lecture hall for the meeting nor did Dr. Malviya attend it. Instead we met under the giant banyan tree on the spacious lawn in the centre of the quadrangular campus complex in the light of a petromax. The large base of the tree served as the dais. Nehru spoke to us about the country's dire need of scholars to take India to the great heights it had attained in the past. He also spoke of ushering real socialism in the nation so that all citizens were looked after. After he had left we discovered a police officer in plain clothes lurking on the premises with a notebook.

Looking back at these small events in my life I feel that somehow they add up to make what we call the personality of a character we are talking about. These were clearly two types of young men in pre-independence India—those who were politically conscious and those who couldn't care who ruled the country. The former were in a small minority. Being politically conscious did not necessarily mean politically active. But most young men of the day, politically conscious or not, were agreed on one thing, that socialism was the only answer to the nation's myriad problems of poverty, caste, discrimination, communalism, dowry deaths, maltreatment of women and so on. Little did we know then that socialism needed dedicated leaders and managers who were not greedy and intent upon lining their own pockets. Events of the last 65 years since Independence have proved that under Indian conditions socialism can prove to be the worst form of government we can have.

The American writer, Pearl S. Buck had only recently been awarded the Nobel Prize for literature for her novel The Good Earth. I read it over and over again. It was so simply written about village life in the northern region of China, that I thought I could write a similar book on village life in India with which I was quite familiar. It would be a great service to the country since the rural social structures and usury and exploitation of the poor in India were similar to those in China as depicted in the Good Earth. With me to think was to act. Immediately, I shut myself in my room in Turner hostel and devoted almost two months to this project. I was so obsessed by it that I took it to a small printing press, called Sewa Press, on Hewett Road, about a mile away and got it printed. It was a small two-room establishment consisting of a straddle machine placed in the front room while the compositors and proof readers sat in the back room. When other students were poring over their course books for the approaching board exams I was devoting my entire time to my novel. In February 1946 I took the first copy to Jawaharlal Nehru to ask for a foreword. He was sitting in his drawing room which opened on the verandah and came out to meet me. I gave him the book. He glanced through it for a minute and said, "to write a foreword I would have to read the book. Tomorrow I am going to Indonesia. Then on coming back I have to be in Delhi for talks with the Government of India. So you see how difficult it is for me to write a foreword for your book." I came back and ultimately got a foreword written by U.S. Verma, head of the English department of the college.

I took a copy of the book to Dr. Malviya. He was very pleased to see it. His bungalow was always open to me. The main sitting room in the house behind the verandah served as both his study and drawing room. Sitting with him and facing him across his large teakwood table was itself an education. Only a few days later I was doing an experiment in the chemistry lab when I heard a loud voice behind me shouting "Roll No. 758". I turned around and saw Dr. Malviya standing next to me in the narrow aisle. "Come with me Mukut

Behari," he said. The chemistry department was at the other end of the campus quadrangle from the main building where the principal's office was located. We walked across the lawn in silence. "Sit down", he said on reaching his room. It was then that he told me that he had just been informed that my attendance in the classes was far short of the minimum required by the UP Board of High School and Intermediate education. He was using his special powers as the Principal to grant me an exemption under the sickness clause. He wanted an assurance from me that I would devote the remaining six seeks before the exams to my studies and studies alone which I readily gave. To say I was moved by his gesture would be an understatement. The portly gentleman had taken the trouble to look into my class schedule for the day and walked the full length of the campus to meet me. I was merely one of his seven hundred students, half of whom would go away from the college like me within a few months and would never be seen again. But ECC (Ewing Christian College) was like that in those days. Its teachers tended to practice what they preached from the pulpit. On two or three occasions I also attended the Sunday morning service at the church adjoining the college campus. The emphasis of the sermons was on the theme of service rendered to the poor being the highest form of service to God. This together with the small jobs we did for the poor under Mr. Gould's guidance have left a lasting impression on me. It enabled me to understand better Gandhi's statement that before he planned any action he thought to himself whether it would benefit the "poorest of the poor" in India.

I think that spiritually inclined people who talk of practicing what they call "non-duality" of creation, while continuing to pursue their individual self-interest, miss the central point. Non-duality is a thing that can be experienced only through actual practice, which means feeling the pain and anguish of the oppressed of the Earth. St. Paul is said to have slept in the same blanket with a leper. To me that alone is truly experiencing spiritual non-duality, or the feeling of one soul, one spirit, one force, pervading the whole universe. Under Gould's influence, though he had not asked me to do it, I once took a bag of wheat to marooned residents of a village which had been turned into an island when the river Yamuna was in flood. Only the boatman was my companion. I still remember the joy that lit up the faces of the villagers, specially mothers with children, on seeing my boat landing on their shore. Dr. Malviya died with his boots on while he was still the principal. In those days heart patients rarely survived long.

While I was thus playing the role of a good Samaritan in public there lurked in the background a little known dark side of my character which no one knew anything about. After getting my novel on Indian rural life printed and collecting twenty-five copies of it from the printer I never went back to him to collect the remaining copies and make the payment. But what was stranger was his goodness in never coming to collect the five hundred rupees that I owed him. He could have pestered me day and night and complained to the warden of my hostel, the principal Dr. Malviya or my father. The huge bundle of five hundred copies of my book that must have sat unclaimed in his limited space for an indefinite period was a constant reminder to him of my perfidy. Five hundred rupees of those days was like fifty to hundred thousand rupees of today. He was a poor man, slept on a Hessian cot in the verandah outside his shop, ate, plain and rustic food from a roadside dhaba and kept his family in his village about a hundred miles away. Though he was himself of short stocky build, his employees were even poorer and looked frail and consumptive. For his two proof readers and three compositors life was a long night both actually and figuratively. They sat on their raised stools at least twelve hours a day in the dark windowless ante-room of the two-room establishment, lighted day and night by a 100 watt bulb hanging in the centre of the room without a shade. The walls were grimy and laden with splashes of ink. A mixed smell of printers ink, binder's molten glue, urine and similar roadside perfumes filled the air of the room. During the rush of work they worked through the night, till two in the morning, partaking of the dhaba meal and tea that their employer shared with them. I spent several such nights at the Sewa Press and quickly established a false camaraderie with them only to betray them at the end.

I have described this incident in detail because this is the stuff corruption in India is made of. We train early not to care whom we are deceiving and cheating. I came across many such people who never complained of non-payment of money that I owed them. As editor, owner and publisher of a weekly student magazine I brought out in Allahabad, I hired a part time secretary, Rao, for three months. He worked as a clerk in the local office of All India Radio. I paid him for two months but not for the third. Later I happened to visit the radio station and saw him. I apologized for not paying his dues. "Oh that! Forget it. I enjoyed working with you," said the magnanimous Rao. I similarly cheated a few others. Once in 1947, I fancied a luxury car worth Rs. 7,200 (equivalent of a million rupees today) and borrowed the money for it from a close friend of my father who readily gave it to me. Of course, my father immediately repaid him. But what if he hadn't? You might say I was a pampered child. This would be only partly true. The fact is that in India a son can do no wrong. His parents and their kinsmen are always ready to support him and protect him from the clutches of the law. Looking back at my misspent life I now feel that all these long years I have played the dual roles of Robert Louis Stevenson's Dr. Jekyll and Mr. Hyde. My only solace is that most, if not all, of my "highly educated" countrymen are like that.

When I joined the Allahabad University in July 1947, a month before India gained its Independence, I was confused about my career goals. Half my mind was turned towards taking to farming as a close friend Vikrant and my maternal uncles had done. At the same time there was the lure of the easy going life of the university where there was plenty of leisure to read what you liked. I was already a member of the Alfred Park public library which contained the choicest classics and the latest fiction of the day and had made friends with the two assistant librarians who were young and cooperative, though their alderfly boss, the chief librarian was a forbidding looking Bengali, whose personality commanded silence in the office the moment be arrived on his bicycle in his dhoti and Kurta. My only other interest or hobby was to loiter on the platform at the Allahabad railway station at least once a week and have tea (British style) and cake, made by a local bakery, in the upper class refreshment room which charged only six annas (thirty-seven paise) for the package. After browsing through a few books and magazines at the station book stall and occasionally picking up a cheap magazine I would return to my hostel on my bicycle. In course of my frequent visits to the railway station I struck a friendship with a young ticket collector, named Siddhiqui (name changed). When the Hindu-Muslim riots broke out in the wake of Independence of India and its partition, Allahabad was relatively quiet. But fear persisted in the hearts of the local Muslims of being attacked by mobs of Hindus from nearby villages. Many of them were itching to go to Pakistan if they could somehow safely cross through Indian Punjab. During the same period I was eager to travel to Bombay to sell my friends Vikrant's raw tobacco to any of the cigarette factories operating there. He had consulted me before planting it. I and Siddiqui struck a deal. I was to escort his father upto Delhi, and say to any rioting mobs of Hindus who might try to kill him that he was any attendant and a Hindu. In return he would give me three tickets to travel by second class (today's first class), the original first class having been abolished soon after Independence) to Poona via Bombay and return to Allahabad by the same route. The tickets were to be given to him to be destroyed.

As it happened, his father who wore a thin beard that made him look a Muslim became nervous by the time our train reached Etawah and he returned to Allahabad. I heaved a sigh of relief. He and I were alone in the whole compartment. All the middle class gentry used to travel by what was called the "Intermediate" class. Only people holding high positions or aristocrats traveled by the second class and the mostly British officers traveled first class. I went to Saharanpur and surprised Vikrant who was only two years older than me. His father sent the family tutor, Mr. Badola to accompany us. The three of us traveled to Bombay. It was our first visit to the metropolis which looked clean washed like a picture post card with horse drawn buggies and tongas plying freely on the roads. We stayed in a hotel on the Strand road along the sea coast near the Taj at Rs.10 per head per day, breakfast included. On the way back we took a day's halt at Gwalior, then the headquarters of the Golden Tobacco Company. This was a free travel by the courtesy of my friend Siddique. We are willing to go to any lengths to enjoy freebies from any one on any grounds, for example colonies getting free lights from municipalities. Ticket collectors in those days had the power to blindly issue tickets to any destination through circuitous routes on their bill books, and make a false "carbon copy", which they kept with them for their accounts department, for a short journey of a few miles by the third class. I have related this experience as an example to illustrate we were, generally speaking a character less people who would not hesitate to take advantage of any situation for the sake of money. Vikrant and his father were rich men by any standards but they too jumped at this opportunity for free travel. Indian middle class has always been, with few exceptions, a corrupt class of greedy, unscrupulous and unprincipled people who would defy any law to make the extra buck if it could be done by bribing some body. I am merely a specimen of it. And, as in my case, our training to cheat other people and the law, begins at an early age.

10

Networking
A Maze No One Can Enter

Come to think of it, heavens would not have fallen upon me had I not used my cousin's husband as a 'source' to get me a college lecturer's job and later the post of a sub-editor in The Tribune. I was not unemployed but holding a respectable permanent job of a teacher of English in a good public school in the salubrious environs of Mussoorie, then known as the queen of the hills. In course of time I could have settled down in that city and married my colleague, the music teacher, who appeared to have fallen for my informal ways, not knowing that all those qualities had been assiduously cultivated as part of my college education. I used to meet her every evening for long walks. The option of returning to journalism was always there. I could any day have gone back to my old paper, Nagpur Times. I am discussing in retrospect these apparently boring details of my life to show that my story is the story of my beloved country, India, more so of post-Independence India. Promoting the interests of family members has been an old tradition in India. In this country a hero is not a person who has done great service to society, specially its poor members. The real hero held out as an example in society is one who props up his brothers and sisters and their children by bending rules. This makes for a strong and powerful family dreaded and respected by society. As a direct consequence of this national obsession for promoting kinsmen the powerful families always remain powerful for generations to come. Independence opened up millions of jobs, contracts, licenses for rationing and liquor shops. Hundreds of new industrial townships came up. Hydro-Electric and irrigation dams were built in a hurry. Wars with Pakistan and China provided an opportunity to equip the armed forces with the best armaments. Nearly all these new opportunities were grabbed by the rich and powerful families. Bending and making rules to benefit the favoured few became the order of the day. Networks of such families sprang up to share in the loot. Building and being part of such caucuses became the primary occupation of every citizen who did not want to be left out of the general melee for wealth and power. My seeking my rich relative's help and his readily obliging me by twisting the employment norms and making an "exception" in my case not only enhanced his reputation as a person who was good at heart but also helped me to gradually become a member of the "network" of the rich and powerful. You go to any office, private or public. You will find it packed with relatives and favourites smuggled through the back door, defying all rules and norms. My case was no exception.

This is how the powerful minority has always remained powerful and the "slaves" of the system who constitute ninety percent of the population will always remain slaves. Over the last two decades the gap between them and us has been widening in geometric proportions. Upward social mobility which is the essence of an egalitarian democratic society is nearly zero in India and will remain so until this networking gridlock is broken.

I find that over the intervening five decades this typically Indian habit has assumed monstrous proportions. One of the charms of assuming even the smallest vestige of power in a government or private office is the right it gives a person not to answer or even acknowledge letters concerning his or her official work. Naturally so. If you want an acknowledgement or action on your request you have to pay a price for it in cash or kind.

The easiest method is to go through a "source", a respectable euphemism for a tout whose job it is to cultivate people in positions of authority from peon to a secretary in the Government. In pre-independence British times they virtually ran the Government and, for their services to the crown, they were awarded titles like Rai Saheb, Rai Bahadur, Khan Bahadur M.BE and even knighthood.

These gentlemen formed a close coterie of the upper castes, Kashmiri Brahmins, Parsis, Kayasthas, Brahmins, Marwaris, Jains, Banias, Patels and Thakurs were the most convenient tools that the British authorities used to govern the empire. They formed powerful networks of their own, each competing with the other for a share in the imperial loot. Though most of the members of these powerful coteries belonged to the upper castes, they formed only a small minority of their own castes. The majority of upper caste people were also poor, but not so poor as the lower castes.

These people acted as hangers on for the titled elite. The common man generally got his work done through these underlings of these dignitaries who had their own networks of peons, clerks, "bara-baboos" and gazetted officers to keep their clients' files moving.

What I wish to highlight here is my own despicable role in this tragic scenario. In the matter of not replying to letters, which I have described above as one of the worst forms of corruption, my name should come on top of the list. My bosom friend in Allahabad University, S.A.Z. Jafri, whose hospitality I later enjoyed for several days in his bachelors' den in Lucknow in 1953 lent me the hand written manuscript of his thesis for polishing up. I promised to return it within a week of my return to Nagpur where I was working as a staff reporter in Nagpur Times. I just simply slept over it. Jafri sent me several reminders over a period of several months and finally threatened to come personally to retrieve his thesis before I cared to send it back to him, unchecked. During the same Lucknow trip I met an anglo-Indian girl who had been my classmate the previous year in the department of journalism at Hislop College, Nagpur and later became a well known writer. She was then studying in the famous Isabella Thoburn College in Lucknow. She lent me her bicycle for several days to facilitate my movement in the city. I offered to get an article by her published in my paper. On my return to Nagpur I did not even care to write to her a letter of thanks, leave alone publishing her article. On receiving an invitation card to my wedding, another co-ed of Nagpur days living in Mysore sent me an expensive ornamental vase of brass. I never acknowledged its receipt nor sent her any gift when she got married. I can never forget how I let down my mentor at Allahabad University,

Prof. R.N. Deb who treated me as a family member and came all the way from Allahabad to Meerut to attend my wedding. I had spent many summer vacations with him at Allahabad and in the hills. When his eldest daughter got married he sent me a card. I did not care to even write to him, leave alone sending a gift or attending the marriage. I can fill a complete chapter with a list of people I have thus betrayed in my life.

The same can be said about my seeking recommendations for higher positions. I was reasonably well employed in Nagpur Times and later in Hitavada in the same city when I decided to quit in a huff and seek my fortunes elsewhere. Eventually I got a decent job of a teacher of English in a Santiniken style public school in Mussoorie on my own merit. It so happened that I could not resist the temptation to exploit a rich and enlightened relative in Ambala Cantt, who was an engineer by training and was also among the pioneers of the scientific instruments industry in India. A great philanthropist, he ran several institutions including Hindu temples and a degree college that had migrated from Lahore after the city became part of Pakistan. He got me the job of lecturer in English in the College in 1954 though third division MAs were not eligible for it. A year later the same relative who was the husband of my cousin helped me to get a job in The Tribune which was then publishing from Ambala Cantt. (after migrating from Lahore and a brief interlude in Shimla). In the act of seeking his recommendation and later the job I misused a letter written to me by N.J. Hamilton, Editor of The Onlooker, a highly prestigious society magazine published from Bombay. In response to my application for a job he had asked me to come for an interview to Bhopal where he was going on an official visit. What I concealed from my relative and later from the Editor of The Tribune was Hamilton's subsequent letter canceling the interview. I had in a brief note thanked him for the appointment and promised to meet him in Bhopal. He immediately wrote back to me "since I find two spelling mistakes in your brief letter there is no point in my meeting you". All the time I was pretending to my relative and the editor of The Tribune that had I not got an opening in the local paper I would have joined the Onlooker in Bombay.

To tell the truth I was trained to be a cheat. In the first job of a tourist guide I got in Delhi after coming out of the university in 1951, I was asked to accompany an old American tourist to show him Agra and Jaipur, cities I had never visited. "Don't worry about that", said the accomplished lady who ran the agency, "you speak fluent English. That is all they want. Tell them anything and they will believe it." She happened to be the good looking wife of an officer in the Government of India. She was right. The 78-year old tourist I escorted was more interested in getting himself photographed in the places we visited, to be shown to his friends in the U.S., than in the history and architecture of the great monuments. I showed him. He cursed himself bitterly for leaving his camera behind in the hotel when we had an elephant ride at Amber palace at Jaipur. "Oh I would have shown my picture riding an elephant back home, if only I hadn't left the camera in the room." He also blamed me for the lapse since I should have reminded him about it. The tourist agency had put us up in separate rooms in a second rate hotel which was, in fact, a guest house. He found this out, moved to the Circuit House which was then the best hotel in town and got a certificate from me that this was indeed the case. I got no further assignments from this agency. "You sunk me with my best international supplier of tourists", the lady said bitterly afterwards.

My next job was with a publisher of directories of important people. The modus operandi of my employer was that of a perfect con man. The firm had a name which sounded very British and had an office in a tiny tin shed on the roof of a block in Connaught Place. What mattered was the CP address, since none of the VIPs we approached was ever likely to visit the office of the one-man firm. "You introduce yourself as a representative of a company publishing directories, take an appointment with the most important people in the city you visit and exalt them to great heights of eminence during the interview. In the end while leaving you casually but pointedly say 'of course, there is small charge for the service we render to cover the costs'. I have never met a man who has refused to pay", said my employer who also took me along with him to one celebrity he was interviewing. Among my victims was Lala Bharat Ram, one of India's foremost industrialists and proprietor of Delhi Cloth Mills, and our former foreign minister Sardar Swaran Singh who was then practicing as a lawyer in Jullunder. Both of them gladly paid up the hefty charges I quoted.

It was not as if it was all rosy and cozy in the "respectable" and reputed" organizations I served in later years. One way or the other, wherever I went I found personal greed of the members of the staff and management overriding the interests of the organization or nation, or the ethical principles we preached as journalists. My suave manners and fluency in English made a perfect blend for any employer looking for a con man, and to my surprise these are the only qualities which all my superiors and numerous contacts liked about me. They had all come up by the same ladder that I was climbing.

Again my own case is the best example of this phenomenon. When I retired from The Statesman in 1988 at the age of sixty I was penniless, my provident found was already gone as loan taken for a flat in a journalist's colony and the gratuity could not sustain me more than a year or two.

I took a job as Editor of a new weekly on a good salary. It ran only for two years and folded up when the political party running it went out of power and its "source" of funds dried up. My health soon deteriorated and a slipped disc in the vertebra in 1993 sealed my fate. I was too weak and debilitated for surgery. I undertook home based small jobs and rented out a three bed-room DDA flat I owned (in addition to the flat we live in) to a private company. Then in 2004, with the coming of the Congress party into power my fate zoomed. The main beneficiaries of the economy were idlers and parasites like me. My wife has acquired a flair for operating on the stock market from home and picking up the right shares. The boom in the share market brought the worth of her stock to eight figures with a sizeable dividend. Within the same period the rental income from my DDA flat has gone up four times and the sale value of the flat has gone up nearly ten times from Rs. 27 lakhs to Rs. 2.5 crores. Besides, the flat in which we live and which came to us virtually free in 1978 is worth Rs.3.5 crores. Plots of developed land which were bought by ordinary people like me for as low as ten rupees a square meter in 1955 are today selling at one million to three million rupee a square meters, a jump of 1,00,000 to 3,00,000 times over the original price. As owners of two flats and sizeable stocks we can count ourselves among the upper middle class elite in India. Without doing anything to earn it our wealth keeps rising. My wife's eternal regret is that in 1965 we gave up a 300 square meter plot allotted to us in Gulmohar Park at Rs. 30 per square meter and bought a car instead. Today that property is worth Rs. 30 crores.

For people like us our rulers have achieved wonders. We are the truly liberated people. We can proudly hold our heads high before the elite of the world. India has the largest number of billionaires in Asia. Its middle class elite has become one of the biggest buyers of luxury goods in the world. We travel abroad for holidays and send our children to the costliest foreign schools. We change cars like children buying new toys. Manmohan Singh, our Prime Minister, had during his first term promised to turn Bombay into Shanghai. His dream has been accomplished in so far as it concerns the five per cent rich people in that city. Their life styles are changing with the rapidity of a rotating top. Every day new designs appear in the air conditioned malls. Theatres and arts have prospered and are competing with the West in every way. Our sleek airports, our gorgeous hotels which keep multiplying like pigs are making their grotesque presence felt in every corner of the big cities of India. Expensive parties and social get togethers are arranged ostensibly for entertainment but actually to cement the upper caste networks. In the matter of defence we have the third largest army in the world. We are manufacturing satellites of our own. In missile technology we are fast catching up with China. We claim to have the capability even to manufacture the hydrogen bomb. A large slice of the nation's resources is earmarked for fighting anti-national forces like terrorists, Maoists, Naxalites and separatists and protecting several thousand VIPs. For the poor millions there are not even public toilets. They still shit on the beeches, railway tracks or marshes in the city.

Meanwhile, our economy is said to be developing at the rate of six to nine percent. The wealth of the upper middle class, in which I include myself, is rising at the rate of 25 to 50% year. Besides, a lot of the imagined surplus generated by this imagined growth is harvested in advance for so-called development projects which is a pseudonym invented by the media for transferring wealth to the private sector and its upper grade officers, contractors and suppliers.

If the national income has grown only six to nine percent and the wealth of the upper classes has zoomed by 25% to 50% a year, it stands to reason that the real incomes of the remaining 90% of the population has gone down proportionately. Take the housing sector as an instance. My income from my extra flat has gone up four times in nine or ten years.

I have managed this by changing tenants every two years or even more frequently. Though there is a provision of ten percent annual increase in rent in the lease agreement I sign with my tenants that does not satisfy me. I want much more rent from my flat. Rents keep rising at fifteen to twenty percent per year. The great mass of population in urban India still lives in rented houses. Till the liberalization of the economy about two decades ago opened the flood gates of greed in India there was hardly any noticeable difference between tenant and owner. A tenant lived in the same house at the same rent as long as he liked even and after his death the tenancy passed on to his successors. Today the tenant is a gypsy. The tenancy laws have changed in favour of the landlord and the latter can have his house vacated after a stipulated period even if he does not need it for his personal use. For all practical purposes, the tenant is a homeless person who has to change his residence every two years at huge expense in increased rent, transportation of his luggage, a month's rent to the broker, change of school for his children. Above all, there is the emotional cost of being rootless and lost in a big city, shunned by neighbours as a bird of passage. Whatever laws may be there for the protection of the tenant they are freely violated by arm twisting of the tenant by landlords, brokers and fellow house owners with the connivance of the government. Politicians, media barons, bureaucrats and industrialists have made acquiring property with their ill gotten wealth their main business. It has emerged as the main means of dumping black money and huge bribes.

Education, transport and medical expenses keep escalating almost every day in some garb or the other. The brunt of all this is borne by the common man who keeps tightening his belt almost every day. He is abandoned to his fate. He is worse off than he was sixty-five years ago at the time of Independence, while the incomes of the ten percent rich and upper middle classes keep rising so they can roll in luxury.

My submission is that this is the stuff revolutions are made of.

Welcoming the passing away of US-baiter Chavez as an opportunity for America to improve its relations with Latin America Time magazine said:

Even if Maduro (Chavez's chosen successor) loses, (in the forthcoming election for President) Washington and the rest of the world need to remember the unmistakable reasons for Chavez's rise to power—chief among them a failure to build the kind of democratic institutions in Latin America that can close the region's unconscionable wealth gap. That flaw still lingers, which is why the memory of Chavez will too.

These lines in the reputed capitalist magazine should be carefully read by every plutocrat and intellectual in India.

The most apt and incisive study of the present situation has been made by P. Sainath, an Editor of the Hindu. He writes in an article in his paper under the caption "Feeding Frenzy of Kleptocracy":

Also getting smaller is the average per capita net availability of foodgrain. And that's despite showing an improved figure of 462.9 grams daily for 2011. (Caution: that's a provisional number). Even then, the five-year average for 2007-11 comes to 444.6 grams. Still lower than the 2002-06 figure of 452.4 grams.

It's scary: as we warned last year—average per capita net availability of foodgrain declined in every five-year period of the 'reforms' without exception. In the 20 years preceding the reforms—1972-1991—it rose every five-year period without exception.

The biggest act of corruption the middle class elite is collectively guilty of with the connivance of the government is the non-enforcement of the Minimum Wages Act which has proved to be a non-starter except for the six percent of the 478 million work force of India engaged by the "organized sector." I am saying this in this autobiography because I am as guilty of this crime as any one else.

The bogey that giving the minimum wage to workers will reduce employment is false. In fact it will generate more employment by increasing the demand for light and mass produced consumer goods. No employer can afford not to hire people. Even now the stingy Indian employer hires the minimum number of workers and makes them work 12 hours a day.

The essence of the economic philosophy presented in this book is that the larger the consumer base the faster the progress of a country. In countries like India, Mexico, Russia, Ukraine, South Africa and others where workers live on a starvation wage and money is hoarded by a few employers unemployment and under employment is 20 to 40% of the work force whereas in developed countries with high minimum wages unemployment is only 4 to 12% of the work force.

A highly respected senior editor of a national daily recently wrote an article bemoaning the diminishing investment in agriculture in India. I sent him a letter I had written to The Hindu stating my theory that all you needed to stimulate the economy generally was the strict enforcement of the minimum wages Act. He wrote back: "I fully endorse your views on the enforcement of the Minimum Wages Act." Our rank in the 2013 United Nations Human Development Index is 136 out 186 nations.

I am reeling out these figures of the gap between the rich and poor in India because I find myself directly responsible for it along with others of my class. I am aware that the economy of the country can immediately revive if, like all Western countries which we try to imitate in living a luxurious life, we give the statutory minimum wage to all workers. What the economy needs is putting purchasing power in the hands of the people. The secret of success of an economy is that money must circulate as it does in Western countries. It must not be hoarded. With a little extra money people will be able to buy their basic needs. Mass production of such goods will generate employment and the economy will grow.

Like it or not consumerism is here to stay. It has gripped the hearts and minds of humanity as no other creed, ideology or religion. capitalism, communism, Hinduism, Christianity and Islam are mere names of only one phenomenon, Consumerism, which the whole of humanity is pursuing single-mindedly. If India wishes to achieve an economic miracle in the shortest possible time-frame it has only to widen its consumer base from a small fraction of its population to the majority. This is how it can be done.

The notorious Indian caste system is responsible for India's black money hordes in Swiss banks which exceeds the combined black money deposits of the rest of the world. Black Money in India is largely the accumulated unpaid wages that should have legitimately been given to the working classes. The workers are not paid their due wages because they belong to the lower castes whose services have been guaranteed to the upper castes for thousands of years virtually free. The upper caste masters horde that money by buying property in the black market or, if it is a large sum, putting it secretly in foreign banks. If you add the vast majority of Muslims and Christians who are equally exploited by the Hindu upper caste you will find 90% of the nation's wealth concentrated in the hands of about 10% of the population constituted almost entirely of upper caste Hindus.

Socialism or communism will not solve India's problems since parties that follow those ideologies are also controlled by upper caste Hindus. What the common man needs is an assured national minimum wage which is at least 33% of the per capita income of the country (66% in metropolitan towns where house and transport consume the bulk of the pay). A beginning can be made with big megalopolitan cities where the minimum wage should be rigorously enforced.

An interesting study by Esther Duflo of the famous American MIT reported by the Economist (London) from a lecture she delivered at Harvard under the title "Hope Springs a Trap" shows how injection of a little extra money over and above the starvation wages they were accustomed to changed the life of a whole community in West Bengal from one of utter despair to one of hope. Even after the aid was stopped they now earn more, eat more and aspire for a better life.

"The results were far more dramatic. Well after the financial help and hand-holding had stopped, the families of those who had been randomly chosen for the Bandhan programme were eating 15% more, earning 20% more each month and skipping fewer meals than people in a comparison group. They were also saving a lot" says the report.

It is my considered view that rigid enforcement of the Minimum Wages Act across the country can bring about just that miracle in India. It will create a consumer class of at least half a billion people, cut down black money transactions to near zero, bring house prices and rents to affordable levels and usher in a new era of prosperity for the whole nation. Economists should examine this layman's theory with unprejudiced eyes. Indonesian offers an example of how this 'miracle' can be achieved.

The Indonesian CEO of a British company in Jakarta told me that in Indonesia the Minimum Wages Act was rigidly enforced on all businesses, shops and establishments-small or big. In the last 10 or 12 years the Minimum Wage has gone up four times. If any businessman proves to the Labour Commissioner that he cannot pay such high wages, he has still to pay the previous year's minimum wage. No exception is made to this rule. The result is the economy is booming, everybody has the purchasing power to buy things. Unlike India, there every body is a consumer. The economy has been growing steadily at the rate of 6.5% a year and the country has faced no recession. From around US dollars 50 in 2001 the minimum wage has gone up to about $200 per month now. Each year the government fixes the wage at a level considerably higher than the rate of inflation in the economy.

When India's Human Development Index is adjusted for gender inequality, India becomes south Asia's worst performing country after Afghanistan. Despite all the boom in women's education and their increasing presence in the job market, they continue to be treated as 'property', or at best as a link in the upper class networks to establish relationships and strengthen the networks.

On the newly constituted Multi-dimensional Poverty Index (MPI), which identifies multiple deprivations in the same households in education, health and standard of living, only 29 countries do worse than India (though data-sets are from varying periods of time across nations). The MPI puts India's poverty headcount ratio at 54%, higher than Bangladesh and Nepal.

The vacuum created by this high neglect is an open invitation to the Naxalites to fill it. Already they are believed to be calling the shots in more than a third of the country. Citigroup Inc, an international financial services company with some 200 million customers in more than 100 countries, has said in its report on 'India in 2007' that the Naxalite movement "has spread to 165 districts in 14 states covering close to 40 per cent of the country's geographical area and affecting 35 per cent of the population".

Ridiculing our tall claims to super-power status, Cait Murphy, Assistant Managing Editor of 'FORTUNE' magazine describes India as the "world leader in hunger, stunting and HIV" since "half the world's hungry live in India."

Quoting UN statistics she writes:
- 47 percent of Indian children under the age of five are either malnourished or stunted.
- The adult literacy rate is 61 percent (behind Rwanda and barely ahead of Sudan). Even this is probably overstated, as people are deemed literate who can do little more than sign their name.
- Only 10 percent of the entire Indian labor force works in the formal economy; of these fewer than half are in the private sector.
- The enrollment of six-to-15-year-olds in school has actually declined in the last year. About 40 million children who are supposed to be in school are not there.
- About a fifth of the population is chronically hungry; about half of the world's hungry live in India.
- More than a quarter of the India's population lives on less than a dollar a day.
- India has more people with HIV than any other country.

The World Bank, which has approved about $3 billion in loans for Indian projects, is among the increasingly anxious foreign backers. "It is easy to be optimistic about India's economic prospects," the bank stated in an India Development Policy Review. "But there is growing concern that the basic institutions, organization and structure for public sector action are failing—especially for those at the bottom . . ."

"The latest family health survey, conducted by India 's Ministry of Health, showed child malnutrition levels even higher than in Sub-Saharan Africa. According to the survey, 46% of children under 3 in India are underweight. (Unicef figures show that 28% of Sub-Saharan children under 5 are underweight.) Anemia, linked to poor nutrition, is prevalent in 79% of India 's children aged 6-35 months, up from 74% seven years ago . . ."

It is a sad reflection on the myopic state of India 's rulers, intellectuals and politicians that even from so close they cannot read the writing on the wall. Umpteen instances can be cited, besides the riots in Bangalore triggered by actor Raj Kumar's death, to show that people's patience is running out. The flash point may be reached any time when they may be forced to take things in their own hands. In large parts of the country we are sitting on a tinder box that can blow up any moment. But, blinded by the razzle-dazzle of the "Market", we see it not.

In a study of the Indian Economy, titled "Seeds of Despair", by Simon Robinson, the American magazine TIME says:

"The income disparity in the new India is massive: there are now 36 billionaires this (figure is of 2007). It has gone up to 103 now in India—and some 800 million people living on less than $2 a day. In the most desperate pockets of rural India, a confluence of factors, from poor rainfall to the new availability of consumer goods, has driven some farmers into crushing debt.

"The financial hardships are so extreme that thousands commit suicide every year. Far from benefiting from the country's new prosperity, whole villages of India's rural poor are being left adrift, eager to join in the boom but unable to afford it. —More than 1,250 farmers committed suicide in Vidarbha's six central districts alone in 2006, up from 248 in 2004."

One can safely assert without fear of contradiction that in the prevalence of inequality between the rich and poor, by any yardstick India not only tops the list, it has practically no rivals, so wide is the gap between the two classes. This unique distinction for the land of Gandhi, the 'naked fakir', is in part the legacy of our deeply embedded caste system which gives us a divine license to be insensitive to the sufferings of the poor ('castes') whom, so the average Hindu seems to believe, God has made as substitutes for animals to carry the proverbial beast's burden for the upper castes.

Or else how can one explain the disappearance, at the hands of professional kidnappers, of nearly 1,00,000 children from the streets of India every year, and every body sleeping over it as if nothing had happened!

The poor parents have to run from pillar to post and move heaven and hell to persuade the almighty city police to condescend to merely record the case of a lost child in their register. Its being pursued and investigated is out of the question.

By contrast, take the case of a top executive of a software multi-national company, in Delhi. The kidnapping of his eight-year-old son became an international media sensation, a prestige issue for the government. Official money in lakhs of rupees was spent by the Centre, UP and Delhi to trace the child who was ultimately recovered after his father had coughed up Rs.50 lakhs to the kidnappers.

In its report on kidnappings in Karnataka The Times of India said quoting a source "we only hope there is not a repeat in Karnataka of the gruesome Nithari" (a Delhi suburb where children were butchered to satisfy the appetite of a few gentlemen cannibals for human flesh).

The only parallel I can think of to such callous indifference towards the anguish of the poor, which has been a typical feature of our Aryan culture for thousands of years, is the treatment of the Black African slaves in America before Abraham Lincoln—one of the greatest men of all times—abolished slavery in that land.

11

How I caused A Sexual Revolution in the University

The person who really changed the course of my life in Allahabad University was Mr. R.N. Deb, then a lecturer in the English Department but later became its head and died while holding that position. He had been allotted a small bungalow, facing the main gate of the University, in Holland Hall, a hostel where I lived. He happened to be my class teacher in the second and final year of B.A. and took a liking to me because I asked too many questions. One day at the end of the class he called me aside and asked me to come to his house at four that evening for a cup of tea. That was the beginning of a relationship that lasted through two decades till he died. He had a friend Capt. A.B. Lal of the political science department who later became Vice-Chancellor of Rajasthan University. I traveled with them and their families to Chitrakoot, the pilgrim hilly town about a hundred miles from Allahabad, where my father was then posted as an engineer in P.W.D. Two years later I stayed with them for a fortnight in a cottage near Ranikhet, the Himalayan hilltown under the shadow of Nanda Devi one of the highest Himalayan peaks. I spent a whole month of June with him when the hostel was closed and his wife and two daughters were away to Mrs. Deb's home town Calcutta, as I had taken up a job in the city. He even traveled five hundred miles to Meerut to attend my marriage. I still cherish the "collected works of Tennyson" that he gave me as a wedding gift.

The greatest favour perhaps that he did to me was that he put me in touch with university girls by recommending my name to the membership of The Friday Club, an exclusive group of about half a dozen boys and equal number each of girls and teachers of the department who sat for two hours in the staff room over coffee and sandwiches every Saturday evening. Its only activity was that its members staged an English play every year. In short, from a coarse country boy he turned me into a gentleman. Boys and girls studied separately till B.A. after which M.A. classes were co-educational. Uptil B.A. girls studied in the Women's college, separated by a high wall from the imposing building of the English department.

Mr. Deb was an excellent painter and short story writer. Every month a longish short story by him would be published in the magazine section of the Sunday Amrita Bazar Patrika, also published from Allahabad. In those days no magazine section of a newspaper was complete without a short story. Mr. Deb held an exhibition of his paintaings in the AIFACS gallery on Rafi Marg in Delhi. I helped him to organize its publicity through art critics I knew then, specially Richard Barthelemew, a Burmese national domiciled in India who had been my colleague in The Statesman before he quit to become a full time art critic and manager of an art gallery in Janpath.

Was it true? An invitation to a professor's house for tea on the first day of the new session. At the stroke of four in the afternoon I timidly entered Prof. Sen's neat little bungalow. It was truly an artist's retreat. The verandah and the small lawn that separated it from the road were studded with plants, pots and cane chairs. Inside, the professor sat in his study which was next to the drawing room along the verandah. Embroidered Bengali tapestry adorned the doors, windows and sofas in the house. Above the bookshelves in the study the walls were decorated with paintings, Mr. Deb's own work. The only bright object in those somber surroundings was a thick purple carpet in the drawing room. Adjoining it was the small dining room where the professor took me after exchanging pleasantries for a few minutes. It was his custom to have a quiet cup of tea there with his wife at four while their daughters did their school homework in their little room on the other side of Mr. Deb's study.

Mrs. Deb received me with great warmth as we sat down. I thought he resembled the ideal Indian housewife on a picture postcard with a big vermilion mark sitting prominently on his moonlike face. I spent a pleasant hour with them. They inquired about my birthplace, parents and my teachers at the Ewing Christian College where I had studied before joining the Academy. Tea and homemade cookies were served by a maid whom I had seen quietly entering the kitchen by the back door as we sat down.

From that day I was Mr. Deb's adopted ward on the campus for my remaining stay in the university. After tea Mr. Deb said, "My dear boy, let me till you why I have called you. The station director of All India Radio has asked me to pick two students, a boy and a girl, to broadcast a dialogue, of thirty minutes on how undergraduates see their future. "You have the right accent for the radio and speak English as he should be spoken", he said offering the assignment to me. My partner in the discussion would be Sujata Patwate (name changed), also a second year student, from the women's college of the university and daughter of a High Court Judge.

Sujata and I were to meet in the drawing room of Mr. Deb's house every day at three to write the scripts. It was a challenging task. There was no TV then. Radio ruled the air waves. The script had to be really good. On the first day we sat on an embroidered purple coloured carpet weaving scenarios of our future, a dream future. Around 3.30 we noticed Mr. Deb walking through the verandah past the window of the drawing room and tip-toeing to his bedroom through the study. Mrs. Deb gave us tea and biscuits. Sujata was bubbling with ideas. We talked back and forth for four or five days before our script was ready to be shown to the director of AIR, Allahabad. Every day Sujata would come punctually at 3 p.m. in a cycle rickshaw while I waited for his sitting in a chair in the verandah and everyday we enjoyed Mrs. Deb's hospitality.

Mr. Deb did not wish to see the script. He said he would hear it on the radio. He did not like to interfere with the naturalness and spontaneity of our effort. The scripts passed scrutiny and were a success.

During my last year in the university I was passing by Mr. Deb's bungalow on my bicycle when I saw Mrs. Deb standing behind its wicket gate talking to the blacksmith who had his workshop in the nearby market. I stopped to pay my respects to him.

"Wait Mukut, I want your advice". He called me into the small garden behind the tall hedge bordering the road.

"I was discussing with this man how to protect my house from these Holi vandals," he said. "Last year they took away the wicket gate and a bamboo chair lying in the verandah for their Holi bonfire, trampled upon flowers and plants, plucked hedges, battered doors and broke window panes. I want to put a removable barbed wire and an iron gate only for that day to stop them. Those ruffians have no sense of shame. They shout the foulest and filthiest imaginable sexual abuses not only naming my husband but also me and our poor daughters. I tell you they are the scum of the earth. They call themselves gentlemen. This university is breeding criminals. They disgrace themselves in this manner even in front of the girls' hostel. Can you think of anything more shocking than such vulgarisation of our sacred colour festival?"

Mrs. Deb had a shrill voice which, when he was agitated, could be heard a mile away. Mr. Deb heard it in his study and came out in his lungi and banyan.

"Mind your blood pressure, dear. This is a small matter."

"I have no blood pressure. It is you who have it"

"That is why I am asking you not to be excited. I do not want you to have it too. It is a minor matter. Boys will be boys. Can we not give them one day in the year to let off steam?" He explained to me that every year the students living in the hostels got drunk with marijuana essence called bhang, the traditional Holi drink, and roamed the streets dancing, singing, visiting houses of all teachers living near the campus and playing what he called "some foolish pranks".

His wife sneered. "They are not mere pranksters. They are rogues"

"Not such strong language dear, they are tomorrow's ICS officers, high court judges, lawyers, professors, writers and ministers.

"May be some precious gems from their lips will enrich your vocabulary which you can pass on to your literature classes", she said.

"There is nothing in it that they can teach me. I used to be in those merry-making groups myself as a student before you made a gentleman of me," retorted the professor. "With our bodies drenched in coloured water and cannabis juice flowing in our veins for one morning we were the lords and masters of the earth," he added nostalgically. He enjoyed provoking her. and went into the house. I and the blacksmith came away.

I was distressed by Mrs. Deb's revelations of the students' levity, and even more by Mr. Deb's approval of it. To my mind there could be no excuse for vulgarity in life even if someone were to tell me that in their youth Gandhi and Nehru too were like that. Surely Mr. Deb was old enough now to recognize that such mass display of sadistic obscenity could not be condoned in any civilized society. I had not heard of it earlier since I used to spend my Holi holidays at home with my parents.

"But why should such shocking things happen at all in a civilized society like ours?" I asked Mr. Deb.

"My study of Nazism has led me to examine social organizations in general. There is no such thing as a civilized society. What we call a society is an organized mass of individuals. Between it and the helpless individual stands the unorganized human aggregate called the mob. Its natural tendency is to stay as it is. You may call it inertia. To resist order it indulges in rowdism and creates chaos. To build order you must be prepared to cope with the revolt from the inherent forces of disorder in us. It happens everywhere. The riots by football fans in Europe and England, and by Oxford and Cambridge students on boat race nights are just stray examples. Other oppressed souls itching to defy order can just walk into a pub, get drunk, break somebody's head and provoke a small riot. Society imposes order upon the individual through fear of reprisals if he does not conform to its rules and norms. The mob removes that fear by giving him the mask of anonymity or a common cause. In it he tastes power, the power to destroy order and be above the society which persecutes and torments him. He realizes that mob fury can bring down the mightiest authority and he is the mob."

"That is quite different from shouting filthy abuses against innocent teachers and breaking their furniture and doors" I said,

He disagreed with me. "There is nothing abusive about language. It merely indicates the state of mind of the speaker. The words which you call abusive, when uttered by a teacher of anatomy or gynecology before his colleagues or students would be considered perfectly respectable."

"But you will agree that in the present case they are plain abuse," I said.

"No, I do not see them as abuse. To me it is plain slogan shouting, a case of the oppressed proclaiming their demands".

"What are they demanding by shouting those dirty abuses?" I asked in disgust.

"Girls, of course. Those are not sexual abuses but sexual demands. They are saying 'give us girls, give us more freedom."

"Restrictions are imposed by society. What can teachers do?"

"The prisoner sees only the gaoler. To break loose he must kill the jail keeper first. These professors are not so innocent either. They have all the sexual freedom one can want, beautiful wives with whom they can live in nicely kept bungalows and move about in style. The students see all this and envy them. How many of those boys can ever dream of such luxury?"

This happens everywhere in the world," I said.

"No, it does not. It happens only in India and the East", he retorted.

"How can you say that? Everywhere the teachers are married and students must stay single".

"It is not so simple. In the West there is no barrier against free mixing of boys and girls. In fact there it is a social necessity and a compulsory feature of campus life. On festive occasions like your Holi you will find their young men and women drinking, singing, dancing and indulging in other revelries together and not separately"

"I suppose we could have the same kind of freedom in India if we really wanted to"

"No, you may never have it", he replied with an air of authority and explained that Indian society was guided by the rules of the Aryan sexual hierarchy whose primary instrument of governance was sex, both in matters of state and religion. "It is a sexual tyranny designed to ensure strict racial purity. Sex here is not a right but a privilege governed by rigid rules and conventions of eligibility. Its sole objective is matrimony to produce children of pure breed and not love making for the satisfaction of a natural emotional and biological need. The rules are harsh on women. Girls whose parents cannot afford a fat dowry shall have no right to sex throughout their lives. Thousands commit suicide because only those women can expect to be fed and sheltered by the bread earning males who give them sensual pleasure in return. This is the blunt, harsh truth. Neglected wives of polygamists face the same faith. Widows are expected to die on their husbands' pyre since their sexual utility to society ends there."

Back in my room in Holland Hall I found myself a changed person. The casualness with which Professor Deb had dismissed the whole issue amazed me. But I realized that what he was saying was the plain truth. What the abusive Holi revellers were asking for was an opportunity to fraternize (call it 'flirt' if you like) with girls. That was the only way to soften and humanise them.

It was in a confused state of mind that a little later I walked into the room of Asif Ansari who was president of the student's union for that year. He happened to be my best friend from our Ewing Christian College days where we had lived in the same hostel Here he lived in another wing of Holland Hall. A polished, soft-spoken wiry little man and a scion of the landed aristocracy, he was a communist and a natural—born leader of youth. I had been to his village with him when his father suddenly died. He had at his command a few dozen dedicated boys and girls of the youth wing of the communist party who had worked vigorously among the two thousand students of the University for his election to the president's post. I asked him whether he was aware of how our fellow students debased themselves in front of houses of teachers on the Holi festival. He said that like me he too had spent his Holi in his village home and had no idea of how residents of the ten hostels around the campus celebrated the festival.

He was shocked to know that such things should be happening in the university and said:

"Will the Women's Hostel Warden allow the girls to attend our function?

"Do not be a sissy, man. The trouble with you, Mukut, is that associating too much with girls and teachers has made you effeminate and servile. You should join our party. We shall make a man of you in

144

six months. We also have girls, plenty of them, but not the boneless types you know. Ours are real firebrands."

I said I accepted his comments about me but that did not answer my question about the Warden. He could still spoil our plans.

"O' that mataji! Do you think the girls care for him? Still to be sure of their presence at our Holi celebrations I shall go to him tomorrow and invite him to be one of the chief guests at our function. That should fix him."

"Yes, he will be flattered," I said and by way of caution I asked

"How will you ensure the safety of the girls without informing the Vice-Chancellor Proctor of our plan?

Asif again admonished me to behave like a man. He reminded me that the and proctor were stooges of the government while he was the elected president of the union. He had more moral authority over the boys than they had. "I am a man of the masses. There can never be too many of them for me at a meeting. I can handle them like a pied piper", he said with confidence.

We used to make fun of Asif for imitating Nehru in everything like dress, mannerisms and style of speaking. He had even cultivated Nehru's quick temper and the ability to give vent to his anger within a fixed set of five or six mildly harsh Urdu words, like 'Jahil, himakat and badtameez'. Nehru's followers would take these as compliments or bouquets from their beloved Panditji. So did Asif's admirers. But it was the first time I discovered that this man had acquired Nehru's dare devil spirit also. Fear was one thing Nehru never knew. Nor did Asif.

He told me that he would ensure the safety of the girls and smooth conduct of the function but I must take full responsibility for organising all the foppery which was his way of describing the music and dance items to be staged on that occasion. I agreed. I was also to arrange advance publicity for the programme to attract the maximum crowds.

Early next morning I cycled down to the Women's Hostel and met the girls who had been contributing news and features to my paper called 'A.U. Weekly.'

I also visited a few music lovers in the boys' hostels. Editorship of the A.U Weekly had given me contacts in every field. We quickly identified teams for putting up Holi dances of Rajasthan, Bihar and the hills.

More than half the space in the next issue of my weekly was devoted to the hectic preparations being made by boys and girls for the union's unique Holi festival. On reading it many volunteer groups sprang up wanting to perform on that day. We selected three of them. Though a Muslim, Asif had been a Holi addict since childhood. As one the biggest landlord families in their district in East U.P. his ancestors had been hosting grand Holi celebrations at their village mansion for their ryots most of whom were Hindu. He rose to the occasion and provided at the union's expense light refreshments, perfumes, colours and tankards full of ice-cooled thandai on the lawn in front of the union hall.

The fateful day of Holi found me all in a twitter. Would our plans succeed? What if the girls stayed away from the function? The boys would then make a holi bonfire of the Union hall furniture. Asif had no such doubts and was calm as he gave orders to the staff and contractors' men to put things in their places before the start of the show.

Being the chief organiser of the music and dance show I was busy looking after the minor needs of the artistes, most of whom were girls, in the rooms behind the stage.

From there I could watch the audience unnoticed. I could see boys entering in groups by the door at the other and of the hall, walk to the staircase and go up to the first floor to stand in the gallery which ran round the hall and was soon packed to capacity. It afforded them an unobstructed view of the dozen or so front rows of chairs on the floor below them which were occupied by about a hundred girls who had trooped in quietly in groups of four to ten. They had come dressed in colourful clothes to suit the mood of the festival and presented a more alluring sight to the spectators in the galleries above than the artistes on the stage. Boys who came late had to be content with the few hundred seats in rear part of the hall or just stood in the passage to the staircase. The president made a short opening speech which was followed by a Radha Krishna dance by Kamala, a student of the University and a noted dancer, and her male partner.

Before returning to our make-shift green room at the back of the stage I paused at the door of the hall to take a look at the audience. To my surprise the maximum concentration of the crowds in the gallery was above the first and second rows of chairs on both side of the hall, From there the performers on the stage were hardly visible but one could get a close view of the audience below. It was obvious the boys were there to ogle at the girls. Professor Deb had proved right. The slogan shouting 'vandals' of previous years had suddenly turned gentlemen. They had got what they wanted.

The performances on the stage kept the audience completely engrossed for about two hours at the end of which everybody came out on the lawns for refreshments and to play Holi. Trays of sweets and bowls full of 'gulal' powder in many colours were placed on about a dozen tables. Girls collected on one side of the ground and boys on the other. Moied asked all of them to come forward and help themselves. After some hesitation the girls moved to their side of the tables and started lightly smearing each other's faces with gulal powder. The boys hesitated and just stood and watched. Slowly about a dozen of them came forward and, like the girls, sprayed the coloured powder within their own group. Sweets were consumed with delicacy. Nobody was pouncing on them.

The most active among the organizers were the female volunteers of the Student Federation of India, the youth wing of the communist party led by Shifaly, a cousin of Asif. He had ensured that the girls would be there.

It was then that I began to see through my communist friend and realized that he specialized in trickery. Taming those unruly student mobs of Holi revellers had been not so much an act of courage as of cunning. He had understood the weakness of the boys and taken full advantage of it. I twitted him. "So that was your secret weapon of crowd control—Shifaly and her gang and the rest of the girls. You knew exactly how the boys would behave before them. I did not. Is that why you keep pretty girls in your party?"

"You are welcome Mukut. I keep asking you to join us. Come and see for yourself. You will meet more Shifalys there".

12

"Our Youth Is No longer young"

—Khwaja Ahmed Abbas in 1948

Khwaja Ahmed Abbas, the legendary film personality and columnist said in the winter of 1948 "Our Youth is no longer young". His words have always been ringing in my mind but it is only now, when our great country has reached the abyss of its moral degeneration, that the full import of his words has dawned upon me. In fact he was politely referring to me and my type of people.

I was then a student of the Allahabad University, called the Oxford of India in those days. At my initiative a group of twelve boys living in Holland Hall, a hostel run by a Christian mission, had formed a club called "The Merry Makers". Two of us had decided to vacate one of our rooms and double up in it so that we could furnish the other with a sofa, chairs, and tea table for the club. We brought out an English wall newspaper every week containing member's writings and poems and, once a month, invited an important personality to have tea with us in Barnett's, the best hotel in town. VIPs of those days did not consider any group too small or lowly to merit their attention. When we learnt Khwaja sahib was in town, on his way to Bombay from Kashmir where he had gone for a short visit, we invited him to have tea with us and he gladly came. It was here that in course his talk that he uttered the axiomatic phrase "Our You is no longer young". It had lost its fire and passion and become too careeristic, he said.

I published a report of his discourse in the A.U. Weekly, founded and edited by me. Perhaps the first printed student weekly in any

Indian university it was distributed free in all the 1500 rooms in various hostels. Small ads from local shopkeepers and cinema halls financed it. A correspondent in each hostel and some part-time staff writers—all working for free—provided the news and other editorial content).

Those were times when students had time to devote to other activities besides their course studies. Since childhood many of us had developed a taste for classics and current great writers like H.G. Wells, Aldous Huxley, novels about the Spanish revolution then at its peak, Sydney and Beatrice Web, Hitler's Mein Kamph, Marx's Das Capital, Virginia Woolf, Herman Hesse, Pearl S. Buck, J.B.S. Haldane, Munshi Prem Chand, Jaya Shankar Prasad, D.F. Karaka and several others. A great many of us took part in various sports. Some were using the university as training ground for politics. Among my contemporaries were men like Narain Datt Tiwari and former Prime Minister Chandra Shekhar. R.K. Garg, the late Supreme Court lawyer and CPI MLA in U.P. was my classmate in Government High School, Saharanpur and later at Ewing Christian College and University. The two of us constituted our school's debating team. I usually got the first prize and he the second because I used to mug up my speeches whereas he always spoke extempore. Naturally, he scored over me in life and became a highly successful lawyer at India's apex court. But his forte was politics. He was close to Indira Gandhi and was the moving spirit behind the Krishna Menon society. Asif Ansari was another close friend. Both of us lived in Turner Hostel in Ewing Christian College. I traveled with him to his village Yusufpur in Ghazipur district of U.P. when his father, a rich landlord, suddenly died. It was my first encounter with a muslim joint family. Mud plastered open spaces dominated the high walled single-storey mansion spread over a large area with plenty of space for hens and cows. The most striking feature of the event was absolute normalcy. But for the pervasive silence in the atmosphere, it appeared as if nothing had happened. His father's death would make no difference to Asif's career. What if his father had passed away. His uncles were there to look after him and his mother as well as his property.

Later we moved to the university and were together for another four years in Holland Hall, run by the same mission as Ewing, an intermediate college. (Classes eleventh and twelfth were taught in what were then called intermediate colleges) Garg lived in Muir, an elite hostel which produced the varsity's largest number of entrants to the I.A.S. But he was made of a different stuff. He and Asif moved together, joined the students Federation of India (the youth wing of CPI) and launched one or two movements in the institution, including a hunger strike which I opposed in my paper. Ultimately, Asif became President of the university union. He never married and died while serving as a judge at the Allahabad High Court. Garg came to Delhi and became a lawyer at the Supreme Court. He died in a car accident a the age of 67. Both remained committed to their cause till the last.

While laudable, their kind of dedication is not what Khwaja Ahmad Abhas meant when he told us that youth was no longer young and had become careeristic. For both of them politics was the public front of their careers as lawyers. Likewise for Narain Dutt Tiwari, Chandra Shekhar and several other contemporaries who later became important Ministers, MPs, MLAs and political heavy weights. Politics was their chosen career. They were each affiliated to a national political party and had no choice but to follow its dictates. They were forbidden from acting together on any issue. If one party took up a public cause the others would remain silent about it. They were incapable of reacting spontaneously in unison to an act of injustice and cruelty by authority or society. When I was ferrying relief supplies to villages ravaged by floods in the Yamuna all of these budding politicians remained coolly aloof and indifferent. Party politics was their sole career aim.

Abbas was a visionary. He could foresee the disaster that was coming—the complete downfall of human character. His phrase "youth is no longer young" could also be interpreted to mean that before they had tasted youth our young people were already old and doing what old men and women normally do—acquisition of wealth.

Sixty-five years and two generations later Justice A.K. Patnaik, a Supreme Court judge, had this to say about today's youth-: "The unusual interest in accumulating wealth on the part of young Indians is weakening their emotional attachment to their nation and they need to be sensitized about their duty and responsibility according to the Constitution of India while our post-independence generation was admittedly interested in obtaining a reasonably remunerative career to be able to bring up a small family, today the yardsticks have completely changed." Life for today's youth is the naked dance of money and nothing else. Before a young man has settled in a job he starts dreaming of a house of his own.

Justice Patnaik's mention of the present-day Indian youth's responsibility to the Constitution apparently clearly seems to question even its patriotism. This is obviously collapse of the values of the freedom struggle.

On the other hand, Khwaja Ahmad Abbas would perhaps give full marks to Jyoti Swarup Saxena, an outstandingly brilliant student who resisted the universal craze to sit for the IAS entrance examination and stuck to his first love; English literature. For some years he taught as a lecturer in the Allahabad University and then moved to Jodhpur University as a Reader. I sought him out in 1973 in Jodhpur where I had gone as member of a Press party on a visit to the Central Arid Zone Research Institute. He lived with his family in a small, sparsely furnished villa at the foot of a hill, a few hundred feet below the four hundred years old Mahal (palace built by the royal family through bonded labour in exchange for food in years of severe famine.) A pipe smoking coffee-house addict Jyoti died of a heart ailment when he was only about 50.

What Abbas meant was a spirit of sacrifice for one's principles and ideals. At times it may call for action on the spur of the moment against an act of injustice or cruelty or a concerted well thought out protest by the common citizenry, irrespective of communal or party affiliations.

I shall never know the secret of how and why I cleared the B.A. and M.A. examinations of the Allahabad University. I was a fluent speaker, a vague reader of all kinds of serious literature except my text-books and above all, had a way of endearing myself to my teachers through involvement in numerous social activities of the university. Bu I know that I fared badly at all my exams and yet I passed, and even had a gold medal presented to me by Governor H.P. Mody at the convocation for the best essay in a university wide competition. All that I can say about it is that without telling me a word about it my teachers at the university must have secretly manipulated the examiners to pass me at both my BA and MA examinations. This only proves the unwritten Indian law, "Favourites must be favoured."

Starting new activities in the university was my main occupation. I launched a printed weekly university newspaper and ran it for more than a year when it attracted the attention of the professor in-charge of the university's annual journal. He was so impressed by it that he decided to find it out of his own allocations and gave me a room in the English department for its operations. I also organized a week-long Wordsworth Centenary Celebration in 1950. The Chief of the British Council in India, an Englishman, came from Delhi to attend it. He brought with him many charts and pictures depicting Wordsworth's life and works, for an exhibition we had arranged on the occasion. It was acclaimed as a great achievement of the department. But my main contribution to university life was stopping the exhibition of extreme vulgarity by students residing in the hostels on the day of the Holi festival. All students of each hostel used to take out separate processions and march to the homes of professors living in the vicinity to shout the filthiest sexual abuses at them and their families. How I managed to stop this display of obscenity is described in another chapter of this book.

It is for educationists to determine whether all these activities of mine, howsoever desirable, would justify manipulating the university results to allow me to pass the B.A. and M.A. exams in the second and third divisions respectively and even award me a gold medal, when throughout my stay I did not touch my course books except the "Keys" that condensed the courses into capsules for passing the exams.

13

The Most Memorable event in my life

During my previous visit to Kashmir two years earlier with the large family of my maternal grandfather I had met Prof. D. R. Suri, a short, bald and elderly professor of mathematics from Sialkot in Punjab. He and his wife lived in a spacious cottage of spartan taste on a hill along the Lidar river. They used to spend their entire summer vacation there every year to rejuvenate themselves with the appetising mineral water of the Lidar. In the evenings they would come down to the grassy plain where the torrential river flowed in two streams and sit down on its bank for a quiet hour. Our tents were close by and occasionally I would sit with them and then accompany them to their cottage. I had an open invitation from the professor to be their paying guest whenever I wished to visit Pahalgam again.

I am not a believer of the maxim "think before you act." Instead "act before you think" has been the motto of my life since my boyhood days. In 1946, two years after my first visit to Kashmir, a strong urge to visit Pahalgaon again overpowered me. I took some money from my parents and left for Kashmir in June.

The main purpose of my second visit to Kashmir was to make another trip to the holy cave of Amarnath, a twenty—six mile trek from Pahalgam across the over fourteen thousand feet high snow peak of Sheshnag. On the previous trip I had gone there in style as a member a family party of twenty-four people. We had travelled on ponies, taken with us rented tents loaded on mules and made three night halts each way, enjoying the food prepared by our own cooks. That was in the middle of July, the official pilgrimage season when thousands of tourists like us were scattered all over the route. This time I wanted to do it alone on foot in the first week of June, when there were no pilgrims or tourists to be seen. The owner of the mule that would carry my tent, bedding and provisions was to be my sole companion on the journey.

The whole of the following day we were busy organising our expedition. We bought spiked walking sticks and snow boots with nails that would protect us while trudging over miles of snow on the slippery descent from Sheshnag peak. On provisions we let ourselves go and filled several bags with fruits, including a basket of cherries, bread, biscuits, chocolates, butter, cheese, cream and whatever else caught our fancy. Hiring a mule and a tent was no problem. Prof. Suri introduced us to a reliable mule owner who could also act as a guide and friend along the way. Every shopkeeper we spoke to had only one unsought advice to give us, "do not go. It is dangerous. The roads have not been repaired and the night halts are totally deserted."

On the day when we were to leave for Amarnath it started raining. We loaded our mule and waited for the clouds to clear. But when by Ten O'clock there was no let up in the downpour we put on our rain coats, canvas caps and nailed boots, picked up our sling bags and spiked sticks and thumping the pebbly ground set off on the journey, disregarding the protests of the mule owner who had to follow us reluctantly.

We walked fast and warmed up within a few minutes so that the rain did not really bother us. The warmth of our companionship more than made up for the cold breeze and the rain drops reaching our bodies through chinks in our flimsy armour. Soon we were walking along a deep gorge of another river called Dudh Ganga because of its milk white water cascading at high speed. This was a new experience for Inder whose mountaineering experience was confined to trekking along streams near hill stations comparatively lower and less steep hills. He was awed by the might and majesty of the Himalayas. The path we were travelling on could not be called a road. It was strewn with stones and broken at several places. The breaches had to be crossed by treading gently on narrow ledges jutting out from the mountains. A slip could mean a fall of several hundred feet and instant death. I told Inder not to worry and walk with confidence and care, holding firmly to the mountain with one hand. It was at such places that one discovered the power and presence of the unseen spirit in us which guarded us from perils with unfailing certainty. I had never heard of anyone fall from those ledges. I told him that the thrill of walking in the higher ranges of the Himalayas lay in living with risks every moment and knowing that nothing would happen to you.

Inder wondered how I could be so nimble-footed over those wild and hostile rocks. I told him that though a man of the plains mountaineering had been in my blood since childhood. Trekking in the Himalayas and boating in the Yamuna at Allahabad were my main sports. Much of the journey lay in climbing steps cut in rocks by nature or feet of men and animals. Most of these were overladen with leaves and slippery pine needles dropping constantly from the surrounding trees that kept swaying with the sharp wind. They were also soaked in water. We walked through scores of swift moving streams flowing across the road and drank gallons of water from tiny water falls spouting from the interior of the rocks.

In three hours we had covered the first stage of the journey and reached Chandanwari after walking eight miles and climbing two thousand five hundred feet. Normally, it was a whole day's work for the pilgrims. On my previous trip we had camped there for the night.

The rain had not stopped but its fury had abated and it had come down to a drizzle. Sunlight was filtering through clouds and trees. In the middle of the forest we found a large tent with smoke and pleasant smell of food emanating from it. A well dressed young Sikh gentleman came out on hearing our gleeful sounds and welcomed us. The tent was a small restaurant and apparently we were its first customers that day. Tourists to Pahalgam often went up to Chandanwari on foot or horse back though we had not met any on the way.

When I told him Inder was a doctor, he made us sit at a table in the centre of the tent while talking to Inder all the time. "Sir, you are most welcome, Sir. Will you have tea first or food? And so on". Inder was most courteous in his replies and kept on thanking him with a smile while asking him to give us whatever he could quickly provide as we had a long way to go. "Food is ready, Sir," and ordered his two assistants to serve it.

"You will like music", he said switching on his large, battery operated HMV radio and tuning in the Colombo station of BBC which was started during World War II.

He told us that his name was Jatinder Singh but we could call him Jatin and added that before starting his own business he had been an assistant manager in one of fashionable clubs in Lahore.

"Why did you leave it and come here in this wilderness?" Inder asked.

"Adventure sir. Love of mountains. We have one life to live and we can live it fully only when we are young."

I could see he was speaking the truth. Nothing but love of adventure could have prompted him to camp alone, six months in a year, in this remote wilderness. When we told him we were proceeding to Amarnath he was horrified and like everybody else said, "do not go. It is dangerous".

Inder countered him. "Remember Jatin what you said just now. We have one life to live and we can live it fully only when we are young".

We told him we had a tent, bedding and provisions on a mule that was following us. He advised us to halt for the night at a shelter for workers just ahead of Sheshnag Lake. It would be lying vacant now and could be very dirty. But that was the only covered space we would find before reaching Panchtarni, the third stage of the journey, which we could not possibly make before nightfall.

We left him and wandered for a few minutes in the surrounding forest. I wanted to show Inder the "bhoj patra" trees whose smooth bark was used in ancient times as paper. Most of our old scriptures were written on it. I plucked off a chunk of it from a tree with my hands and peeled it layer by layer. It made several glossy cream coloured sheets of writing paper. On my previous visit I had spent hours among these trees writing love poems to a girl on those crisp barks with a Parker pen.

As we emerged from the grove Jatin came running and panting behind us. He was carrying a paper bag full of spiced hot pakoras freshly cooked in his kitchen. Pressing these on Inder he said, "Take these doctor. Do not depend too much on your mule man. You may be stranded." We were touched by his gesture and moved on. Soon we came to a permanent snow bridge. A little beyond was a white board, which said, "You are now at 10,000 feet above sea level." This pleased Inder immensely. I told him we had another four thousand feet to climb before going down into another valley.

The food, tea and the encounter with Jatin had buoyed up our spirits and we climbed with swift steps. This portion of the trek was uneventful but packed with the most breath taking spectacles of shimmering snow and cragged ranges towering one upon the other while innumerable varieties of flowers carpeted the hill slopes around us. The road was bad and rocks slippery but these hurdles only provided more stimulus to our zeal for adventure. The sharp wind kept recharging us with fresh energy. Rain had stopped, the sky was clear and colourful. Dazzling multi-coloured bands of sun beams were being shot back prismatically into space by miles and miles of towering snow peaks. We were both looking at all this, enraptured, and walking as if in a trance. We stopped again and again to capture those memorable views and record them in our memory. To this day those gorgeous scenes are large canvases in the picture gallery of my mind.

Now and then, after a steep climb, we would lie down on a patch of grass and arrange our hair ruffled by the breeze with a comb. We had taken off our rain coats and jackets and shoved them into our sling bags. Such halts were few and brief. Within a few minutes we would come back to life, take a few deep breaths and open our eyes with a smile. Next moment we were charging up the hill with renewed fury. I wished such exhilerating stoppages were longer. We should have travelled in a more leisurely style.

Three hours' trek from Jatin's tent brought us to a high rock overlooking the Shishnag Lake. On it, protected from storms by a crevice, stood the workers' shelter that Jatin had told us about. It was a long room of stone with a single door which was open. We walked in. Inside it was a row of twelve stone settees covered with straw to sleep upon. The floor was littered with crumbs of food, smoked bidis and half-burnt wood and ash. It was not clean but not particularly dirty either. Cool breeze was blowing into the room through the small window in the opposite wall bringing in the fragrance of the pine trees on the hill. Mingled with the smell of burnt wood and tobacco that permeated the room, it made the place look quite cosy, though a bit untidy.

Outside it was bright and sunny, the time Five p.m. Deep down the hill, about three hundred feet below us the huge lake lay still, clear like a crystal, reflecting the sky in its celestial water. Beyond it on the other side rose another range of the Himalayas capped by the snows of the famous Shishnag peak which shone majestically in a golden light at height of sixteen thousand feet. From where we stood at a height of around twelve thousand feet we could see far away in the opposite mountain, on the other side of the lake, the thin white mule track that would take us to the fourteen thousand feet high shoulder of Shishnag. From there it was a straight descent over nearly two miles of snow after which a brisk hour-long walk along a gorge would bring us to Panchtarni, the third night halt on the pilgrimage to Amarnath.

Our mule was nowhere in sight and spending the night in that wilderness without the provisions it carried, without even a candle, was unthinkable. A thought struck me and I shared it with Inder.

I told him we still had three-and-a-half hours of daylight before us. We were not tired and could easily make it to Panchtarni before night fall. We had only to climb another two thousand feet to the shoulder of Shishnag and from there it was all down hill journey, I said pointing to the snowpeaks. He jumped from his seat on a rock overlooking the lake on which we were perched for a short rest and said, "good idea, come let us go". We ran down the hill to the bank of the lake and walked along it to reach the other side. The climb to the top of the mule track was free from hurdles and within an hour we had reached the shoulder of Shishnag. Now came the difficult part. The other side of the peak was like a mountain pass, shaded from the sun on all sides. More than a mile of our path, perhaps two miles, was covered by snow. It was for this stretch that we had equipped ourselves with nailed boots and thick walking sticks with long spikes. Inder was overjoyed at the sight of so much snow though I felt depressed by it. We had to fight against the setting sun. After a bright and sunny climb we had now entered the twilight zone. The top layer of the slope was soft and fluffy. We had to be careful while negotiating it. Inder stayed close to me and asked me to put my free hand on his shoulder for mutual support against slipping down the hill. In this fashion, with slow and steady steps, we reached the bottom of the slope in another hour.

I screamed with joy as we touched plain ground. "Inder, we have done it! It is only seven and we have another ninety minutes of daylight before us. Panchtarni is over there beyond those hills. We shall reach the priest's house rolling down the hill in no time now." He was happy too.

"What a wonderful day we have had, Mukut! I wonder why everybody was advising us against it. Imagine what we would have missed had we listened to them." We sat down on the stony ground and surveyed the scene around us. It was stark, narrow and desolate. We were surrounded by mountains. A little ahead roared a swift stream with a bridge across it. We had to cross it and then go along its course.

I disagreed with him. "Our advisers were not wrong Inder. I now realize we have taken a big risk. All the while it has been touch and go for us. Come let us hurry up and get out of here as fast as we can. I have heard that this is the hour when snow bears come to the streams for water."

He laughed away my fears and we set off again. In thirty seconds we reached the bridge. To our utter amazement it was broken in the middle. A five—foot span of it had collapsed in the stream. I was stunned. We were stranded and trapped. There was nowhere to go, backward or forward. For nearly fifteen minutes we fretted about the place trying to see if we could somehow get across the stream. It was not very wide, couldn't be more than fifty feet across. But it was swift and could carry us away in its current. It did not appear to be very deep but in that limited light we could not be sure of it.

In my desperation I put my stick in the water to attempt a crossing. Inder pulled me back with a jerk. "Do not be a fool Mukut. We have no choice but to spend the night here. Be calm. We shall survive and find a way in the morning" My face turned pale. I sat down on the bank perspiring despite the extreme cold and started crying. "I have wronged you Inder. I should not have exposed you to this danger. Please forgive me for this folly if we survive this night and never see me again. I am not worthy of your friendship," I said with tears streaming down my cheeks. I was in a real fright then. Inder sat down by my side, took out the rain coat from my bag and put it gently around my shoulder, hugging me while doing so. "Nothing will happen to us Mukut. It is only the matter of a night in the open. So what of that? It is peak summer time. Why do you worry?"

There was no rancour in his voice. He spoke in a matter of fact manner as if we had merely missed a train and would have to spend the night on a railway platform in the certain hope of getting another train the next morning. I reminded him that we were at an altitude of over twelve thousand feet amidst snows where the night temperature could plummet to several degrees below freezing point. We were sitting in a deep hole in the mountains, at the bottom of a huge inverted cone, from where there could be no escape from weather or wild animals. By the morning both of us might starve or freeze to death if we were not devoured by bears, I said. It was getting dark where we sat surrounded by high ridges though there was still some light in the sky over the peaks. As I spoke of wild bears I looked furtively in all directions and indeed did see shadowy figures in the snow covered slopes some distance away. "Look", I said showing them to him. He gazed into the dark vacancy above the hazy snow line and said, "There is nothing there. It is only your imagination. Come let me take you away from the water to a place where you will feel safer. He stood up, put his hand under my arm and helped me stand on my shaky legs. Our immediate surroundings were still clearly visible upto about fifteen feet. We walked around a bend in the hill, away from the water, and selected a patch of stony ground strewn with pebbles for our night halt.

There Inder took out the bag of spiced pakoras Jatin had given us after lunch in Chandanvari. The pakoras were heavily spiced and had an electric effect on my jangled nerves. We ate, drank water from the stream and praised Jatin for his kindness. "What a good soul", said Inder. "Yes, today he has saved my life," I replied. By the time we finished the pakoras my spirits had revived and I was less apprehensive of my fate though not completely restored in my self-confidence. We were now in near total darkness but for the light reflected by the snow around us.

Inder told me that I was feeling nervous because it was the first time I was spending a night on snow. "Your snow bear is the snow not bear," he said.

After a nap of about an hour I woke up in the middle of the night, shivering. The cold stones under me were cutting into my bones. Chilly breeze had pierced through my clothes and was numbing the body. There was more light now. The sky was packed with millions of stars whose light together with its reflection from the snow in our vicinity made the surroundings clearly visible. In this state of utter helplessness in this lonely wilderness I was gripped with fright. With great difficulty I managed to sit up, but could not stand. I pulled my knees into my chest with both arms and sat crouched over them. It did not help and the shivering continued. I remembered seeing a beggar on a road one wintry night, trying to warm himself by clapping his hands. I tried the remedy first slowly so as not to disturb Inder, then louder.

He woke up, saw me and sat up. "What's the matter, Mukut?", he asked.

"I am shivering with cold. Clapping warms up the blood a little," I said.

Inder had an inspiration. He remembered another life saving technique he had read about in an adventure magazine. "Come I shall warm you. Lie down close to me" he said. Unbuttoning his raincoat and mine he inserted the buttons of each into the holes of the other. Thus joined, the two raincoats together became a sleeping bag for two. He held me tight throwing one arm round my back and the other under my neck.

For about half-an-hour I lay passive and motionless in his clasp with my heart and breath battling for life. Slowly the numbness was gone and normal sensations returned. Evidently Inder's body could generate enough heat for two and he had taken every care to pass on all the surplus to me by wrapping himself so closely around my body.

It was bright daylight when I woke up. Inder had awakened earlier but kept lying still till I opened my eyes. He unbuttoned our sleeping bag of raincoats and we stood up. The first thing that caught our attention as we looked around was a box-like hut of wood sitting on the ridge barely fifteen feet away from us towards the snow. The blue and green paint on its planks suggested it was being maintained for stranded travellers like us. How both of us missed seeing it the previous evening was a reflection of our nervousness and despair. Its door was ajar but we did not care to look in. Our only concern was the river and how to cross it. We jerked our knees to restore circulation of blood in our half-numbed legs, picked up our bags and sticks and walked to the bank. It was an amazing sight. The water was not more than one foot deep and its stone strewn bed was clearly visible. The current was swift but not strong enough to carry us away if we stuck together. As an extra precaution we decided to walk along the bridge so that we could hold to its frame if we slipped. The paint marks on the pillars of the bridge were another foot above the water level. This could mean that normally the river carried twice as much water as it contained now. Apparently its level had come down overnight.

Our physical condition notwithstanding it was a moment of extreme jubilation for us. Without wasting a minute, we took off our boots and socks. Putting on our boots again we waded the gurgling stream and crossed it with slow and firm steps, holding each other's hands and balancing our body weight on the sticks, in about five minutes.

On reaching the other bank we sat down on the stony ground and dried our feet and legs with our sling bags. I stood for a minute facing the river with folded hands to offer a silent prayer to God for his great mercy in saving our lives. This duty done we set off towards Panchtarni.

Within a few minutes we came to a small colony of itinerant shepherds who had set up about a dozen tents along the path. Their sheep scratched the hills for grass and leaves. Two of the men who were standing by the roadside watched us from a distance with a fixed stare. As we came close to them their mouths gaped and eyes bulged with wonder. We greeted them with a smile. They did not respond but kept looking at us. After we had gone past them a few steps the elder of the two hailed me. "Wait brother" he shouted. We looked back. He came forward with his companion and asked "Where did you spend the night? How do you happen to be here so early in the morning?"

"We couldn't cross the river at night. So we stayed on there"

"In the hut?"

"No, in the open. We did not see the hut"

The man joined his hands in prayer and lifted his head to the sky "Allah be praised for saving your lives, brother. You must be hungry. Come with us."

He took us to his tent and asked us to sit with him on the ground outside it. His wife gave us two glasses of hot salted tea and freshly roasted gram. He told us that the stream flowed from a high snow peak close by. In the day, specially in summer, the snow melted and by the evening the stream was overflowing with water. At night there was no melting, only freezing. Even part of the river froze and it was reduced to a small stream by the morning. That was why we were able to cross it. We thanked our stars for this fortuitous phenomenon. The tea was invigorating. We ate part of the gram and stuffed the rest in our raincoat pockets. The shepherds walked with us for some distance.

Man and sheep were hardly distinguishable. Herdsmen and their children scaled the cragged ridges around us with perfect ease as if they were running on plain road. Except for a bit of barter and cash trading they had little to do with the outside world. This gorge was their territory and they treated us as their honoured guests.

We reached the house of Gobind Ram, my family's Amarnath priest, in an hour, after crossing a vast mile-wide plain of sand and gravel, named Panchtarni because it is shared by five mountain streams as their common bed, a rarity on those snowy heights. He remembered the gifts of gold and cash my mother had given him on my previous visit. His mind was like a calculating machine. It remembered every amount, small or big, that his patrons had given him all through his career as a 'panda.' He gave us warm sweets to eat and then took us to the legendary Amarnath cave on horses over a narrow, precipitous route atop a deep gorge. It was frightening to both of us. Over a large part of it we felt that every minute our lives were in peril but the priest and the owner of the horses who walked behind us talked and laughed as if they were loitering merrily on a hundred feet wide road. This reassured us.

We thoroughly enjoyed the icy marvels of the huge cave. It is a massive awning in the mountain, a dome shaped cube about fifty feet in length, width and height. Pilgrims were bathing in the ice cold water flowing from the cave, wearing a long white garment provided by the priest. "If this water is holy it must be holy for all. We contented ourselves with washing our faces, hands and feet with some drops of the sacred water the mere touch of which sent shivers down our spines.

We returned to the priest's house in Panchtarni by lunch time. Our mule man was waiting for us and started ranting and raving the moment we alighted from our mounts. Accusing us of being heartless he described in detail how he and his animal had a scrape with death on the snows during the night. We told him we had been in the same plight, gave him money and pacified him. The priest gave us a delicious lunch of hot khichri with ghee, potato and pickles. We decided in consultation with him, to move on and spend the night at the road workers' shelter on the other side of Sheshnag Lake. It seemed quite simple now that our beddings and provisions were with us. The panda arranged horses that would take us to the top of the Shishnag snows and thus save us from the treacherous stream crossing and the slippery and slushy snow-covered slopes of the peak. The horses would put us down on dry ground on the sunny side of the mountain from where it was an easy descent up to Shishnag Lake with no hassles like streams, bridges and landslides.

The mule owner readily agreed to the proposal and promised to meet us at the shelter beyond the lake. Before starting he wanted to give the animal rest and food. The priest accepted with folded hands and a deep bow the generous tip we gave him for his services. We filled our bags with bread, butter, biscuits and fruits from our provisions on the mule's back and started off. Our mounts were sturdy and tall and made good speed throughout the ascent to the peak. Crossing the stream at the spot where we had spent the previous night gave us a feeling akin to the nostalgia that one feels for a great experience of bygone days. It had been an immortal moment in our lives. We were traveling on a narrow path along a gorge. On reaching the wide snow-covered climb our horses could move two abreast.

We reached the shelter at a leisurely pace at about eight in the evening. On the way we sat for an hour by the side of Shishnag Lake, a sprawling sheet of water spread over a vast bowl under the snows. For the first time in two days since we left Pahalgam we tasted real peace. If the gorge where we had spent the previous night was a playground of the gods, this place around the lake must be the higher heaven, abode of rishis like Narada. It exuded calm. The contrast between the two places was striking. It was the same hour of the evening but the scene on the other side of the peak was dark, desolate, narrow and noisy with the roar of the stream, while the lakeside was bathed in the reflected glow of the sun shining on the neighbouring mountains. Birds sported near the water and there was no breeze. It appeared that even the god of the wind flying over this place was struck by its serenity and got lost in contemplation of its beauty like the other invisible rishis who, so I imagined, were scattered around the lake. Sitting there and watching the landscape we refreshed ourselves with the fruits and other eatables we had retrieved from our food stocks on the mule's back. There was still no sign of the animal and its owner but we had no doubt that they would come and join us shortly.

The workers' shelter was occupied when we reached it. This cheered us as it meant we would not have to spend another lonely night in this rocky wilderness. In the space facing the entrance sat a man cooking food over a fire made by burning jungle wood. Inside on the stone settees sat seven other members of the party offering 'Namaaz', the Muslim prayer. The man welcomed us with a 'salaam' and asked us to join him near the fire. We sat on the floor and closed our eyes in silent prayer.

After the worship the men rose and gathered round us to hear of our adventures. They were all between twenty and thirty, fair, slim and of medium height. Each of them wore a dusky shirt, pyjama, light sleeve-less jacket and a thin beard. Hameed, the man who was cooking and not praying, was their leader and did most of the talking. He said they would be happy to give us a blanket and a place to sleep. "Allah is great. He has sent you to us. You are safe here. You should not have come in this season. But it was His will that brought you here. Who are we to judge His ways?"

Hameed's philosophic tone impressed me. "You were not offering 'Namaaz' with the others. When will you pray?" I asked him. He kept quiet. One of his colleagues said, "He is always praying. The name of Allah is ever on his lips and He thinks of Him while working on the road, walking, talking or cooking. His mind is only on Him, nothing else. Namaaz is for those who have to be reminded of Allah at least once a day in the midst of other occupations. He is a Sufi, a vairagi." Hameed smiled keeping his eyes on the fire. The food they gave us consisted of corn bread and salted tea in a bowl which served as curry. We emptied our bags of the bread, biscuits, butter, fruit and jam and offered it to them. Hameed refused to take it. "You are our guests. Allah has sent you to us. How can we take food from you?"

It became clear to us that we would have to spend another night without our beddings, there being no hope left of the mule arriving with our baggage. The sleeping arrangements in the shelter were simple. Taking us to be a married couple they gave us one settee by the wall and a blanket. The light of the fire was beginning to fade. Soon it was pitch dark. Hameed closed the door of the room but kept the window open for some more time to let everyone settle down in the faint light from outside.

In the morning we were early. Refusing to accept payment for their hospitality our hosts bade us goodbye in a matter of fact manner. To these hardy hillmen experiences like ours were part of life. In those rugged altitudes one could never be sure that a member of the family journeying to another place a few miles away across the mountain would hit home by nightfall. They had enough faith in Allah not to spend a sleepless night worrying about the traveller's fate, be the person a man, woman or child. They knew that some kind samaritan or mother Nature herself would shelter the wayfarer who was sure to turn up, safe and sound sooner or later, none the worse for the wear and tear of the journey. This spirit showed on every lineament of his face as we came out of the road workers' hut and surveyed the azure splendour of dawn over the hills and its reflection in the Shishnag lake below. He was ecstatic about everything and in no hurry to resume our downward journey. Regretting that he had not brought his camera along Inder was using his sub-conscious mind as a substitute, shooting into it through his laser sharp eyes images of Himalayan beauty that he would like to preserve for the rest of his life.

He was not exaggerating. The lightness of the breeze at those high altitudes combined with his bubbling enthusiasm was making him run down the slopes with springy steps that seemed to barely touch ground. By contrast I was in low spirits and straggling behind him with measured, thoughtful steps. Weighed down with remorse by the dangers and hardships to which I had exposed Inder I was labouring under a guilty conscience as I walked. After a steep descent of about half-an-hour he stopped in a pine grove to let me catch up with him. After a good lunch with our friend Jatin in Chandanwari we reached Pahalgaon the same evening.

14

The Years with Master ji

Guliver of Jonathan Swift, Ichabod Crane of Washington Irwing and W. Cowper's Alexander Selkirk are some of the names that come to my mind when I think of Rama Pati Banerji the man who influenced my life in a nascent manner during the most formative years of my life. When I first saw him he was a dashing young Bengali intellectual who chose to spend his life in a no man's land, that was kota village, the ancestral seat of my mother and her parents. It was like an island in a sea of jungles, bullock cart tracks, shrubs and bushes in which it was easy to get entangled and, here and there, some open fields. Distance wise it was not far from civilization, just six miles away from the district town of Saharnpur on the western tip of the vast province of U.P. in British India, bordering what was then Punjab that extended upto Rawalpindi (now in Pakistan) and beyond. An island six miles off the coast of Bombay has nothing to do with Bombay. I have visited such an island near Bombay. So had Kota nothing in common with Saharanpur, not even language or food. In Kota they spoke a dialect with a vocabulary of a few words of one or two syllables while in the city they spoke proper Hindustani with a lot of Urdu words in it. Being a Bengali Banerji took time to understand it.

In Saharanpur ordinary people ate food made of wheat, pulses, potato and mill made sugar. In Kota on the other hand, except a few families of the rich, they ate thick chapatis made of coarse grains like jowar and bajra sweetened with gur or jaggery. Their dresses were also different. In the city you will hardly see on its roads a person without a shirt and some kind of footwear. In kota, on the other hands, most of the males wandered about bare cheated and bare footed. The halwai and the grocer wore banyans which they occasionally took out when it became too hot. Their only dress was a short dhoti tied up to the knees. While women in the city wore dhotis and saris village women from poor families wore long skirts a blouse and a long scarf. In winter men and women wore thick jackets stuffed with pure raw cotton balls.

Masterji was perhaps the only educated person I have met in my whole life who can be said to have led a normal life without any ambition, family attachments or even friends. A life-long bachelor, moderate smoker and crossword addict, he took life as it came from moment to moment. His entire baggage to his last day could be assembled in two suitcases. When the youngest of his three pupils, Prem Nath, got afflicted with tuberculosis, a near fatal and highly infectious disease in those days he volunteered to stay with him in the family's garden house and kept the patient in good cheer.

I have often wondered why Banerji chose to apply for this position in response to an advertisement in the Hindustan Times some time around the year 1930. And having accepted it, why did he decide to spend his whole working life in the job beset with so many hardships and practically no rewards? He was an M.A. in history from St. John's College, Agra, by far the best college in U.P., apart from the Universities of Allahabad, Lucknow and Benares. Besides, he was son of a divisional inspector of schools, a post that was rarely given to Indians then. Why should a promising young man with this background, made illustrious by the fact that in those days there were very few educated families have chosen to live in such a godforsaken place?

His being son of an Inspector of Schools meant that he could walk into the best schools in the province for a teacher's post. Under British rule pedigree and recommendation mattered a lot. Was he a revolutionary like Sri Aurobindo who fled to Pondicherry to escape harassment by British authorities after his acquittal by the courts for alleged involvement in a conspiracy case? What could be a better place to hide from the clutches of the law than the house of a rich but virtually illiterate family of a small village in the midst of a vast jungle? The only educated member of this family by marriage was Om Prakash Gupta, a brother-in-law of the younger brother of my maternal grand father and a civil engineer in the irrigation department of U.P.

He rose to be its engineer-in-chief and member of India's Irrigation Commission, thirty years later. The two brothers, Asa Ram and Shiv Charan Das, lived jointly in one haveli without any division of assets or income among them. Between them they had three sons. Gupta suggested that instead of roaming around like vagabonds with nothing to do, the boys should be given proper education.

Though the family owned a large mansion in the heart of Saharanpur, moving out of the family seat was not feasible. So an ad was placed in the newspaper and Benerji was selected. He was housed in an abandoned hundred-year old haveli of which he was the sole occupant. An attendant used to bring him food from the family kitchen twice a day. A glass of one pound of buffalo milk was served to him morning and evening in the class room, along with the boys, it being only additional nourishment available in those days. The attendant would also visit him for a few minutes in the evening to light divas in the passage and the kerosene lantern in his room. An eerie silence prevailed inside the haveli and also outside it during the night. Bats who kept fluttering their wrings at night were his only companions in this haveli.

I hesitated to enter its dark passages even in day time. It was surrounded by undulating heaps of mud. On one side of it, across a sloping uneven track for passers by was a mud hut with a large compound wall where levied Kabool master, the village school teacher who had himself not studied beyond the fourth or fifth class.

At his request the Hindustan Times was subscribed to. It came by post. Kota had no post office then but a postman visited it everyday from the nearest post office to deliver letters and collect all letters posted in a letter box that was hung in the verandah of the mud house of the village chowkidar built on a plinth of about two feet. It was not more than fifty yards away from our haveli. After his school hours Banerji, called Master ji by everybody, used to sit on a bench placed on the large tiled and polished platform in front of the mansion with my grand father who did not know English, and translate for him for a few minutes the main headlines of the day in simple Hindustani tinged with his Bengali accent. On days when the chowkidar was delayed in delivering the paper Master ji would walk down to his hut to collect it.

Throughout his stay of about 30 years in the service of the family he preserved a reserved profile, keeping his distance both in his dealings with members of the house and the residents of Kota village. Everybody respected him and greeted him but he hardly ever stopped to have a long chat with anyone. In fact, he is the only person of my acquaintance that I can recall, in my whole life of over eight decades, who did not have even one friend and no family of his own. Yet he was aware of all the goings on in the village. He even knew who was sleeping with whom in the village community. I suspect he got all his information from the servant who took food to him from our haveli twice a day and also the servant who lighted his entry, stair case and room at night. He sometimes shared spicy bits of village gossip with me when I used to visit Kota during my long vacations.

Nor was he interested in religious festivals or rural folk arts. It involved mixing with rustic rural crowds which he avoided. Sitting on the floor with villagers to sing devotional songs or celebrate a festival was repugnant to him. My grandfather and his younger brother were fond of inviting itinerant minstrels to give late night performances on the wide uneven space between their residential mansion and a larger building opposite it that housed their small secretariat on the ground floor and a guest house, wide terraces and a free kitchen (called 'langar') for visiting tenants on the first floor. Using a rustic garage like room attached to the opposite building as the green room and putting up a make-shift stage of large wooden settees, these groups of folk actors would reenact heroic deeds by past warriors in the light of a petromax. A colourful screen was hung between the green room and the stage and another between the stage and the viewers.

The all male audience sat on rough jute carpets spread on the floor. The stage was so located that the ladies of our family could watch the whole show from the windows of their rooms in the upper storey of the haveli. The strong points of these wandering troupes were their colourful screens and costumes and their loud voices that could be heard clearly at a distance of a hundred yards. They included men of all ages, including boys of the age of 10 or 12 years, but no females. Boys had to don the clothes of women and with their piping voices some of them performed their roles beautifully. Though illiterate they had learnt their parts by heart.

I happened to be in Kota during two of these performances. One was a one-night show of the Alha-Udal saga. Alha and Udal were two great Twelfth century warriors whose valour and sacrifice has been enshrined in an immortal verse by a great court poet. The long poem is recited in a particular style which was very popular up to world war-II years and many a minstrel or bard made their living by singing it to the accompaniment of a guitar or similar musical instrument or even an orchestra.

The other show that I remember seeing in Kota was 10 day long Ramlila, enacting the our greatest epic Ramayana, the story of Rama, God incarnate and prince of Ayodhya. The shows used to go on till two in the morning and such was the devotional fervour and dedication of those times that no member of the audience left any of the shows till it was over. Instead of sitting with the ladies in the windows I watched it squatting on the ground near the stage with my grandfather and uncles. The following day some young members of the audience, including me, would try to reenact the scenes we had seen the previous night. It helped me in performing the minor role of Manthra, the woman who misled queen Kaikayi at the very start of the epic, in a Ramlila we staged in a middle school run from a dharamshala in Nehtaur, a town like Gangoh where my father was posted for a year.

Later, around the year 1975, I had opportunity to see the dance drama form of the epic staged in Lucknow by Rukmini Devi Arundale's famous Kalakshetra of Madras. A thing that struck me most about the South Indian dance version was that it showed Sarupankha—Ravana's sister to avenge whose insult by Ram and Lakshman, he abducted Sita—as a beautiful Aryan princes while in all North Indian Ramlilas that I have seen Sarupankha is shown as a hideous woman.

For the wandering actors, performing in Kota estate was a great honour. They slept on the settees which served as the stage, went to the well near the family temple for a bath when they cleaned up all the grime of crude paint and coal ash which they used to smear on their bodies to play their different roles. They were served free food in the 'langar'. When performing elsewhere, they had to live in the jungle under trees or in the verandah of a temple and cook their own food. Most of the time they performed on open ground without a stage or green room.

Though Master ji did not actively cultivate friends in Kota he was not averse to translating for them in Hindustani language any communication that they might have received in English. He was the only person in the whole village who could perform such a feat and he was only too oblige anyone who came to him with such a letter.

In the evenings after the class Masterji would take a short walk of about two hundred yards to the family's pleasure garden. Spread over an area of four acres it was surrounded on all sides by a ten feet high wall and looked like a fortress or prison from outside. It had a big gateway, large enough to house on its first floor a Sanskrit School for children of Brahmins financed by my grandfather. Attached to the park was a row of three small temples, presumably built by my grandfather or his ancestors. We could also visit the temple by a side door in a wall of the park. Opposite the temples was a well and a Peepal tree under which sat the only halwai (sweet maker) in Kota. I remember his jalebis which I used to relish, though he made other sweets too. For us the whole village was one grand haveli of my grandfather and his younger brother, complete with a huge cattle yard, a pond, a carpenter and a grocer, Benarsi, who sat on a thin sheet spread on the floor of his tiny shop along the rough track to the park. All his merchandise was contained in small rusty tin cans placed near his seat.

I remember the grocer's name because I used to buy from him lolly pops, lemon drops and spicy (Khatta-mitta) churan which he kept in small rusty boxes of tin. Adjoining our two mansions were two havelis of second and third generation cousins of my grandfather. They were minor landlords and maintained very good relations with us. The haveli adjoining ours was connected to ours by a window in the common wall so that women and girls in the two houses could chat with each other whenever they liked. The window was fitted with iron bars and doors. Opening such doors or windows into adjoining houses built by the same owner was a common practice in my childhood days. It enabled housewives and children to socialize. Gossiping and sharing what was cooked in the Kitchen was largely confined to immediate neighbours.

Colleagues of the same sank at the work place also because family friends. Behind our haveli was another large house also owned by our family, which was kept empty and to which there was a secret passage through the bathroom. My mother told me in whispers that all the wealth of my grandfather and his brother was kept in an underground cellar in that house. There were no bank lockers then to keep your money and jewellery in safe custody. The empty house also provided us with a safe hideout in case robbers raided the haveli.

Though armed with a gun one Gurkha watchman who patrolled outside the haveli at night would be no match to a gang of robbers, like Sultana Daku gang that was a terror specially to the rich in the villages of the entire region.

In the center of the park was a small bungalow with a large room, two attached rooms and a verandah which was built by my grandfather to serve as his court. Though he knew no English and had no formal education, he was appointed by His Majesty's Government as the honorary magistrate of the area to handle patty disputes between villagers. Two of my other relatives had been similarly honoured.

Around the court were four large lawns with high hedges. These were maintained by gardeners and were used by Master ji and his three wards for playing football, tennis and volleyball. Master ji had been a good sportsman in his school and college days. He was also a gymnast and often used to display the muscles of his arms to his pupils. I tested them too once. They were hard as a stone. Evidently, he was taking physical exercise in the morning to stay fit. Being too young to join the big boys and I used to play in another lawn of the park with my four aunties who were younger than me. But it was Master ji who taught all of us the importance of playing games in open spaces. On his advice my uncles also bought board games played with a dice like "monopoly" which was a British pastime and had become very popular in India.

Another landmark of Kota was the family's oldest employee, Pachauri ji, who was 95 years old when I first saw him in 1938. He was then leading a retired life with his children, grand children and great grand children. I was told that he was a young man of 14 or 15 when the Sepoy Mutiny of 1857 broke out which the British managed to crush ruthlessly. He never saw an Englishman but had seen a battalion of Indian soldiers passing through the area and had hidden himself from them.

My first intellectual interaction with Master ji happened in my twelfth year in Mussoorie. I and my mother used to spend my summer vacations in Kota or whereever the family went for a holiday. In 1940 they decided to spend two months in Mussoorie. Master ji accompanied them where ever they went as the only educated person in the party. The hill town was quite a contrast to our life in Kota. Those were days when the British Empire was at the peak of its glory. Royalty of the country could be seen in all its splendour in that small city. To my child's eye everything looked gorgeous. All motor traffic stopped at King Craig, over a mile below the city. From there one had to walk or take a horse or hand pulled rickshaw to come up to the city. Some years later, cars were allowed upto a point below Mussorie's famous Library.

Hand pulled rickshaws plied in the city. They signified the status of the passengers as cars do today. Normally a rickshaw would have four pullers, two to pull it from the front and two to push it from the back as they went up and down steep slopes. The rickshaws of royalty and aristocracy had six to eight pliers, dressed in liveries and taking turns to put the vehicle moving at a trot. The Maharaja of Kapurthala had built a palace in Mussorie called Kapurthala House. The rickshaws of the family looked like sedan cars with the royal insignia embossed on the doors. Other princely families usually stayed in special suites of rooms in the Savoy Hotel. Jawaharlal Nehru also stayed there with his father Motilal Nehru who was one of the most successful lawyers of his time and practiced at Allahabad High Court (Sir Tej Bahadur Sapru was his 'junior' lawyer). Birla, the second largest industrialist of India after Tata, had built a bungalow there. Nabha, Kasmanda and many other small potentates had built large houses. Charleville, the second largest hotel in Mussorie after Savoy was a favorite of rich Englishmen. So was the small Hakman's Hotel in the middle of the mile long Mall Road which runs from the Library to Kulri market. The hotel and the children's park adjoining it have been built by flattening a lower part of the hill. While walking past Hakman's on the Mall at night after 8 p.m. we could hear the tunes of the orchestra playing in the dance hall. The British were very fond of musical bands and had built a band stand opposite the library where a band would play music at the umbrella like "Hawa ghar" every evening at 6 P.m. for the entertainment of tourists.

It so transpired that princess Nilofur, daughter of the Nizam of Hyderabad and acclaimed as the most beautiful woman in the world, happened to be staying in a mansion two bungalows away from the small five room house called Rishi Cottage on Camel's Back road that we had hired for the season. Because of its long drive way her house was located on a hill almost directly below ours. We used to watch her taking tea with her family on the terrace of her bungalow. It was quite exciting for all of us to view real royalty at such close quarters. I still remember her flowing hair and long blue gown. Her face was only vaguely visible to us because of the distance between the two hills. My younger uncle Prem Nath suggested we should buy binoculars to gaze at her, but my elder uncle, Dhan Prakash who was studying Law at Lucknow University, snubbed him. "You will go to jail if you do that and no one can bail you out," he said reprimanding him for the very idea of buying a pair of binoculars to secretly gaze at a princess in her private moments.

It was in Mussoorie that Master ji became friendly with me and had long talks with me about the war which was then raging in Europe. Hitler had already captured France and was turning his attention to North Africa to open another front there. I used to go for long walks with him taking a full circle of Camel's Back and Mall roads, a total of about three miles. On the way we would stop by at one of the two skating rinks in the market. I used to stake on the polished wooden floor of the hall while master ji sat in the gallery around it to watch the performers collide with each other or lose their balance and fall on the floor. I went to the rinks only a few times and merely walked wearing the skates in the hall holding the railing of the galleries. A chienese young man used to perform fantastic feats with his skates in the rink He was the son of the local Chinese shoe maker whose clients were mainly the British elite who came to Mussoorie for long stays. In those days China Town in Calcutta was known for its shoe makers. I had better luck with horse riding which I also learnt in Mussoorie. Horses were freely available for hire by the hour and their keepers ran along with them till the rider was fully trained after which they left the customer free to take the horse where he liked and bring it back at a fixed time.

Master ji would stop at a book shop and collect a few magazines, specially the Illustrated Weekly whose crossword puzzles he used to solve. Its crossword puzzler was a great institution then with a prize of Rs. 13,000/—(equivalent of Rs.2.5 millions of today) for the best entry and a large number of consolation prizes or free entry coupons for upto three mistakes. A new puzzle was announced every three weeks. Numerous small magazines sprang up which discussed the clues and suggested the answers, and did a thorough post mortem of the previous puzzle. I picked up this habit from master ji and applied my mind seriously to it for about three years and won a few consolation prizes. One advantage of buying the Illustrated Weekly was that it got me into the habit of reading short stories. The magazine was then styled on the Saturday Evening Past of America and was full of short stories, some of which ran into a series in two or three successive issues. For a school student it was a great learning experience.

Being an M.A in history Master ji would often talk to me about the earlier wars in Europe and the French, Spanish and Italian revolution. He introduced me to the American Civil War which Abraham Lincoln fought to liberate the Black Slaves and keep America united as one country by defeating the secessionist forces. The Russian revolution led by Lenin, Stalin and Trotsky did not appeal to him. As a student of history he believed in a strong aristocracy to take a country forward. "Could a small country like England have built such a huge empire if it did not have its dukes and lords?", he would ask. He felt that rule by the working class could not succeed become it consisted of "all brawn and no brains". Master ji was also a believer in a strong middle class. "England is strong because it is known as a nation of shop keepers and country squares". He always held out England as an example of what a country should be. Would Gandhi, Nehru, Subhash Bose and Sri Aurobindo be what they became if they hadn't had British education, he would ask. It was England that had made India a nation and given it democratic institutions and modern education, he would tell me.

When going for a walk on the Mall in Mussoorie he would dress like a perfect Englishman from toe to top, His attire included a felt hat slightly tilted in the front. He also carried a fancy walking stick after the fashion of English gentleman who would not be seen on the roads without a walking stick or umbrella. I had a walking stick with a double handle and pointed like a nail at the bottom end so that it could be used as a seat while trekking. The two handles had a wide leather strap fastened between them which could be turned into a crude chair for rest while walking up a mountain. Mussoorie has several steep walks and rough hills on which one can climb with ease provided one is armed with a stick. The same is true while coming down. You need a stick to check a fall.

Summer trips to Mussoorie became an annual feature for the family. Master ji was always there. He made me buy several books, mostly classics by well known English and French authors. He was indifferent towards the freedom movement launched by Gandhi ji but quite effusive about the various revolutions against tyranny launched in Europe. You could call him an arm chair revolutionary. The books he recommended were cheap.

Some of the best classics could be bought in Penguin and Pelican paper back editions for only six annas (about 40 paise and the equivalent of today's eighty rupees). When in the summer of 1944 the Kota family took a two month holiday in Kashmir Master ji made me buy Sir Fraucis Young-husband's "Kashmir—the playground of Asia". It was a large bound volume with a lot of pictures in it. The Kashmir visit was memorable in many ways. I was in my sixteenth year then and had read quite a lot of revolutionary literature, which was an achievement at my age. We had taken two fully furnished house boats and parked them near a lawn along one of the channels of the Jhelum river that cris-crossed the city of Srinagar, quite close to the main market of the city, called Mira Kadal. The smaller boat was allotted to the three of us, me, Master ji and uncle Prem Nath. A third still smaller boat made up our little flotila. Our boat had three rooms and the bigger one had four large rooms.

The small boat was the permanent home of Rahman, owner of the houseboats. It had two unfurnished rooms with a common sloping roof. I can never forget his name because he was one of the five husbands of his wife. Other co-shares of the lady's favours were probably his brothers and cousins. They all lived in the same house but plied their different trades. I had read about the prevalence of polyandry in Kashmir but this was the only example I actually saw. The five men lived peacefully together. It they ever quarreled about small things we never heard it. We dealt only with Rahman who brought us delicious meat dishes prepared by his wife every day. That was the first time I tasted meat. The family's all vegetarian meals were cooked separately in a tent pitched the adjoining lawn. We belong to Vaishya Caste. Ours used to be a strictly vegetarian community.

Now every thing is changed. My grandchildren in India and abroad can not live without it. It seems our whole clan is slowly becoming carnivorous. My uncle Prem Nath who was four years older to me had had tuberculosis when he was sixteen and had to be treated in the Government's TB Hospital in Delhi. The doctors had recommended a meat diet for him. Master ji was a gourmet. He loved meat and taught me to relish it too. But I soon gave it up and did not take it even during my trips to foreign lands, including Saudi Arabia, where they used to serve vegetarian soup by picking out pieces of meat from the soup in the kitchen before serving it. I used to quietly swallow it. The other vegetarian in our Press Party, lived only on bread and butter and other tinned snacks throughout the week long trip, when he came to know to this practice.

The trip to Kashmir has left memories far too numerous to recount here. It included a fortnight long stay in Pahalgaon in tents pitched on the lawns of the boisterous Lidar river, a week long trip to Amarnath, a three-day journey by house boats to Ganderbal where the Jhelum meets a branch of the Indus, two quick trips to Gulmarg and Baramula lake which looked like a sea and a night's halt in the house of our family priest in Mattan who arranged the five day trip to the Amarnath shrine. In Srinagar we saw Mahammad Ali Jinnah, the founder of Pakistan, taking a stroll like a common tourist, accompanied by his sister, in the market along the Jhelum river. Master ji at once recognized him by his pins-nez and pointed him to us.

Throughout the two-month long trip the three of us, me, Master ji and Uncle Prem Nath were always together like the Three Musketeers. It seems Master ji had read several books of travel and adventures in odd places like Tibet, Africa, North and South Poles and Amazon, and would often talk to us about it. As I grew up and became almost an annual visitor to Mussoorie, I discovered some rare books on travel in the Mussorie library I became its permanent member.

Apart from the long stays with my mother's family during the summer vacations I made at least two more visits of a week or two to Kota village every year. If there was a marriage or child birth my mother was required to spend at least a month in the village to participate in the various ceremonies connected with the great event. I had to tag along with her. In fact I used to love it because it gave me a good excuse to stay away from school and wander in Kota like a vagabond. A terrible tragedy struck the family in January or February 1942 when Dhan Parkash its main hope, died of food poisoning in Lucknow University where he had gone to do a combined course of M.A. and L.L.B(law). He was the only bright star of the clan who, it was hoped, would bring the huge estate out from the bleak waters of a small village and place it at par, if not superior to, the titled nobility of the district.

For Master ji it was a personal loss. He had always been proud of the fact that he had trained a rustic village boy to the level of a university where he had performed so well. His two other students failed in their matriculation exam conducted by the UP Board of High School and Intermediate examination, got married and settled down to the life of their ancestors and tried their hands at modern faming. Prem Nath uncle even went to America in a young farmer's exchange programmer arranged shortly after Indian independence. He was accompanied by his brother-in-law, younger sister's husband, Lakshmi Sharan who lived in Mirapur, a Gangoh type small town. He was a Khandsari(raw sugar) magnate and he led a movement to remove the duty on Khandsari which the government had imposed to help the sugar industry in 1958. With my help and that of a professional PRO who had many contacts amongst M.P.s he organized a publicity campaign which forced Morarji Desai, then Finance Minister of India, to cut down the duty by half. That was when I discovered that you could pay journalists for carrying favourable stories by making them part-time employees of a campaign.

Narrating their experience of the three-month long farmer's exchange programme both my uncles, Prem Nath and Lakshmi Sharan used to be more effusive about American women than about American farming, specially women and girls of the farmers' families they lived with. They were most impressed by the completely informal treatment they got from them in their homes. They came back starry eyed as if they had been to the Moon. Unfortunately uncle Lakshmi Sharan, who was emerging as a Khandsari tycoon, died young, around the age of 45 from a heart attack.

Both Prem Nath and Lakshmi Sharan bought large tractors and started reclaiming barren lands. Prem Nath was a brave man. Around 1965 when he was about 42 he lost a leg in an accident. He carried on with an artificial leg for the rest of his life as if nothing had happened. He could drive a car and do all rough jobs of a farmer like a normal villager. In his younger days too he was fond of playing pranks and experiments in which he used to tag me long, I being only four years younger than him. Once he tied a donkey to a small make-shift cart and tried to make it move. On another occasion I and he floated on an air filled rubber bed in a small tank near our haveli. Had the air leaked out we would have both drowned in the tank. When his mother came to know of this adventure she promptly confiscated the air bed.

The first act of the Congress party government when it came to power after Independence was the abolition of the Zamindari system and giving full ownership of land to the tiller. The landlords could keep barren or forest lands which had no tenants on them upto a limit of thirty acres. These limits varied from state to state and were violated on a large scale by almost all landlords through devious means to acquire holdings of hundreds of acres. Earlier, in 1945-46 the family moved to Saharanpur into a spacious bungalow built in the middle of its 20-acre compound along the railway line on the outskirts of the city. It bought this property from an English man, a barrister who had decided to return to England in his retirement.

In Kota my aunts who were younger to me had started learning the three Rs from Masterji. My youngest uncle, Prabodh Nath, younger brother of Prem Nath and junior to him by twelve years, had also joined the group. With the move to Saharanpur all of them joined schools for boys and girls but continued to do their home work under Masterji's guidance who also gave them extra coaching. Gradually, the next generation of sons and daughters entered Masterji's class room one by one. The first was Arun, the posthumously born son of Dhan Prakash. He was followed by Kusum and Arvind, daughter and son of Rajendra Prasad, elder step brother of Prem Nath.

On watching these developments in the Kota family I was reminded of the two sequels Pearl S. Buck wrote to her Nobel Praze winning novel Good Earth on the rise of a Chinese peasant to a great landlord, "Sons" and the "House Divided". As the family grew it broke up. New buildings came up on the spacious grounds of the bungalow to accommodate the new members. Instead of one there were three kitchens now. Walls came up to partition the inner paved compound. Though in their mutual relations they still behaved as one family, my grandfather and his brother split up the property into two halves. My grand father and his large family of three sons and five daughters had to squeeze into half the bungalow. The only common rooms were the drawing room and Masterji's class room which also served as his living room. Due to shortage of space a bed was put for him in the same room where he taught his pupils with an almirah for his clothes and other belongings. Though he was still respected and looked after well, it was clear that as times changed his role in the family was changing. Prabodh Nath, my youngest uncle and about eight years my junior to me in age got selected in the national military academy, joined the Indian Navy, married Helen, an Irish girl and rose to the rank of Rear Admiral before he retired. Fond of owning big imported cars at a time when such cars were a luxury, he turned out to be the most successful member of the Kota clan. One by one my aunts, Kamla, Bimla, Urmilla, Uma and Usha (the only daughter of my grand father's younger brother) got married and went away to the homes of their husbands. Masterji had to now coach the school going children of my uncles.

My contacts with Masterji were no longer intimate. I would just say hello to him, chat with him for a minute as he sat in a chair under a tree along the drive way and slip into the house. Whether he would want to talk to me like old times was also not certain. He looked detached and aloof, a lonely figure, perhaps a misfit in the current social environment. His former pupil Prem Nath, had now become his employer. Both lived in their own separate worlds. With so many worries on his head, Prem Nath was always in a hurry, Masterji had practically nothing to do but to while away his time in just sitting and watching members of the family moving almost their business. Occasionally, he would pick up a novel or a thriller and read it. Once a week he would get dressed up and go out to a restaurant to have a meal of fish and meat curry, alone.

Like Kota, in Saharanpur too he made no friends. Occasionally he would go to an elderly Bengali doctor, also a Banerji, and talk with him. The old man loved to talk to young people as he walked. He was fond of solving arithmetical puzzles. He once taught me how to calculate the square of any two-digit number ending with five, eg 35. "you multiply 3 and 4 and place 25 before it to make 1225", he said. His son had taken an MD degree in Germany and taken over the medical practice from his father in a big way. Banerji senior had placed a seat for himself in the long dispensary hall where he would sit and read newspapers and religious books in Bengali, while keeping watch on the compounders and the cash they collected from the patients of his son.

Masterji would drop in for a while, in a month or two, to have a chat with him. Other than this contact, to the best of my knowledge, Masterji was a lonely person. His value to the family continued till the last day of his life. Being the only educated person in the house he could look after the progress of each child as he or she grew up. Every body respected him. But it was clear that as time passed he was losing interest in the affairs of the world. He had no inclination towards religion though he loved to read about mystics and the miracles they performed. Till the last day when he died suddenly of a heart attack at the age of about 50 he remained as aloof and detached from the affairs of the family he served so devotedly during his entire working life of nearly 30 years as on the day he arrived in Kota. That, I think, was his greatest achievement.

15

Another form of Slavery

The most memorable aspect of life in India in the late Nineteen Twenties and early Thirties perhaps was the near total absence of electricity in all towns and villages. Though city streets were dimly lit by kerosene lit lamps posts, the 24-hour-day was neatly divided into darkness and light. During summer nights all life shifted to roof tops or the streets, lanes and bylines. In middle class families the male members took early meals and sat on cots and reclining bamboo chairs outside their homes to spend on hour or two chatting and smoking a hookah (hubble bubble). Women generally moved to roof tops to gossip, sing bhajans (devotional songs) or just go to sleep. Not being allowed to go out of their homes by their men folk it gave them an opportunity to chat freely with females of the neighbouring homes across the roofs. From the roof of my haveli (a large joint-family house) in the small town of Gangoh in Saharanpur district of U.P., where I was born in 1928, on moonlit nights I could see the whole panorama of night life in the neighbourhood. I distinctly remember a neighbour's daughter aged about eighteen, whom I fancied when I was only seven years old. I told my mother I would like to marry her. My mother told this to every one including that girl who greeted my childish remark with a hearty laugh. "Do you really wish to marry me", she asked me. I was too young to blush.

On dark nights people carried a lantern or a diya (small earthen lamp) to the roof. It is amazing how far a little light can go. People sitting close to it were clearly visible from afar. Students used only lantern light for their studies. Fortunately, the type fonts of books in those days were not so microscopally small as they are today. A small kerosene lamp at every 100 yards in the streets could illumine the whole town adequately. The traffic consisted mainly of a few pedestrians and, rarely, a bicycle or two.

In this environment, with every member of the house sleeping on the roof, burglaries were not uncommon. There were no bank lockers and you put your money in a private bank at your own risk. In 1939 an uncle of mine lost all his savings from a thriving practice as a lawyer when the Benares Bank failed. It happened the eve of his daughter's wedding. People kept all their money in secret pockets made by them by digging a small pit in the walls of their houses. There being no cement concrete the walls made of bricks had to be very thick. Burglars operated singly or in pairs and were usually unarmed, but for the hammer they carried with them to make an entry hole in the wall. If some one in the house woke up the burglar usually made a quick exit without turning violent.

By now I believe you have guessed what I am driving at: In those times, seventy years ago and beyond, every thing happened on a small scale. Houses were small. Even big mansions were located in small lanes. Markets were small and narrow. You could cover the whole length of a district town on a bicycle in five to ten minutes. Schools, libraries, hospitals, cinema halls were small and neatly kept.

Everybody seemed to know everybody else. Even servants and labourers became known by name in my small habitat, Gangoh, which with on population of about 13,000 enjoyed the status of a Town Area. Wives of barbers and pujaris (brahmines who performed sacrificial rites) were permitted by their husbands to visit the homes of well to do people to perform their professional duties.

Gangoh is where I was born. My father's name was Jagdish Prasad and my mother's Vidya Vati. My two siblings having died in their infancy due to the bad quality of my mother's milk it was decided to hand me over to a wet nurse, Sahbo by name, who came with her husband from the Solan hills near Simla to fetch me. I was a year old when I was brought back by the couple to Gangoh. They say much of the wiring of neurous in the brain is done during the first year of man's life. This probably explains my extreme founders for the hills. Sahbo lived in a village, perhaps cluttered with all kinds of dirt and animals. But those days hygiene was not an issue and one who survived developed an immunity to all kinds of diseases. A daughter was born to my mother two years later. The family patriarch, my grandfather Bul Chand, who took decisions in such matters perhaps decided that they could take risk with a girl's life. Sure enough, she too died like my other siblings. I have never heard of a girl being given to a wet nurse in the hills—a thriving business in days when bottled milk for infants was unknown in India.

The barber's wife came ostensibly to do the ladies hair by massaging it with oil and tying the hair into pony tails. But the actual purpose of her visit for which she was eagerly awaited by all the ladies of the house, who were not allowed to step out of their homes except to attend ceremonies in other homes, was to bring news of the town, particularly spicy stories about the goings on in neighboring houses which were generally occupied by descendants of the same lineage, mainly first or second generation cousins. From each house there was much to report. Married brothers always shared the same house with their parents. Locked in, the women had no option but to watch each other closely and brood over little things that happened in the house. Fights between mother-in-law and daughters-in-law and amongst the daughters-in-law were common.

I was privy to such talks along with my mother, Vidya Vati, upto the age of about eight. Once in a while these women, specially the family barber's wife, would talk about ghosts of dead relatives appearing in houses of families to which they had belonged when they were alive.

These spirits were believed to be seeking revenge for the injustices done to them, such as being deprived of their property rights. But they did not act silently like the ghost of Hamlet's father that spoke to him in complete secrecy. They believed in making their presence felt by the clanking of utensils in the kitchen or upturning some piece of furniture during the dark hours of the night. Nobody dared to get up from bed to find out what was happening. There was no electricity and, so the story goes, if any one did get up and light a diva with a match stick he was slapped by an invisible presence or the diva in his hands was extinguished instantly.

Not all ghosts, however, were inimical. In my childhood days in the Nineteen Thirties the story was widely prevalent in our circles that on a totally dark night, around the hour of midnight, some burglars were trying to enter our haveli. They were chased away by a hefty chowkidar standing before our door. Since my grandfather never kept a chowkidar the general belief was that this must be the doing of our family's patron saint, Hari Das Babaji, who had died about a century earlier and in whose memory we had built a small temple on our lands on the outskirts of the town. He was venerated by about a hundred families of our clan of Baniyas (Vaishyas). He must have appeared in the garb or a watchman to protect our haveli from burglars, it was universally believed in the whole town of Gangoh.

While his wife attended to the hair of ladies of the house, Punna, our family barber took care of the cosmetic needs of my three uncles and two cousins, both older than my father, and supplied them with the latest gossip in the local market. Both he and his wife behaved as if they were performing a ritual. Time did not matter to them. Shaving with a long razor used by barbers in an art. Sometime a shave would last half-an-hour or even longer depending on the person Punna and his client were talking about. He would apply soap on a rich customers' face and continue the dialogue till it was over without touching the latter's face with his razor. Meanwhile the soap would dry up and he would apply it all over again. There were several such interruptions during a shave. As in the case of his wife, Punna's arrival was a social occasion and one or two of my uncles and cousins drew their chairs close to the scene of action and join in the conversation in his chhaprauli village, about sixty miles to the south of Gangoh along the Yamuna river. Like every one else in our area he must have and later switched to razer blades but retained his old habit of chatting with his coterie while showing. He gave a whole interview to me when he was shaving and yet his shave continued.

Writing about the shaving ritual reminds me of Charan Singh, who later became the Prime Minister of India. After Mrs. Gandhi's defeat in the Parliamentary elections in 1977, fallowing the lifting by her of the state of Emergency, there was much excitement over the formation of the new Janta Party government. Homes of all top leaders were open to correspondents who were rushing about to get a scent of the composition of the new Government. When I walked into Charan Singh room where he was surrounded by his advisor and some newsmen, he was shaving. As was usual with him he was squatting on a carpet spread on the floor, with a desk in front of him on which he had placed a mirror. When I left his room about half-an-hour later, he was still shaving. His home in a village of Baraut tehsil of Meerut district in U.P should be about sixty miles south of Gangoh along the Yamuna river. In his younger days, like everybody else in the region he too must have acquired the habit of chatting while shaving or getting shaved by a barber.

Among the group who sat with him that day was Raj Narain, the socialist leader with a wide base in Eastern U.P. and Bihar. He took pride describing himself as Charan Singh's Hanuman. It was he who fought in the Rai Bareli constituency against Mrs. Gandhi and lost. He then filed an election petition against her in the Allahabad High Court which he won leading to her disqualification to hold office and the ensuing developments.

The razor blade had not made its appearance in the towns and villages of India and everybody had to go to a barber shop or call a barber to his house to get himself a shave. Old habit die hard and many people continued to use barbers long after razor blades had become popular. My father took to it haltingly and would shave on alternate days. As for as I remember my uncles continued to use Punna for shaves and haircuts till their death in the Nineteen Forties and Fifties. We lived in two havelis on two sides of a huge open quadrangle which was used for marriage parties and children's games. My eldest uncle, who was twenty years older than my father, lived in one haveli with two of his three sons and their families. Two cousins of my father lived in the other haveli which opened on a large drawing room that was meant for the common use of male members of both homes.

By the widely accepted concepts of those days there was a vital difference between the occupants of the two havelis that was the cause of much jealousy between them. Each family had three brothers. Our haveli was occupied by my eldest uncle Lala Hirdey Narain and his three sons, daughters and grandchildren. My father, Jagdish Prasad was educated in the Roorkee's Thomson college of Civil engineering be a junior engineer (then called overseer. His first job was that of Secretary, District Board Muzzaffar Nagar. He later joined the P.W.D. His elder brother Babu Maharaj Singh, passed his law examination from Allahabad University and later settled down as a lawyer in Saharanpur. He had two daughters I was the only surviving child of my parents. Thus, while our family was overflowing with children and grand children my father's three cousins had between than just one child and that too a girl who would go away when she got married, leaving the estate without a heir.

This was a major cause of silent heart burning between the two families that nevertheless behaved as one. Babu Kedar Nath, father of the girl, was a forward looking man. Besides being the founder and moving spirit behind the only boy's high school in Gongoh he had built on the edge of the town, about half-a-kilometer's walk from our house, a pleasure garden, complete with a fountain, walks or rate hedges, a variety of flowers and a tennis court. The fountain was powered by water flowing from an adjoining factory whose chimney was always. Spewing out a smoke from the coal it was burning and producing a pip-pip sound. Babu Kedar Nath had a share in its ownership. I do not remember now the product it was manufacturing though I had visited it once or twice. Rooms in its upper story were let out to students or teachers. Kedar Nath younger brother, Rishi Ram, was a Mukhtar (an unqualified but licensed pleader who handled petty cases) in Saharanpur district courts.

It is a hard fact of life, but sad all same, that the same cousins who probably played together and met each other every day while living in Gangoh, never met to say hello to each other when they moved to Saharanpur. My uncle, Babu Maharaj Singh, rose to be the leading lawyer of Saharanpur district and even had the honors of having a degree college named after him, while his cousin, Rishi Ram, remained a mere Mukhtar all his life, pleading petty cases in junior courts. Money and status come first in establishing relationship. Blood comes last and is often a negative factor, for, the closer a blood relationship, the deeper the resentment on one side and arrogance on the other over the difference in wealth and status between the two parties.

Every day the male elders of the clean would being out their "moodhas" (easy chairs made of case) and place them over it or in front of their garage shaped drawing room along the lane.

One of their favorite pastimes was to pass remarks in whispers on passers by who used to be people known to them and usually wished or saluted them with greetings like "Ramram" or "salaam". Eyebrows were raised whenever a known upper caste women passed by. Though veiled ladies of this class had to have a good reason to be seen on the road. As a rule men were not supposed to enter the upper storey which was the domain of women of the house till much time. Those who did were branded as sissies or slaves of their wives. Chewing pan was a good way of whiling away time. Every haveli had a small alcove like shelf where it kept all the ingredients that event into the making of a delicious paan. Beside most people kept a "paan daan" an or note metal box in which they kept a few hours supply of beetles which they occasionally shared with visitors. Paan was the old form of hospitality which has now been replaced by tea and coffee. Large hubble-bubbles (hookahs) could also be seen outside some houses around which people of the same would sit on easy came chairs and chat. The smell of tobacco smoke pervaded the atmosphere. Members of different castes could not smoke the same "hookah".

After lunch too men retired to the outer room, separated from the women's compartments by a staircase or a courtyard. Woman of all castes had to keep their faces covered with veil while walking on the road or when a man senior in age to their husbands entered the house. No opportunity was spared to make women feel inferior to their menfolk. This attitude was somewhat relaxed among the lower castes whose women went out to work. Lady teachers who taught in schools were exempt from these restrictions. They were treated as a class apart. Wife-beating was not uncommon. One heard a number of stories about upper caste women being brutally beaten in a routine manner by their husbands.

It was considered a husband's right to occasionally thrash his wife and no one was supposed to interfere in his performing this ritual no matter how much the victim cried for help. The practice of wife beating was not confined to villages and small towns. It was widely prevalent in cities too. Women who were loaded with the finest saris and jewellery by their husbands too had to bear it. I saw a few cases of this kind in the capital of India. I have brooded over this phenomenon and analysed it. In my opinion it is some kind of an epileptic fit when a person loses control of himself and becomes violent. I have seen highly educated and apparently sophisticated men indulging in this crime against which there is no recourse except divorce, which is a cure that is worse than the disease, though these days it is an option that is being exercised by quite a few young women who are capable of standing on their own feet.

On the outskirts of Gangoh stands what I call the "hall of shame" of our community. It is a row of tomb like monuments, attached to each other, cemented and painted white in memory of 'satis', or women of the clan who died on the pyres of their husbands, offering themselves to be burnt alive with their corpses at their cremation. The practice of "Sati was widely prevalent in India till Raja Ram Mohan Roy pleaded with the British rulers in the first half of the Nineteenth century to put an end to this barbarous crime. It had taken hold of the Indian mind so completely in the medieval era that even The great saint Kabir eulogised it. I have read his praise of his poems titled "Hundred poems from Kabir". Whenever there was a marriage in our family the bride and bridegroom were escorted to these shrines by a large number of women of the community to offer ceremonial prayers and gift by way of homage to the "sainted souls" of women who had thus sacrificed their lives to be united with their hundreds in the other world (or were made to do so). I and my wife had to go there too when we got married in 1955.

In short, Gangoh of my childhood days was a fossilized town, where all taboos and superstitions which evolved in the middle ages were religiously practiced. Marriages are a classic example. There ceremonies began months in advances and ended months after the wedding. I vividly remember the scene the family scavenger and his friends made after each feast was over. Several hundred guests were served food on the quadrangle in front of our haveli sitting on long carpets spread on the ground and eating from half plates and small earthen pots delicacies prepared on the spot by expert halwais (sweet makers). After the feast the leaf plates and earthen pots with the left over food were deposited in a huge drum placed in a corner of the quadrangle by volunteers from among the hosts and their friends.

A crowd of scavengers and their children were already collected near the drum. It was the privilege of our family scavenger to distribute the left overs of the feast amongst his kinsmen and friends. As a child I used to watch the scramble among them for sweets, ice-cream cups and other items of left over food. Within moments the drum was emptied. In modern times in big cities this function is performed by vultures who fly over vast dump yards created by municipalities to collect and process the city's waste. I wonder if in Gangoh and small villages and towns of North India this obnoxious practice is still continuing. There was no dearth of social workers and reformers in Gongoh of those days. Arya Samajists, Gandhians, Sanatan Dharma enthusiasts and other organization and individuals who believed in ridding Hinduism of the junk of rituals and superstitions it had accumulated over centuries and milleniums of its prevalence on earth. But not one of them thought there was something wrong and dehumanizing in this abominable ritual reserved for the lowest caste of Hindus, for eating food fit only for dogs, cats and other animals and birds. I am pointing to this practice as an example of the main theme of this book, that is, the supreme indifference of Indian society to social evils of all kinds.

(That I am not above it and am not speaking from lofty heights is proved by what happened a moment ago while I was writing these lines of this chapter. Suraj an optician's delivery boy, a young man of about 25, came to deliver my new reading spectacles. I asked him for the bill. He said "in that case you will have to pay sales tax and the price will go up substantially". I just kept quiet and did not pursue the matter any further. In observing complete silence at this moment I was only doing justice to the title of this book "autobiography of a corrupt Indian". This is true Indianness. Whenever any thing goes wrong in the family, community or society, we just keep quiet. It is not becoming of a "respectable gentleman (or gentle woman) to be seen getting involved in petty squabbles. The accumulation of these "petty things" in due course becomes a social evil of vast proportions which no one can control).

As I said in my "case study" of housing complexes in Delhi, the universal upper caste perception of the lowest castes is that they are animals and should be treated as such. We must remember that our ancestors lived in villages where these distinctions were religiously observed. Though our generation has moved into cities our social attitudes towards the lower castes have not changed. Even Jawaharlal Nehru, the great socialist and democrat, was proud of being a Kashmiri Brahmin. He took on the title of Pandit and was known as "Pandit ji" throughout the country. If any one said "Pandit ji is coming" or "Pandit ji said this", it only meant one person, Jawaharlal Nehru. In such an atmosphere it is not surprising if even in bit cities of India the lower castes are treated as a species apart, some where between human beings and animals. They should never be allowed to claim equality with the upper castes.

The only ray of hope in this bleak prospect was the local high school. The mere presence of a school enlivens a rural or semi urban community. One of my father's cousins who lived in the other haveli was the founder secretary of the school. In its existence of almost a century it has brought the light of wider awareness of our world in thousands of homes in and around Gangoh. During one of my father's numerous transfers to far flung town in U.P. I studied in this school for three weeks in the seventh class. My uncle being all-in-all in the school management, he had merely to tell the head master that I should be allowed to sit in the class for as long as it took my father to find a house in his new town he was posted. The school was housed in a small but neatly kept building in the city. Classes were held from 10 a.m. to 4 p.m. we had to go back to school at 6 p.m. each class forming a row in the small quadrangle, and march to the playground on the outskirts of the town about half-a-mile away. My uncle was extremely punctillious about the morning prayers and the games in the evening. He also took care to appoint the best available teachers. I still remember the middle aged Muslim history teacher who used to come wearing a sherwani and pyjamas and made the class extremely interesting with anecdotes about historical characters. I still remember the lesson he taught us about how Chand Bibi (also known as Chand Sultana) defended the Ahmednagar fort against the forces of Akbar, the great Mogul emperor.

The school has now grown big and has been functioning for several decades in a large new building or a part of the former playground. More than the luminaries it has produced at the national level, I am impressed by the light the school has brought into the lives of ordinary people in Gaugoh and surrounding rural areas. My uncle had hired a small double-story house and converted it into a hostel for boys from the villages and appointed Gobind Ram Badola, the scouts and drill master as its warden. I remember the name because, though a man from the Garhwal hills in the Himalayas, he settled in Gangoh after retirement and was the constant companion of my father who also returned to Gangoh to look after his orchard and property when he retired from government service as an engineer in P.W.D. The caste and class composition of students in the period 1930 to 1950 would make an interesting study. Most of the students came from the Brahmin and Vaishya communities. Lower caste people avoided educating their children.

"If we send them to school they will want to become babus, demand bicycles and wrist watches and clothes to wear. Who will plough the fields then?" They would ask.

One heard the same story from people of all crafts. At best they would make them literate by sending them to a village school master who ran a one man school and taught the rudiments of the three Rs, that is reading, writing ad arithmetic. Writing was taught on a "takhti", a light wooden board which a child could easily place on his lap while squatting on the floor. It was plastered with a muddy paste after each exercise. Writing was done with a pen made of thin bamboo shoots with their tips sharpened into the shape of a nib with a sharp knife. We would dip these pens into ink bottles each time we wrote a letter of the alphabet. It was believed that writing on a "takhti" was essential to learn good hand writing.

One reason for the choice of takhti as a medium writing, besides its cheapness compared to paper, was that under British rule Urdu was the official language of North India, apart from English. Written from right to left, its alphabet has long strokes which are best learnt on a large canvas like a takhti. I was perhaps the first male member of my large joint family who chose Hindi as my medium of instruction and learnt writing the alphabets of both languages on a 'takhti'.

Likewise, slates were used to practice arithmetical exercises of addition, subs traction and multiplication. Small sticks of a special type of chalk were used to write on slates which formed an integral past of the essential stationery kit of every school child. One was considered to be an educated person once he had learnt the three Rs. Since government aided schools began with class three most people did not go to school at all. Yet many of them were able to read books, write letters and do simple sums to maintain their business accounts.

A large number medicine of shopkeeper and other businessmen in Gangoh were content to get their sons educated only upto this level. But still many of them, specially Brahmins, used this skill to read big books like the Ramayana and Mahabharata epics and short story magazines which were very popular those days. Even without schools it was a literate middle class.

Likewise, my eldest cousin used to subscribe to Tej, an Urdu newspaper published from Delhi and delivered by post. He would read out spicy items form it other elders of the family when they gathered for their morning session.

It was specially true of girls for whom there were no schools at all, except in big cities. Most people taught their daughters at home. The rich, who could afford, hired lady teachers to come to their homes to teach their daughters so that they could appear for the high school board exam as private candidates. Girls had the option of taking another set of exams run by a private organization recognized by the government as equivalent of high school, intermediate and BA exams. Unlike boys whose main language was Urdu, girls were educated in Hindi. They were mainly responsible for the extra-ordinary popularity of Kalyan, a religious Hindi monthly published form Gorakhpur which at one time was the largest circulated publication in India. But since early marriages were common and good looking girls who brought large dowries in great demand, most girls were taught at home notionally upto class seven or eight and then married off.

Thanks to the women of the town, Gangoh was buzzing with religious fervour. They were allowed to go to temples as often as they liked. Both, Sanatan Dharma and Arya Samaj were strong. My eldest cousin, Lala Sumer Chand who was seven years older than my father, was the only Arya Samajist in the family. He was also General Secretary and chief organize of the Arya Samaj in Gangoh for a long time was in constant touch with Gurkul Kangri, an Arya Samajist university in Kankhal, near Haridwar. He used to organize big sessions lasting two days of speeches and prayers by the high priests and scholars of the creed. Not to be left behind the Sanatan Dharmis too organized similar functions. I remember going to both types of celebrations with my mother and sitting in the galleries above the main hall reserved for women and children.

16

Cooling without power

How I invented an "Ice Energy" air conditioner

By a rough estimate Delhi consumes about one thousand Megawatt additional electric power for heating and cooling during peak summer and winter months. This chapter is an attempt to show with a concrete example backed by facts and figures how this extra burden on the power starved metropolis could be reduced by half or more by overhauling and simplifying our cooling and heating systems. On a national scale the saving in our peak load capacity may be as high as 25000 MW or even higher.

In my Snowbreeze the only source of power is a 50-watt fan which needs less energy than the electric bulb in your room and can be run for a virtually unlimited period on an inverter or a car battery to bring down the room temperature by at least seven degrees centigrade.

Apart from being a permanent standby against power breakdowns in the homes of the elite in metropolitan cities, it would be an ideal cooling device for small towns and villages throughout the country that usually have an indifferent supply of electricity.

Its movability from room to room makes it most suited to small hotels, guest houses and nursing homes that rarely have wall air conditioners or hundred percent occupancy.

When I was posted in Lucknow to cover the state of U.P. for The Statesman, I had a lot of leisure on my hands. Not being a coffee house or Press club edict I could devote all my time to reading, writing and cultivating artists. I had a friend who was the regional manager of a foreign firm that made electrical goods. He had made a desert cooler with Khas twigs and a large fan that kept his whole bungalow cool and comfortable throughout the summer though it had to be shut down during the monsoon season because it only added to the humidity. In the summer of 1976 I bought some books on air conditioning and learnt how air conditioners and refrigerators were made with the use of ammonia gas. English translations of Russian text books published in Moscow on all subjects were being sold cheap by the People's Book House through pavement book stalls in Hazrat Ganj, Lucknow's elitist market. I bought two books and ignoring the technical and mathematical parts read about the general principles underlying air conditioning. The literature I read also told me that ice condensed the air while water humidified it.

This meant that instead of water if we used ice in a desert cooler it would not only cool the room but also dehumidify it. My inheritance of an orchard in my home town, Gangoh, in Saharanpur district of U.P., had provided me with enough money to waste on a hobby. I sat about designing an ice-based air conditioner and finally decided to build a unit that could fit under my bed so as to air condition a cabin of about sixty square feet. I put a plywood partition in the covered verandah on one side of my bungalow and put a ceiling of the same wood at a height of six feet. Lucknow was a small town then and an ice-factory was about two kilometers away. I got a covered box of tin of 4'x6'x1' made to fit under the bed and got the open sides of the bed covered with plywood sheets. A powerful 12" exhaust fan was fixed on the feet side of the bed while some holes were made on its head side to suck room air. An ice slab of 40 kg was placed in the tin box which was placed on iron pipes to allow air to pass through its bottom also and prevent the coldness from passing into the earth below. The box was covered and sealed with a lid so that the air could not touch the melted water. I used to bring a slab of ice every evening from the factory in the boot of my car.

It worked. The temperature and humidity of the cabin came down sharply because the unit was mostly recirculating the air of the cabin. I then started working on a model that would fit in a window. I now realize that it was a mistake. I wrote and published an eight page pamphlet on the subject and sent a copy of it to the President of the Indian Science Congress who lived and worked in Bangalore. He sent a very encouraging reply along with an invitation to attend as a delegate the Indian Science Congress that was to be held in the Agricultural University premises in Ludhiana in the following month. He asked me to bring my gadget along. Having been posted in Chandigarh for four years to cover Punjab and Haryana prior to coming to Lucknow, I was quite familiar with the university. Mr. K.S. Virk, its chief public relations officer had become a personal family friend. I and my wife had made several two-day trips to Ludhiana and stayed in the university guest house.

I took leave from my office and left Lucknow for Ludhiana with the enthusiasm of a real inventor. At the conference one of the first persons I met was Dr. Gobind Swarupe Agrawal, who was then the director of the astronomical laboratory in Ooty which possessed the biggest telescope in the country. Gobind and I had been classmates in the Ewing Christians College at Allahabad. We both lived in the Turner hostel on the second floor. Gobind's room was two rooms away from mine. He thought I had come to report the science congress for my paper and I did not dispel his illusion. But his presence at the conference made me nervous and develop cold feet. I realized my folly in coming to the conference without a paper on my research, and with a poorly performing gadget. It might have worked well under my bed but the window prototype I had built was no good. I sat through the full conference and its seminars without uttering a word about my invention and without meeting the president of the Congress who had invital me. The same year, after completing a three-year term in Lucknow I was promoted and brought back to Delhi as an assistant editor. I brought the tin box and exhaust fan with me as a memento of my great folly during my stay in U.P. and discarded them after a few years.

The experience was completely forgotten and erased from my mind until 31 years later circumstances forced me to revive it. In the summer of 2007 I sat smugly in my study, a cosy nook in a spacious flat, with not a care in the world. I am one of those fortunate few who enjoy the luxury of having a full grown, lush green forest overlooking the study and bedroom windows of my house in an upper middle-class quarter of the national capital. My other luxury, of course, was my 1.5 ton conventional window air-conditioner of which I was very proud since I could barely afford it. For me it was a medical necessity.

I watched with poetic detachment the spectacle of a sizzling loo tearing and whistling its way through the jungle while the trees swayed wildly in its wake like a wounded tiger gasping for breath. The clock had just turned the hour of noon on this hot day in early June when the gentle purring of the air conditioner stopped. I was not perturbed because, unlike the rest of Delhi, power breakdowns in my housing colony seldom lasted longer than an hour or two and the fans in the flat could keep running on an inverter during that period.

But this was a special day. The fans could dry the sweat from the body but they were unable to stop for long the strong hot blizzard outside from warming up the room to levels that were unbearable for my old worn out frame. After about two hours, when electric power showed no signs of returning. I began to watch the prospect through my window with a different eye. The sight was not half as attractive as it had seemed to be little while ago. I could now perceive the agony of the leaves on the trees that were shuddering and withering in the heat and finally dropping dead on the ground. The birds sat silently or flew into deeper shade to escape the blast. A few of them sat huddled beneath a cluster of trees sipping water from a puddle, remnant of a recent shower by a passing cloud. I knew that soon my fate would be no better than that of the leaves and birds I was watching.

I asked my obliging wife, Saroj, thankfully several years younger than me and much more agile, to get me water in a washtub and place it on a table under the fan. When it arrived I moved closer to table with my head bent over the water and hands stretched out to feel the touch of the moistened air. But it gave only marginal relief, if at all, from the heat which seemed to be getting hotter in those afternoon hours.

Just then the good woman had a sudden brain wave which was to prove to be an event of momentous importance not only for me but perhaps for many others in a similar predicament. She rushed to the two fridges in the kitchen and dining room, put all the ice cubes and cold water bottles stored in them in a bucket and brought them to my study. After emptying the washtub she filled it up with the cold contents of her bucket.

The effect was electric upon my frayed nerves. Slowly I could once again begin to behold the view from my window with a poet's eye. I could see nothing but beauty in it. The leaves seemed to be dancing and the birds singing. After all they were Mother nature's own children and she knew best how to look after them, I now thought.

Fortunately for me, my air-conditioner started humming the familiar tune in another two hours, just when I was once again beginning to lose my sense of appreciation of nature's beauty beyond the glass panes. My wife beamed with joy for my sake and heaved a sigh of relief.

Saroj told me that my torment had reminded her of her childhood days in her home town, Meerut. On such occasions of extreme heat her father would order a large slab of ice from the ice vendor round the corner of the street where they lived. He had it placed directly under a fan in a large brass tub, used for kneading dough in the kitchen, in a room on the ground floor. It took care of the heat for the whole afternoon and evening for the entire family of ten. Similar ice slabs were placed by first class railway passengers in their compartments before the days of airconditioning.

Saroj's childhood tale brought only a frown on my face since I had grown up as a village lad who had not used a fan till I was twenty-five. When at college I would spend my summer vacations in my mother's village roaming in the fields and groves with my local friends in the mid-day heat and even playing open air games with them. Winter or summer, weather watch had never been on the minds of members of my generation and they never talked about it. This was a vice we picked up in later years from our British rulers who, we noticed, must compulsively spend the first quarter of a social get together discussing weather. It only reminded me of the vast reservoir of energy that once seemed inexhaustible and had seeped out of my system unnoticed as the years rolled by, largely due to my changed life-style which has, step by step, made me a new man, a cripple sustained by modern props like the air-conditioner.

"So, Ice is the answer to our power woes", I muttered.

"For short breaks, yes", said Saroj.

"Why not always?"

"Because if you use too much of it for long hours, the ice will become water and the room will become too humid. It will be worse than under a desert cooler which diffuses the moisture inside it by constantly drawing fresh and dry air from outside at high speed." Our conversation ended there because Saroj had to rush to her kitty party which she never missed. But the event sat me thinking and, as always, with me to think was to act.

Initially I borrowed a tin can from the kitchen, placed ice in it and put it in a box of wood specially made for it by a carpenter. I fixed a small 4" exhaust fan on the box to suck air coming through a one-inch wide slit in the box. It cooled the room but not much.

Finally, with the help of two carpenters, an electrician, an ice vendor and number of others we managed to produce within a few weeks the prototype of what we finally called "Snowbreeze" air conditioner. My experience with ice based air conditioning in Lucknow had assured me that I could not fail to bring down the temperature and humidity of my room through such a gadget if only I persisted long enough in my efforts.

It took me three months of trial and error before giving my invention a final shape. I called it Snowbreeze since it was based on ice. My friends liked it and advised me to patent it. I thought it would be better to make the know how completely free and sent a short note about my discovery to all newspapers. Indian Express picked up the story and sent its science telecast and photographer to my house to cover it. Soon after the story appeared with pictures and a graph of how Snowbreeze worked, I got a call from CNN-IBN TV channel. They wanted to do a report on my invention. It was a complete surprise to me since I had never thought of contacting any TV channel about it. Their crew spent three days recording every aspect of Snowbreeze and took my gadget away with them in a van to see it worked in their office. After they were fully satisfied about its genuiness they did a seven minute telecast on it with much advance publicity. They came back again the following year and did another feature on it. The Hindu and The Statesman did long illustrated features about

Snowbreeze. Finally I published a book giving a detailed description in twenty pictures of how Snowbreeze could be manufactured by any one in his house. Some enterprising people in Kolkata even tried to make it but failed. It needed a precision which could not be explained in a book. This venture could not have succeeded without the active and willing cooperation of a team of three carpenters led by Shahid and his assistants, who included his son Hasan and colleague Rehmat. Eventually, Hasan who has studied upto the 12th class, stayed on with my project through thick and thin and is still available to me whenever I need him.

But for Hasan (full name Mushahid Hussain) I would not have toyed with about thirty models of Snowbreeze, adopting different techniques each time. He was doing all the work and contributed several valuable ideas to the variegated units. Many of these models are displayed on our website called www.greenairconditioner.org. Come winter, and we started toying with the idea of using Snowbreeze as a humidified room heater. My idea was to put a 500 watt electric heater under the aluminium drums in which some water could be put. Naveen Nigam, my electrician, suggested placing of a halogen bulb above or inside the drums. I had never heard of a halogen bulb but decided to try out Naveen's idea. Initially it did not work. Here Ganga Ram, my all purpose man, came to our rescue. He suggested a design that has worked beautifully all these years. In fact some people prefer to use Snowbreeze only as a humidified room heater in winter. A relative who lives in Dehradum got it made only for this purpose. Its advantage is that it uses only 500 watts of power, is humidified by putting a litre or two of water in the drum and can run on an inverter for a few hours. I put this additional use of Snowbreeze also in the book in which I described the various advantages of air conditioning with ice. On seeing our website which declared that the know-how of Snowbreeze was free to everyone, a big Chinese firm Zhe Jiang More started manufacturing and selling Snowbreeze. It displayed my original models on its website. My son, Professor Akhil Kumar, who teaches in America noticed the site when he was surfing the web and informed me about it. I tried to contact the firm to thank them for using my invention under its original name but all my efforts to contact the company failed.

Then several entrepreneurs, small and big, tried to start manufacturing Snowbreeze but they put in meagre resources in their projects. A young U.K. educated man came flying from Hyderabad and started manufacturing Snowbreeze. He called Hasan to Hyderabad and kept him with him for two months, but he gave up half way and never put his product in the market. We got excellent results from circulating chilled water in copper pipes by using a tullu pump. But as the cost of copper doubled we had to give it up. Now, finally, we have settled down to a simpler model without a tullu pump which uses only aluminium pipes as a cooling medium.

Air conditioning with ice has a bright future in India too but it needs a big company or the government to launch it on a large scale. It is already being tried on whole power grids in America. There they call it "ice energy" cooling because power is first stored in ice. Accoridng to the Economist, London, five percent of all offices in Southern Europe spanning from the Atlantic Ocean to the Black Sea are air conditioned with ice. Ships and submarines use it too. When my younger son, Ankur, went to Taiwan to attend a conference as the Nascom representative he saw a mobile telecom unit of two buses, one mounted with the electronic equipments and the other with an ice run air conditioner to cool the system.

Broadly speaking the original model ran a one inch stream of air about 120 times around two aluminium cans through grooves also made of aluminium which was ejected into the room by an exhaust fan fixed at the bottom of the unit.

One may argue that it is naive if not dangerous to jump to generalised conclusions on the basis of a single experimental effort of an amateur non-scientist trying to grapple with his own petty personal problem of keeping his room cool in summer and warm in winter. But why not? The malady is as universal as common cold. If a medicine is effective in one case it should be equally so for many others suffering from the same disease. Since the stakes are high a thoroughly proven remedy cannot be dismissed out of hand without being given a fair trial. The nation is facing a perennial power crisis. Generating more power beyond certain limits is not only prohibitively expensive it brings in its train more pollution, global warming, disease and deprivation.

The whole world is searching frantically for cleaner, cheaper, alternative sources of power.

It is this author's humble submission that, in a small way, Snowbreeze, is one such alternative insofar as it contributes to cutting down power consumption on cooling and heating homes and commercial establishments and releases no pollutants whatsoever. My layman's experiments with it suggest that water and its byproduct ice offer a cheaper, cleaner and more energy efficient medium of heat storage and exchange than any other chemical agent. Mukesh Agrawal, owner of Jaswant Cold Storage and Ice Factory in Delhi, said that his plant produced 21 tons of ice in 24 hours against a power consumption of 1,119 units, averaging an output of 19 Kg ice from one unit of electricity. A 21 ton plant manufactured by Metalex, advertised on the company's website, consumes 1080 units in 24 hours, giving an even higher average.

The figures speak for themselves. A 1.5-ton room air conditioner consumes 1.5 units of power in one hour, which is sufficient to produce 30 kilograms of ice in an ice factory. With that much ice Snowbreeze can keep a room almost equally cool and dehumidified for eight hours. One might say there are distribution losses in ice deliveries. Under Indian conditions electricity transmission losses are no less, for which there are a variety of reasons including technical deficiencies and massive "thefts", committed in the open, mainly by the richer power guzzling sections of society such as big factories and large bungalows and flats. Add to that the colossal investments in the shape of electrical energy and finance to create the giant-sized infrastructure of power houses and transmission lines for every additional megawatt of power. If you take all this into account you will arrive at the sobering conclusion that a gadget which consumes one unit of energy per hour is in fact using two, the other half being invisible.

The issues raised by Snowbreeze that need to be investigated in depth are:

1. Are our popular electrical heating and cooling devices indeed energy efficient? Can we get better results by modifying them or replacing them with simpler mechanisms that offer more direct storage and distribution of heat, both for cooling and heating?

2. Can water and its by products, ice and steam (or water vapur), be the medium of optimising heat transfer due to the unique property of water of storing and releasing latent heat?

3. An important consideration in cooling and heating systems is their dependence on uninterrupted supply of electric power or other external inputs, such as sunlight for solar power and a strong breeze for wind power. How does Snowbreeze compare with all other systems considering that all that it needs to keep running cheerfully through the worst and longest power breakdown is 25 to 50 watts an hour of electric current which it can get from an inverter or even a car battery? Does it not make it the ideal option in areas where power is not available but ice is?

4. Every new option in creating an alternative source of power requires large investments, including even the apparently free solar, wind and ocean energies. A cost-benefit comparison of water and ice based cooling and heating devices with these sources of additional energy is necessary because it will perhaps show that this is one area which needs more common-sense than science, more attitudinal than physical adjustments, more application and promotion than finance.

5. How does the ice-and-water option compare with the other choices in environmental values? Is it not the least hazardous simply because it is the simplest? It is a well known concept of Entropy that the more complicated and intricate a process the more is the residue it generates.

6. Flexibility: In a vast country like India, which happens to be socially, culturally, politically and economically the most complex in the comity of nations, every system, mechanism or gadget that seeks universal acceptance by the public, must be amenable to an almost infinite number of modifications and customized applications. How does the ice-and-water cooling and heating technique represented by Snowbreeze stand the test? Our experience shows that it can be developed in any shape or size, in any environment, and can be conveniently moved to any place without pre-requisites. It offers similar flexibility in capital and running costs so that everyone whether from the lower middle or the upper classes can derive as much benefit from it as suits his purse.

7. Lastly what can we do to automate air conditioning? Our chilled water models are one way of achieving this objective.

This ice-based air-conditioner has been named 'Snowbreeze' as a dedication to Siva, Lord of the snows of Mt. Kailash and symbol of the lofty, icy Silence of heaven.

Heating: One thing leads to another. It would be only natural to assume that the inventors of Snowbreeze would not allow their favourite hobbyhorse to hibernate during the long winter months. The result of their ruminations was to convert it temporarily into an eco-friendly room heater which reduces energy costs by at least fifty percent and humidifies hot air before blowing it into the room, establishing once again the greater efficiency of home-made Snowbreeze over factory produced conventional domestic cooling and heating appliances in conserving and distributing heat.

Perhaps this is so because air is a poor conductor of heat and much energy goes waste while heating it directly inside a blower. On the other hand, Snowbreeze compresses the air and heats it repeatedly (twenty times) in the grooves around the drum before releasing it into the room. Simultaneously, surface water inside the drum, when exposed to a halogen bulb, evaporates in moderate quantity and humidifies the air before it is sucked into the grooves.

Dr. T.C. Goel A People's Scientist: It gives me great pleasure to dedicate Snowbreeze to the late Dr. T.C. Goel, Director of Birla Institute of Technology and Science (BITS) Pilani, Goa campus, till his death in July 2008. But for him by now Snowbreeze would have become extinct as an inventor's pipe dream. The several hundred 'orders' that have poured in for Snowbreeze units from all over the country and the several hundred thousand 'hits' on the Snowbreeze website, www.greenairconditioner.org, from all over the world since the publication of news about it in the last week of February and first week of March in newspapers and on Google and Yahoo, are a tribute to Dr. Goel's visionary imagination, a faculty not typical to his scientific community in India.

Nearly a year after the discovery that one could save oneself from dying of heat exhaustion during a long power breakdown by this crude home made device, I sent letters to a large number of eminent

Indian scientists and environmentalists, along with a copy of my book "Make your own Air Conditioner-cum-Heater" (see full text on my other website www.gandhionline.org), describing my experience and suggesting that a properly developed Snowbreeze would bring relief to millions who could not afford an AC. It would also cut down the running cost of air conditioning to about ten percent of what it is today. Dr. Goel was the only one who responded to my plea. He not only acknowledged my letter but also phoned me from Goa and said, "you have invented the people's air-conditioner of tomorrow. We must together do more research on this." I couldn't believe my ears. "But I am not a scientist", I protested. "So what!" he said. "Inventions are not produced by science but by necessity. Science only gives them a practical form without which they cannot function. Driven to the wall by dire need non-scientists have often made great new discoveries."

Dr. Goel lost no time in forming a three-man research team with himself as one of its members and Professor Dhananjay Kulkarni, a colleague, as the coordinator. Dr. Kulkarni worked tirelessly for months to formulate a project proposal by studying a working unit of Snowbreeze that I shipped from Delhi to Goa, and worked out a few mathematical modeling formats for it. The proposal was submitted to the Union Governments' Department of Science and Technology for a grant. It sailed through smoothly through a number of expert committees of the Ministry. Then disaster struck. A few months before its presentation to a selection panel Dr. Goel died of cancer and, as was to be expected, deprived of the moving spirit behind it the proposal fell through. But the ground prepared by Dr. Goel was enough excuse for me to cut across the maze of technocracy of the Union Ministry of Science and Technology and appeal directly to its Minister and Secretary as well as to the Director General of the Council of Scientific and Industrial Research (CSIR) for re-opening the case in view of its great importance to the whole country. All three of them saw the merit of my plea and suggested that I seek the assistance of the Technopreneur Programme (TePP), a marvelous facility promoted by the Ministry for encouraging and bringing into the market new inventions. Without this help I would have floundered long ago and there would have been no Snowbreeze-4 and its startlingly cheap and effective 'bucket' model today.

It is to be noted that at the time when Dr. Goel offered to take on the challenging task of producing a common man's air conditioner based on ice and chilled water he was in the thick of a host of new projects in the fast expanding Goa campus of BITS, Pilani, as its founding Director, negotiating a few high tech research projects with foreign universities and, at the same time, battling with a fatal disease though he did not know the end was so near. Only the desire to do some thing to meet the dire needs of the poor classes prompted him to shoulder this extra burden so cheerfully.

If proof was needed of Dr. Goel's far sight in choosing Snowbreeze for the service of the people of India it is there on this website. No sooner had news about the invention of Snowbreeze-4 appeared in a few newspapers all over the country, specially Mail Today which also gave my web address in its report on March 5, there were 192000 'hits' on my website on a single day followed by several thousand of them every day from all over the world ever since. Nearly five hundred email 'orders' poured in from every corner of India, half of them on the first two days for non-existent Snowbreeze-4 units. My website server had to increase his bandwidth ten times to accommodate so many hits.

But will it or can it do so unless people who can deliver the goods take over the task in earnest? Or, will Snowbreeze fade out like a falling star? That is the million dollar question.

Clearly, India needs more persons in authority like Dr. T.C. Goel with an instinctive empathy for the common man, not only in science but in every walk of life.

Indian environmentalists and academics took no interest in Snowbreeze, mainly perhaps because the suggestion came from a lay man whom they perhaps equate with a madman, unless he happens to be a celebrity of some standing. But, like the big Chinese company which has been manufacturing and selling Snowbreeze models an American Professor, showed great interest in my invention and even introduced a special course of the simple technology of Snowbreeze in his mechanical engineering classes. Of all the responses I have received his was the most encouraging. He wrote two letters to me in two consecutive years which read as follows:-

Thanks: Snowbreeze
Saturday, 25 April, 2009 1:33 AM
Dear Mr. Lal,

I am writing to thank you for your detailed information on the snowbreeze you sent to Prof. Sinha, and to tell you I have used it in my undergraduate Thermodynamics class of 85 students. Professor Sinha has an office down the hall from me and shared with me the snowbreeze details. I presented to the class the design, the video, and explained about the background to why the device is especially useful in India. As the students were taking a thermodynamics class, it was a perfect example of an engineering system that used our textbook material in an applied application. Actually, I also used it to demonstrate a basic principle I try to teach my students that often, if they are creative, a simple solution can emerge that is better than conventional approaches. I have recently found out that I will teach this class again next Spring, and I hope that you do not mind if I continue to use this in my classes in the future.

Thanks again and congratulations on such an interesting design.

Matthew

Wednesday, 28 October, 2009 8:45 AM
Dear Mr. Lal,

Thanks so much for the update, I am very glad you sent it. I will be teaching a class of over 130 engineers in the Spring, I will plan to add this into their lessons. It is a really good lesson, actually. There is some great engineering with basic principles, and it shows them that a solution need not be complex, only to work. In the US, engineers tend to over-think many things, I think, and go for really complicated and energy-intensive solutions too much.

With best reagrds,
Matthew

17

On remaining fit and healthy

Vidyasagar's Legacy for the Sick and Poor
—Free Homeopathy

A little known fact about Ishwar Chandra Vidyasagar, one of the greatest social reformers produced by Bengal in the Nineteenth century, was related to me by a direct descendant of his family who has continued the tradition set by the visionary Sanskrit scholar.

Oxford trained Dr. Kushal Banerji the 28-year old son of Dr. Kalyan Banerji, a leading practitioner of Homeopathy in Delhi, told me that his great grand father on his mother's side was a nephew of Vidyasagar from whom he learnt and picked up the habit of distributing homeopathic medicine free to poor villagers. In reply to my further queries he sent me the following email:

"Vidyasagar found homeopathy as a safe, affordable way to help people without any danger of harming the patient. He was married and his son was married to a child widow thus setting an precedent where widow remarriage was established. He worked to abolish sati and to rehabilitate widows into society.

"Similarly my great grand father continued this tradition. Vidyasagar was my great grand fathers paternal uncle.

"My great grandfather Dr. Pareshnath Banerji and his team of doctors were treating 2200 patients a day for free. His only source of income was through the sale of medicines to others and from his invention of Lexin—the medicine for snake bite victims to other countries etc."

Continuing the tradition started Vidyasagar Kushal and his father treat about a hundred poor patients, many of them suffering from serious ailments like cancer, free of charge every evening, while treating only paying patients in the morning.

Recently I had high blood pressure which persisted for days. A cardiologist was called. He charged me Rs.2000 for the visit and prescribed a few blood tests which cost me another Rs.9000. I was lucky he did not suggest my admission to a hospital or nursing home for a complete check up of my heart which I haven't got done all my life. The doctor is a kind man whom I call once a year or so. Had he advised a thorough check up in a nursing home as modern medical science requires the packet would have cost me about 1,00,000 rupees.

A neighbour told me that the spectacles he was wearing had cost him Rs.25,000. Cheaper specs can be bought for about Rs. 2000/. My hearing aid is worth Rs.35,000 but causes resonance of external sounds in the car. I seldom use it. My ear specialist tells me that if I wanted smooth hearing I would have to shell out at least Rs.1,00,000.

Adjoining my colony are two fully air conditioned super speciality hospitals with comforts of five star hotels. Patients from all over the world come to them. A neighbour took his wife on an evening for emergency care and brought her back in the morning. He had to pay Rs.21,000 for the nights' treatment. Another resident of our colony got admitted to one of these hospitals for a boil on his hip. Three days later he came back home poorer by Rs.75,000. Within a few days another boil appeared near the same spot. He cured it himself by spending only about one thousand rupees.

Just across the road from our elitist residential complex is a slum where our maids, servants, drivers and other "menials" live. Being old and retired people I and my wife, Saroj, have all the time in the world to listen to the stories that our maids and drivers bring to us about their families and neighbours. Most of them relate to sickness. Some months ago Poonam, a middle aged maid was killed when a part of the ramshackle roof of her nephew's house she was visiting fell on her head. The matter was soon forgotten and no action was taken against the landlord nor any compensation paid to her children. Every other day we hear reports of some one dying in that colony of natural causes. A few of the dead were quite young.

There is hardly any family in that slum, one or the other of whose members is not going to visit a doctor or a quack to get his ailment cured. A curious case I heard a few days ago was that of a teenager who had high fever and started behaving strangely like a grown up neighbour whose voice he imitated. It was said that some spirit had got into his body. An old woman, also a maid, who lives in the same slum was called. She recited a few mantras for an hour on two consecutive days and the boy's fever went away with the spirit that had got into him. I know of another successful cure by what doctors will call "witch craft". Arjun Pal who was driver of our car till about ten years ago was down with jaundice which used to recur again and again despite treatment in the best hospitals nearby. In desperation he went to his village in Bihar for treatment by a "witch" doctor and came back fully cured. In north India cases of jaundice are often cured by a "witch craft", called "Jhardna" in Hindi. (Its literal meaning is dusting)

According to practitioners of modern medicine the quacks whom these people visit and the woman who cured the boy by her "witch craft" should be arrested and prosecuted. But then where else are they to go? The nearest government dispensary, more than a kilometer away, is doing a good job but is always over crowded. Serious cases are taken to Safderjung hospital, which serves a few million people living in the whole of South Delhi. Its services are stretched beyond belief. I cannot blame the doctors and nurses there for their apparent indifference to individual patients who get admitted there, howsoever serious their condition might be. The fact is that only serious cases are admitted. The others are turned away, there being no room for them. Yet patients are littered all over the place.

The average combined income of husband and wife in the slum is about Rs.10,000 of this at least Rs.3000 goes as house rent for a one-room tenement, with shared toilets, of the type in which the maid Poonam died of roof collapse. Another thousand or so goes in buying country liquor to which almost all male members of these poor families are addicted. That is their only entertainment after a hard day at the work place. Their wives work harder but poor women are trained not to complain. Their children are their solace and wealth. They try to educate them as best as they can, spending an average of Rs.1000 to 1,500 per month on their education Medical expenses are also fairly high. They cook meagre meals once a day which the family eats at noon and night.

The scene in the rural areas where the bulk of India's population lives is even more gloomy. A 46year old doctor, who practices medicine in America and is a graduate of the Lucknow Medical College, told me that she would not dare to work in a rural dispensary even if someone gave her a million dollars for it because there she would always live in fear for her life from rival gangs of criminals. They fight and the injured are brought to the doctor who has to give a medico-legal report. The criminals get the report they want on the point of a gun or dagger. If the doctor does not oblige they kill him. She cited cases of several doctors who were killed by these gangs.

There are, however, some brave hearts in the profession who face these risks and opt for serving in rural areas. Besides, some charitable hospitals and dispensaries work in urban areas like Delhi. Dr. V.K. Gopal, secretary of the Rural Medicare Society of India told me that The Rural Medicare Society stands firmly by its commitment to deliver affordable quality medical treatment to those who are economically marginalized and are unable to bear the ever increasing cost of modern healthcare. The Society continues its journey of service to mankind with the singular belief that 'The best way to serve God is to serve mankind'.

Rural Medicare Society established the Rural Medicare Centre, currently a 30-bedded multi-specialty charitable hospital. The center houses modern medical care infrastructure with comprehensive diagnostic facilities. With 25 visiting consultants covering 12 specialties, the center conducts over 80,000 outpatient consultations and 2,000 surgical interventions annually.

He also told me that there was a 450 member organization called Association of Rural Surgeons of India. It was affiliated to the International Federation of Rural Surgeons. But all such efforts are a drop in the ocean of disease and deprivation that we see all around us.

America spends $ 2.8 trillion which is 20% of its GDP on health care. This amount is 60% higher than India's total GDP of $ 1.8 trillion. America has less than five percent of the world's population. If the same standards of health care were to be applied globally we would have to spend perhaps more than the world's GDP on health alone. We have no choice but to look for alternatives to reach health care to the poorest people in the remotes areas of the country. China developed the institution of bare foot doctors to serve its vast population. When talking about health care why should we only think of the rich and well to do and ignore the poor?

Most of the common diseases can be cured by the body's own healing powers if only we know how to use them. Why should we not encourage and promote practitioners of such cures instead of treating them as quacks? Homeopathy is an advanced science though medical scientists do not recognize it as such. Though occasionally I have to take shelter in modern medicine and surgery, I have survived for more than eight decades on homeopathic medicines. Anti-biotics just do not suit me and modern medicine cannot do without them. In the 1980s a leading dental surgeon told my wife that two of her teeth, would have to be extracted. An appointment was fixed with a dental surgeon who had come on a visit from Australia, to perform the operation. Some one suggested that in the meantime we might try homeopathy also. We went to Dr. Jugal Kishore, a leading homeopath whom we visited quite often. He gave us a medicine to be taken four times a day. The tooth infection disappeared within a week and we did not have to go through the ordeal and expense of a surgery. Our present dental surgeon, Dr. Ashoke Deshpande, himself recommends homeopathic treatment in certain situations.

This noble science has been let down by the greed of its practitioners who do not disclose to the patients names of medicines they are being given. I have dealt with about 25 to 30 homeopaths in different cities during my life. With the exception of Dr. Kalyan Banerji in Delhi and his son Dr. Kushal Banerji I have not met or heard of a single homeopath who would reveal the name of the medicine. Doctors indulge in this unethical practice for fear of losing patients. They do not know the harm they do to homeopathy. Dr. Banerji has a roaring practice. He charges a fee higher than that of my allopathic consultant in Delhi and yet patients have to wait for months to get a 10-minute audience with him. He is also a cancer specialist and visited China in 2003 to cure a senior Chinese official of pancreatic cancer. He was invited there on the recommendation of a patient living in Australia.

Homeopaths are accused of mixing steroids with their medicines to get quick results. Unless they name the medicine which a patient should be free to buy from any source, the charge cannot be refuted. In the summer of 1973 we decided to spend the whole month of June in Nainital which used to be the summer capital of U.P. during British rule. In this hill town there was only one homeopath, a young man in his 20s who had taken a small shop at the far end of the large maidan along the Naini Lake. I went to him for treatment of my chronic abdominal problems. At the end of the month I felt much better and asked him to disclose the name of he medicine which I would use if the disease reappeared. He willingly obliged. I had a similar experience in Mumbai in 1991 where we stayed for a year. Homeopaths give you the name of the medicine they prescribe only after they are convinced that you are leaving the city and would never see them again.

Homeopathy's basic approach lies in curing the body's "vital force", by administering minute doses of substances that would cause the same disease if given in large quantities as Dr. S. Hahnemann, the founder of this science, described it. However, Professor Parimal Banerji, Director General of the Mihijaim institute of Homeopathy in Kolkata, traces the source of this concept of a "vital force" to Vedic times and calls it "Pranashakti". In the preamble of his book on homeopathy he says, "While studying the ancient but ahead of modern scientific thoughts found in the Sanskrit Hindu Vedic literatures about life, I could gather that the very expression of what I wanted to mean about life, which I realized, needs the most comprehensive name as "Pranashakti" as revealed by the ancient sages, which is more explanatory than what is meant by "Bioforce".

He further claims that the practice of dilution of curative substances on which homeopathy relies completely was also known to Indian medical science in ancient times. He says, "When such a minimum dose of a toxic substance as mentioned above is further reduced, this may be by 10,000 times (10^{-4}), by diluting it in a medium. In many cases, it developed a peculiar property of being able to reverse and extinguish the same signs and symptoms of a disease, which could be produced by the toxic effects of the undiluted substances. This was first observed by the ancient Indian scientists in about second millennium BC. That means, such diluted substances affect the activities of the life."

What Dr. Banerji says conforms to my own views and I have myself been thinking along the same line for a long time. Dr. Banerji's book only confirms my own theory that the human body is essentially pure energy without a physical form. It has tremendous powers to heal itself. Also, numerous other substances like herbs, plants, and chemicals found in nature and not in use by modern medicine have curative powers that have been discovered by other systems of medicine. The two systems which have developed sciences of their own are Ayurveda and Unani treatment, the former developed in India and the latter in West Asia. All these systems should be encouraged in the service of the masses who cannot afford the cost of modern medicine.

Gandhiji also developed and practiced 'nature cure', a discipline of medical treatment widely used commercially today. He started a nature cure clinic in Urli Kanchan in Maharashtra and gave simple health tips to people in his weekly Harijan. He was totally devoted to improving the life of poor villagers and teaching them elementary rules of hygiene and sanitation. Perhaps half the diseases we suffer from in India are caused by the insanitary conditions in our cities and villages. Ultimately, we should also recognize that the basic source of disease is the mind and the thoughts we think. It works wonders because it enables you establish direct contact with the source of the mind, called "super mind" or "super consciousness." which is pure energy. Homeopathy also says that disease travels from the centre outwards. In my view that centre is the mind or super mind, the main seat all the diseases that mankind suffers from. Induced by the extreme sufferings of the poor Gandhiji discovered the sovereign remedy of "Ramanama" (repetition of any name of God) as a cure for most diseases.

Here I must relate a personal experience. In February 1966 I went for a thorough health check up to the all India Institute of Medical sciences for abdominal pains. Being a special correspondent of The

Statesman I was given special treatment. The director himself examined me and sent me to Dr. Hari Das Tandon, head of the gastro-enterology department who later became Director of AIIMS and earned worldwide fame in his speciality. After a cursory check up he said "Most probably there is nothing wrong with you but since your company is paying your medical bills we shall put you through all the tests." As he expected nothing wrong was found in the tests. Dr. Tandon smiled and told me "It is the thoughts you think that have created this problem for you."

Lately some doctors in the USA have realized that the cure of heart diseases which take 2500 American lives every day and causes 6,50,000 cardio-viscular strokes every year lies in the mind. The most health conscious country has one of the highest rate of heart problems in the world. In his book the heart speaks Dr. Mini Guarmeir says "healing the heart can have more to do with healing the mind and soul than we ever knew". Dr. Andrew Weil, a pioneer in the science of healing the heart through mind-cure has opened a large clinic for this purpose and authored books on the subject. To remain fit and healthy we shall have to combine the old and new ways of thinking and living and choose the best among them.

Sooner or later science is going to recognize that we have an invisible 'mind' which is separate from the brain and operates it. The whole human body is 'intelligent energy', call it intelligence or consciousness if you like, with tremendous cognitive powers. We are aware of only a few of them. When the famous Tsunami earthquake came a few years ago in the Andamans and Sumatra there were only human casualties. All the birds and animals had fled to safe places. They had advance warning of what was coming through a faculty which we have not cared to acquire or develop.

18

When Knowledge is Free

In Celebration of the legacy of Aaron Swartz

The Economist of London rarely features on its widely read Obituary page a celebrity who dies before the age of 80. One has to be really one of the 'wonders of the world' to die at 26 and within a brief life span accumulate achievements so startling as to merit a full page coverage in that acclaimed weekly. It is an even greater wonder that he had earned notoriety for doing things that are normally frowned upon by the conservative Press of which the Economist is an icon. Moreover, in the eyes of the US laws he was a criminal guilty of a crime punishable with thirty-five years in prison, which seems to be the cause of his suicide on January 11, 2013.

Why I rejoice in the fact that such a man ever walked on earth, and so recently, is that he made an actuality of what I had been merely dreaming of. He gave us a glimpse of what it would be like when education, that is, knowledge, becomes freely available to the poorest man in the world. I rejoice in Aaron Swartz because he was the first modern age martyr to the cause of free education. He was a freak genius in his own right. At the age of nineteen he developed in collaboration with three others Reddit, now the web's most popular bulletin board. In 2002, at the age of sixteen, he wrote what reads like his own epitaph. He would be content to die, he had said, "as long as all the contents of his hard drives were made publicly available". To me Aaron Swartz looks like an angel come to earth. Because of the young age at which he performed his miracles I would compare him with Sant Gyaneshwar, who is said to have written his famous classic Gyaneshwari at the age of fourteen. He too died young. By making public millions of records of the MIT library and an equally vast data from the Library of Congress he foreshadowed a world in which knowledge is free.

The main reason for my enthusiasm for Aaron Swartz is my own background. Born in 1928 in the Gandhian era, I belong to an age when education was the greatest gift one could give to the poor. It was called "gyan daan" (donating Knowledge). At the age of eight I was teaching the Hindi alphabet to my family's servant and the cook, both illiterate young men. The cook, a Brahmin who knew a lot of mantras, picked up the language fast and was soon able to read my mother's religious books. In 1945, as a student of the Ewing Christian College, Allahabad, under the guidance of a young American missionary teacher I was running a literacy class for the servants of the hostel mess. The class was held in an empty garage. There, squatting on a jute mat spread on the floor I and another student from the hostel would conduct a class of about a dozen people, the mess servants and their children, in the dim light of a kerosene lantern. Elder members of my family founded and ran schools and Colleges. A cousin of my father founded and ran till his death the first school in my small home town of Gangoh in Saharanpur district of U.P. Starting from a small building, under his stewardship the school became a high school and later an intermediate college with a large playground on the fringes of the city. A cousin of mine started a school for girls in Gangoh and had it raised to the level of a high school. My father's elder brother founded a degree college named after him in Saharanpur. The owner of an orchard adjoining mine in Gangoh was the main trustee of a large fund bequeathed by a childless rich man for building a degree college in Gangoh in his name. The young man struggled for several years to clear numerous hurdles and finally succeeded. He ran the college for almost two decades until his death. Starting schools was a passion with landlords of yester years. Often wealthy persons with no male heirs would give away their money to start a school or college in their name. They freely gave money and time for the cause of education. Before independence there used to be only one government high school in a district. But each district had dozens of privately funded and managed high schools recognized by the board of secondary education.

Today's urban landlords have commercialized education. But ultimately these institutions have no future. Their owners may make quick money but eventually they will have to wind up as free education becomes available on internet, complete with class room courses, assignments and test. My maternal grand father established a small Sanskrit school in his village Kota in the same district. Spreading free education for all was the main slogan of those times. The tuition fee was nominal and always waived in the case of poor students. Several one-man schools sprang up in mud houses in the villages. The teacher charged no fee and like Ishabod Crame, a famous creation of Washington Irwing depended on doles from the parents. I studied in one of them for a month or so in my mother's village. That was the age when Tagore wrote his famous poem. "When the head is held high and knowledge is free."

I rejoice because I can see before my own eyes the poet's dream coming true, Men like Aaron Swartz have proved that no one can stop all knowledge from being freely available to every one. It may take time but it will come. A time will surely come when the whole world becomes a global university and not only Indians but all humanity can sing with Poet Tagore his poem:

"Where the mind is without fear and the head is held high, where knowledge is free. Where the world has not been broken up into fragments by narrow domestic walls. Where words come out from the depth of truth, where tireless striving stretches its arms toward perfection. Where the clear stream of reason has not lost it's way into the dreary desert sand of dead habit. Where the mind is led forward by thee into ever widening thought and action. In to that heaven of freedom, my father, LET MY COUNTRY AWAKE!"

When, in the far distant future, the history of global university of tomorrow comes to be written, you will find the name of its founder, Aaron Swartz, written in letters of gold on the title page.

Belatedly, the US Congress is considering passing a bill to be called Aron's law which will dilute the provisions of the present laws against cyber criminals that would have put Swartz in jail for 35 years. Aron's father has welcomed the move.

"Aaron's Law" is designed to rein in prosecutors who have used the CFAA to threaten security researchers, journalists, and activists for violating online terms of service contracts. The bill would establish that terms of service violations are not automatic breaches of the CFAA, punishable by decades in prison. Aaron's Law would also limit the ability of prosecutors to "stack" charges on top of each other, compounding the penalties the U.S. government wields to pressure defendants into plea bargain agreements.

"This bill is good news, because it deals with the issue of criminalizing violations of terms of service," Aaron's father, told TIME. "Terms of service violations should not be felonies."

19

Nature And Human Nature

Genesis of our family centred selfishness

This book is being written in the shadow of one of the greatest natural calamities India has faced in the last 65 years since Independence. The cloudburst that hit the Kedarnath shrine and its surroundings at a height of over 12000 feet on June 16, 2013 left over five thousand dead, thousands missing and about 1,00,000 homeless. The media gave various names to this tragedy like a Himalayan Tsunami and man made disaster. Till a century ago such cataclysmic events would be accepted as an act of God. But today armed with the latest technology man can mitigate much of the losses caused by a natural catastrophe. About 20,000 people were evacuated by helicopters of the Indian Air Force supported by some civilian airlines and roads were restored in record time for stranded people to travel by motor vehicles. Food and fuel supplies were rushed to the stricken people. As happens in all such disasters in India, the criminal minds of numerous politicians, businessmen, government officials and professionals saw in this event an opportunity to make a 'killing' from the distressed people. In our country of 1.2 billion people this is not a new phenomenon. Such black sheep abound in hospitals, police, railways, holy shrines and all other places where innocent and helpless people are in a state of panic and fighting for life.

In the Tulsi Das version of Ramayana, India's greatest epic, when Lakshman asks Lord Ram, God incarnate and his elder brother, to reveal to him the very essence of life on earth, Ram answers it in two words "Me and mine." They were living in exile in a forest, far away from their home in Ayodhya, when this dialogue took place. Ram explained that the whole universe was permeated by these two words, me and mine. In this context 'mine' is a greater value than 'me' because 'mine' is the cause of the me. Like Lord Krishna in the Gita, Ram the earlier incarnation of God, is also indicating that there is nothing more precious to a person than his or her children. Kaikayi sent Ram to fourteen year's exile in a forest so that her son Bharat, could be the King of Ayodhya. Dasratha, Ram's father gave up his life saying "Ram, Ram . . ." because he could not bear the separation from his favourite son, Ram. What is more there is a history behind Dasrath's tragic fate. In an earlier incarnation as a king he had gone out on a dear hunt in a forest. In those days bow and arrows were the main weapon of a warrior. The King was an expert in archery and could shoot a prey by its sound. The royal personage heard a sound in a nearby stream. At once he thought it was a dear drinking water. He shot at the source of the sound. Next moment he heard the sighs of a dying man and rushed to the spot to find a young man, Shrawan Kumar, crying in his death agony. He pleaded with the king to carry some water to his old parents in a nearly hut. The old couple was none other than the saint Shantanu and his noble wife Gyanwanti. The two died in anguish on hearing about what had become of their son, and cursed the King, "In the next incarnation king thon shalt suffer the same fate and die, as we are dying now, due to separation from your son". Dasrath was now paying for this sin that had committed in his previous birth. In one of the holiest Hindu scriptures, Yoga Vasishth, there is a story about a saint who was about to curse Brahma, the Creator of the universe when he saw the emaciated body of his son. A voice from heaven dissuaded him by telling him that he had been in meditation for hundreds of years and showed him his son in his present incarnation. Firdaus's epic Sohrab and Rustum points once again to this central theme of parental love. When she heard of her son's death in battle Sohrab's mother burnt down her palace and died of grief within a year. All these stories point to one thing that the desire to have children is a universal passion. But do we ever consider that the poor woman loves her child as intensely as the rich:

The fact is that more than the recently discovered God's (or Higg's) particle, the principal raw material which our objective world is made of is "blind passion" to recreate its own living image. And passion is blind. It has no intelligence of its own. It is just a force, directed by Nature, a form of energy without any attributes or restrictions whatsoever. This is why we have so many wars and conflicts all over the world and amongst smaller groups, even within the family. This energy creates and destroys what it creates in an ever renewing process. But the end result of its creativity is pain. We try to gloss over this fact in a mad pursuit of our passion without trying to understand the root cause of our madness. If a neighbour is hungry or sick we do not care to ask ourselves why is it so? The same applies to torture of men and animals in a routine manner. Have we ever asked ourselves why is it that we are by and large, totally indifferent even to the sufferings we inflict on others by bending or mending the law in our favour because they are too weak and meek to protest?

Why is it that we are prepared to extract the last drop of blood of the poor so that we and our progeny can be comfortable though we are fully aware that tomorrow it may be our turn to meet the same fate of exploited humanity? Is it not a blind force directed by mother nature's intelligence that makes us behave in this fashion? Sigmund Freud described it as sexual attraction to which he and his followers attributed all human activity. But he ignored a vital factor; intense attachment to one's children who are the direct product of the passion for sex. More than sex perhaps motherhood has been the dream of every female of any species. Look at how a cow cares for its calf and is prepared to fight and die for its safety. Or look at birds trying again and again to build nests so that they can breed and bring up their off spring in relative safety. They bring the material sprig by sprig in their beaks and build nests in safe places near the ceiling of our homes. If we destroy the nest they build it again, twig by twig, such is their passion to breed and multiply. Lord Krishna says in the Gita "who ever mothers a mortal form Brahma conceives I am the father sending seed" In its role as the creator Nature is worshipped as Mother Kali" Each unit of creation is directed by her intelligence like a puppet in the hands of a puppeteer. Thus motherhood is the primary function of Nature which it performs through its agent, blind passion. Every species is engaged in a mad rush to multiply. To me this is the meaning of Charles Darwin's great discovery, his theory of survival of the fittesh. The more you breed the more chances your race has to survive. Parsis in India are a fading race because they breed less children. If you walk into a forest you see all around you a wanton waste of vegetation and living beings, the big animals devouring the small ones, birds preying on ants and insects, big beasts eating up cows, buffaloes and dear. If you enter the ocean the picture is the same, big fish swallowing the small ones. In this panorama of creation and destruction on a grand scale, homo sapiens have survived because they have bred more people than nature could destroy. Breeding is the creative force that keeps a species alive. Hence the universally recognized natural urge to love one's progeny and he loved by them. This shows why we love our children so blindly and are prepared to do anything for their sake. Our affection for them is the result of the same blind force (or passion for survival) working in us internally over which we have no control.

Nature does not seem concerned about saving or destroying a particular species. It is an automated force which keeps creating new species and destroying old ones. Each individual unit of life it creates is concerned with its own survival. We call it his ego but in fact it is the primal force of nature driving it. In this sense you may even call Nature a breeding machine.

Hindu mythology sees Brahma, the Creator, as the Sun god who 'illumines' all life with its intelligence. This fact is beautifully enshrined in the Gayathri Manthra, the Rig Veda hymn which is prescribed as a necessary ritual at the beginning and end of all prayers. Individual units of life like me and you can be compared to the rays of this Sun God. Thus each living being is directly connected to its Source, the Creator, even as the Sun's rays are connected to the Sun and nothing else. The Creator Sun is a ball of intelligence, pure illumination. The "divya rupa" that Krishna shows to Arjuna in the eleventh chapter of the Gita points to the same phenomenon. Each ray or unit of life is a stream of creativity. It functions independently and forms social organizations with the limited intelligence given to it.

Birds of a feather flock together. This applies in varying degrees to most species. Many of them carve out territories in which they would not allow entry to other members of their own species. Dogs and monkeys are examples of this phenomenon. But it is amongst human beings that consciousness of territorial rights is more pronounced. Nature has made us independent entities. We come together mainly to kill other members of our own species. It is only rarely that awareness of our common origin makes us conscious of our unity as a single species. Step by step we attain new heights of consciousness and develop the faculty of compassion which is dormant in all of us but awakens only in a rare few human beings. That compassion itself is God awareness. It was that compassion which awoke in Abraham Lincoln and his fellow Americans. It made them sacrifice their lives so that other human beings, with whom they developed a feeling of oneness (spiritualists call it non-duality), could live with dignity. But such compassion is rare and least to be found in the land of Gandhi which is also the home of half the officially listed "slaves" in the whole world, though 40% of India's population leads a life that is only marginally better than that of "slaves".

This is the best explanation I can give of why we are so indifferent to other people's sufferings including those that we inflict on them consciously. Mystics and philosophers describe the primal force as a symptom of "non-duality of the spirit but they are as much slaves of their egos as any normal human being or any other unit of life. Like every creature on earth, our whole civilization is ego-driven. All efforts to supplant ego with reason or violence with non-violence, war with peace have failed. Brute force rules the world. Whoever holds the slightest power uses it ruthlessly to his advantage. Might is always right.

Thus, holding such beliefs in his emotional and spiritual life an Indian is congenitally incapable of looking beyond the interests of his immediate family.

How can an Indian in trouble ever trust another Indian? In one of the greatest disasters that have ever struck the country when the whole pilgrim town of Kedarnath was swept away by the flood a large number of people saw in this tragedy an opportunity to make money. It was a case of saviours turning killers. A bottle of water sold for Rs.200/-, a rice bowl for Rs.500/-, a roti for Rs.180, a seat in taxi to go across the chasm Rs.6000 and a ride to safety in a government owned helicopter which was supposed to be free, Rs.1000 to Rs.3,00,000 as bribe to the officials or private employees operating the service and there were numerous reports of women's jewellery being snatched from them. Till a few decades ago such acts would have been impossible to commit. Public opinion would have revolted against them. Today we are all silent spectators of such tragic happenings. Similar horrendous acts of exploiting the distress of poor people like war widows and patients in hospitals, prisoners injustly put in jail and so on are endlessly repeated all over the country. As in Kedarnath, the government and the Press always look the other way when such things happen. In a survey conducted recently by a national daily only four percent of the respondents said they would stop their cars to take an accident victim to the nearest hospital.

Even without loss of life floods can cause much devastation. As a reporter I have seen whole villages demolished and their cattle swept away by swollen rivers. If I was asked to name the most exciting night that I had spent during my sixty years in journalism, my mind would immediately fly back 58 years in time to an October 1956 night when I joined an intrepid team of about thirty student doctors and nurses of the Christian Medial College, Ludhiana, who were engaged in rescuing and providing relief to people in flood-ravaged villages not far from the city. Army motor boats as well as smaller craft were plying over flooded fields and roads in complete darkness relieved by a *petromax* or lantern that could barely enable us to see each other.

The young medicos led by a professor, a man of unbounded zeal, had set up a tent on dry ground near a large open air camp the district administration had created for people who had fled their villages to escape the flood. The only luxury in the tent was a kerosene stove placed on a table where you could take tea or coffee served in a beaker. The Bhakra and Beas dams had not been built by then to contain the surplus water and all Punjab rivers and their tributaries had drowned half of Punjab. I toured the whole state without a photographer. Everyday, my stories were splashed on the front page of *The Tribune,* then published from Ambala Cantt. My reports on the poor relief work in Amritsar which I contrasted with Ludhiana created a furore and I had to face a barrage of contradictions. It was there that I learnt that in great calamities voluntary agencies can do little unless the administration provides them with the necessary infrastructure.

The most touching scene I saw was in a flooded village about thirty-five kilometers from Amritsar. An old woman was lying on a broken cot amidst the ruble of her house demolished by the river. She was the only member of the family, along with some other villagers, who had refused to be evacuated by boats provided by the government. Being on higher ground many houses were untouched by the flood. "If I had also gone who would look after this mother?", she said pointing to a cow standing in the small cow shed on a raised platform where the water of the river had not reached. I began my story on this visit for The Tribune with the lines: "A three-legged cot can sometimes be a luxury. It is certainly so when the only alternative to lay your body on for a night's rest is the fallen debris of your own house." I remember those lines because my coverage of the Punjab floods got me a reporter's job in The Statesman in Delhi a year later.

In my new job, it fell to my lot to cover the floods in Rohtak town in September 1960, this time with a photographer. For about 20 days the Rohtak flood was front page news. Reporters and photographers from all English dailies of Delhi drove out to Rohtak about 70 kilometres away, and returned in the evening to file their reports, including box items and side stories of human interest. For a few days we had to take a 30-kilometre detour each way when the direct route was cut off by the flood.

For lovers of nature such calamities do not impair its eternal beauty. Atheists equate nature with God. Holy men of all faiths retire in its bosom to silence thought and contemplate on God and His creation. Wordsworth, the poet of nature, saw in it intimations of immortality of man's soul. Our own poet laureate, Kalidas, was so enraptured by it that he wrote out his Meghdoot (cloud messenger) and gave an imaginary description of the region from the Himalayas to Central India as seen from a cloud. In the Nineteen Forties traveling in a low flying Dakota plane Lord Wavell, then Viceroy of India, found the entire route to be an exact replica of Kalidas's Meghdoot. Lord Wavell was a great scholar of Sanskrit. Evidently, while contemplating the beauty of the landscape Kalidas had been transported into the domain of extra-sensory perception.

In ancient times sky watching at night was a favourite pastime of poets and mendicants. Living in forests, along the side of a river, lake or sea and on snow clad hills, they could see the star-studded sky as clearly as one sees it today with the help of a telescope. This is how the ancients developed the sciences of astronomy and astrology. The fate of an individual, they believed, lay in the stars. The whole firmament was part of their natural world. Today our concept of our planet Earth has shrunk to the sights around us that we see on the ground.

The question arises who is it that has given man the aesthetic sense to appreciate beauty? Is it not the same power that has given us the faculties of love, hate, anger, lust and attachment to kinsmen and property? Are these qualities not present in varying degrees in animals too? In fact experiments have proved that they are to be found even in plants. Maharishi Raman once said that we should regard a tree as standing man and man as a walking tree. In his much quoted book The Magic of Findhorm, Paul Hawken has shown how a green oasis of flowers, fruits and vegetables has been grown in a snowbound wilderness of Scotland by the dedicated efforts of plant lovers. In addition to normal inputs of water and soil they gave the plants love and even talked to them. When a poet or mendicant appreciates nature's beauty nature is merely manifesting its narcissism through him.

This reminds me of the time I spent sitting on the lawns of the Rose Garden in Chandigarh when I lived in that city for four years from 1969 to 1973. Reputed to be the largest rose garden in Asia and spread over 27 acres it has 17,000 rose plants of 1600 varieties. The combined fragrance of all these roses in maddening. It greets the visitor as soon as he enters the undulating lawns of the garden interspersed with water channels over which small sloping wooden bridges with railings have been constructed. All this is the creation of M.S. Randhawa, the first Chief Commissioner of Chandigarh, an ICS officer, born in rural Punjab who dedicated his life to the service of the nation in a variety of ways, including the discovery of priceless Kangra paintings. In addition to what we see in the Rose Garden there would be an equal number of varieties of roses that cannot be grown in the soil and climate of Chandigarh. Rose is just a name that man has given to one of the millions of plant species that mother nature breeds in its bosom. Nature makes no such distinction. It breeds life in a bewildering variety of forms.

The next question that arises from this deduction is that is man not just one of the millions of species that nature has produced? Is man's capacity to destroy all other species also not a gift of nature to him? Nature has given man the faculty of possessiveness which it has denied to all the other species whom it wants to live on its mercy from day to day. Each living form has to feed on whatever it can find by its own efforts at a given time. Can the scientific civilization man has enscoused himself in save him from the clutches of nature which is a single wholeness? It makes no distinction between one living form and another and sends out the same life current to run through all its creations.

According to Hindu mythology Nature is that elusive phenomenon which we call Time. After revealing his cosmic form to Arjuna, Lord Krishna (God incarnate) tells him "Thou seest Me as Time who kills, Time who brings all to doom, the slayer Time, Ancient of Days, come hither (the Mahabharata war) to consume." Whether or not we believe in God, we all believe in nature and the supreme power it holds over us. We also totally accept that nature is ever changing, ever moving with Time. Fifty thousand years is but a moment in nature's time scale of billions of years. This is all the time that our species has spent on earth. During this period many civilizations have come and gone. And ours will meet the same fate eventually. Swami Vivekananda put it beautifully by relating a legend from the epic, Mahabharata. When the victorious King Yudhishthira was asked by Dharma (faith incarnate) to tell what was the most wonderful thing in the world, he "replied that it was the persistent belief of mankind in their own deathlessness (or immortality) in spite of their witnessing death everywhere around them almost every moment of their lives."

What we call modern civilization is but a passing phase. By accelerating Time through its new technology which now moves fast and measures Time in terms of nano-technology, which splits seconds into quadrillions of units, our modern civilization is perhaps accelerating the process of its own destruction. Or, is it that this vision of mankind's eventual doom through its phenomenal greed may be a passing phase and, as I have said in another chapter in this book, the knowledge revolution that is sweeping across the world will change man's character and make him less hungry for money and power and more appreciative of the common needs of all living things on earth?

Man is credited with having destroyed millions of species in nature. But it is not known how many sub-cultures of homo sapiens our modern civilization has steamrollered. Greed, pure greed, is our ruling deity today. Till barely a century ago habits and customs of people varied from village to village and city to city. Even in England this was so. In Pygmalion, one of George Bernard Shaw's plays, a linguist standing with strangers in a church portico to escape pouring rain in the street identifies the localities to which each person in the group belonged by his accent. Today variety has given place to uniformity. If a rose can have several thousand varieties how many times more types of human beings can nature produce? Every place, small or big, is capable of producing its own heroes and villains, saints and sinners, artists and craftsmen and businessman of all types. When I go to my small home town of Gangoh a visit to the shrine of Hari Das Baba ji, the patron saint of our extended family, is a must. Some two hundred years ago he was a sadhu revered by our whole community. The site of the small temple is so picturesque that it at once transports us into the bygone era of peace and tranquility. The humming of a Persian wheel pulled by two white bullocks provides a soothing background to the scene. Its water runs in earthen channels and irrigates the surrounding vegetable fields. Such small lingering attachments to our home towns arc fast disappering now. I can relate many such cases of sub-cultures growing under the umbrella of Indianness. Religion makes no difference to it. Begum Samru's church in Sardhana tehsil of Meerut district, a Christian shrine made by a Muslim lady, draws lakhs of visitors and devout pilgrims from Delhi and other places every year. Our cook, Marie, is one of them. Every year she goes with a bus load of other maids to pay her homage at the shrine and have a nice picnic with her friends.

Have you ever wondered why is it that we are often entranced by the beauty of nature? In my childhood we used to watch the sunset and sun-rise almost every day. Today, all such pleasures have been demolished under the giant bull dozers and cranes of massive urbanization, even like the night sky under which, before the advent of electricity, we used to sleep eight months in a year and watch the star studded sky or enjoyed playing simple games on our terraces in the moonlight. All these experiences which were the common heritage of all mankind for 50,000 years have been lost to us in the civilizing process.

But we have lost some thing deeper about which the present generation of human beings can have no clue: that precious treasure is the quality of "contentment" which has now been replaced by "greed". I have said above that we have lost thousands of sub-cultures. What was the distinguishing characteristic of all of them? According to me it was "sharing" everything that we had with our brothers and sisters, neighbours and friends and even strangers. There was nothing that we would not willingly share with others. Our hearths and homes were always open to all. Charles Dickens portrays a similar picture of 19th Century England in his Pickwick Papers. We did not need to be formally invited to the house of a friend or relative to spend an evening or even several days with him. Friendships once made stayed for life without consideration of the change of status and incomes of the concerned parties. Laws were simple but were faithfully honoured and never circumvented for small gains. All this was so because this is the way that nature wanted us to live. It was what philosophers would call a natural way of life. Closeness to nature was its secret. One drew silent strength from nature. Afterall we are mother nature's children and she looks after us if we take shelter in her bosom.

Every culture has a flaw and if it didn't living in it would be heaven on earth. Our culture of Indianness is no exception. Since this book is an autobiography I would perhaps be justified in illustrating this point with my own personal experience. I have made a case study of various residential complexes in Delhi.

The state government in Delhi has based a law called the Minimum Wages Act. The government fixes the wage and upgrades it every six months to keep pace with the rise of prices of essential commodities.

Similar laws operate in every state of India. It is a paper law which has never been applied except in respect of the six to ten percent of India's labour force of nearly 500 million men and women who work in what is called the 'organised' sector. On paper it is mandatory and provides for a jail term of one year for any employer who violates it. But in practice no body follows it. Most employees everywhere in the country get half to one-third the "minimum wage'. Their condition is what Martin Luther King, the American Gandhi, said about his country's Negro workers of about a century ago. Quoting Paul Laurence Dumbar he wrote in his book "Strength to Love" the following lines:

A crust of bread and a corner to sleep in,
A minute to smile and an hour to weep in
A pint of joy and a pack of trouble,
And never a laugh but moans come double;
And that is life!

This is exactly the lot that our tradition of Indianness has cast for the poorest classes for the past several thousand years. It cannot and must not change if our Indianness is to be preserved, say the pundits and intellectuals who run the philosophy and way of life in India. Even the communists who held power in West Bengal for 30 years, did not speak a word about implementing the Minimum Wages Act any where in their state though it is on the statute book throughout India. At least they should have treated the Minimum Wages Act as the magna carta of the working class. But how could they? Almost all the leaders, of the CPI (M) and CPI, specially the chief ones, belong to the upper castes. They have been educated in the best Indian and foreign universities and often have an aristocratic background. They have all the traits of what Karl Marx contemptuously called the "bourgeosie". Though they have gone through the motions of familiarizing themselves with poverty, and have even gone to jail for the sake of their creed of socialism, they have not themselves experienced the anguish of a person whose pockets are always empty and who is not sure where the next meal will come from for himself and his family. Like the capitalists and our novo riche middle class they also think there will be chaos in the country if the

Minimum Wages Act is applied uniformly all over India. With more money in their pockets the masses will buy more food to eat. This would lead to a larger investment in the agricultural sector which the communists would not like because the industrial worker is their main constituency.

To the extent the employer is forced to share his profits with the workers, his horde of black money will be depleted. Indian economy essentially runs on black money. Small industries making goods for poor people will thrive giving a jolt to big industry which produces consumer durables and luxury items for the rich middle class. With variegated production of small man's needs employment will increase, as has happened in ALL those countries where a Minimum Wages Act is rigorously enforced. But to that extent large industry will suffer and so will investment in projects that will determine India's rank in the Great Powers of the globe, such as the race for building powerful long-range missiles and satellites. It will be an entirely different model of economy that will benefit no one but the poor man of India. But this is not the objective worth seeking for a great country.

Lord Krishna has said the final word about this phenomenon in the Gita: "I made the four castes and assigned them a place. Whoever does his caste duty goes to heaven. The duty of the upper castes is to rule and enjoy life according to law and the scriptures. The duty of a Shudra (untouchable or lowest castes) is to serve". In Lord Krishna's time there was no money and service of a shudra came virtually free. He sustained himself on the fruit and roots of the jungle and whatever little his family could grow on small plots of land adjacent to his hut. He also kept pigs and goats and, according to the Gita, ate dog's meat. He received nothing by way of charity. All charity was reserved for Brahmins if the giver aspired to attain heaven. Suffering was the shudra's lot through eternity in the Hindu scheme of things.

All desert coolers in residential complexes in Delhi have been replaced by air conditioners and split ACs resulting in huge power bills of Rs.5000 to Rs.15000 per month per flat. Each flat owner's income ranges, generally speaking between Rs.50,000 and Rs five lakhs (or $ 1,000 and $ 10,000) a month. It will mean a mere extra burden of Rs.100 (one dollar and seventy cents) a month per flat to give the 'minimum wage' to the workers each colony employs. Yet none of the flat owners I interviewed support the workers' cause. Several of them who are highly paid senior executives of charities of various kinds to benefit the poor, shied away from this issue and kept quiet about it when I put a direct question to them on this issue.

More than 65 years after Independence the Planning Commission has recently released data which describes 65% Indians as being poor, or below income levels of Rs.50 per day (Rs.60 in urban areas). The figure of 65% is a gross underestimate according to a study published in The Hindu.

Its author Utsa Patnaik, Professor Emeritus at the Jawaharlal Nehru University in Delhi, points out that poverty in India is actually increasing. It says "All official claims of low poverty level and poverty decline are quite spurious, solely the result of mistaken method. In reality, poverty is high and rising. By 2009-10, after meeting all essential non-food expenses (manufactured necessities, utilities, rent, transport, health, education), 75.5 per cent of rural persons could not consume enough food to give 2200 calories per day, while 73 per cent of all urban persons could not access 2100 calories per day. The comparable percentages for 2004-5 were 69.5 rural and 64.5 urban, so there has been a substantial poverty rise."

If the Minimum Wages Act was strictly enforced on employers all of whom have the capacity to pay but do not pay for selfish reasons, the figure of actually deprived people would come down sharply. But this will never happen and the poor will always remain poor because Indian tradition wills it so. This was followed a few days later by an official report that the gap between the rich and poor was "rapidly" increasing. All this proves one thing that it India's growth process poverty is a fact of life, even as corruption is. In fact the two are inter-related. All anti-poverty laws and systems have to be implemented and enforced by middle class people who want to eat up every penny of the resources set apart to remove poverty, such as higher wages under the minimum Wages Act. Before removing poverty we have to remove middle class corruption.

Jean-Jachques Rousseau, the famous 18th century French philosopher, once argued that man was inherently good but got corrupted by the evils of society. In my opinion it all depends on your definition of corruption. A universally accepted tradition cannot be called "corruption". Non-payment of the statutory Minimum Wage to workers is a universally accepted tradition, sanctified by the scriptures and one of the leading hallmarks of the culture of Indianness. Convention is more important than law. England, once the largest empire builder in the world, has no written constitution and is ruled by convention. Under the Indian convention the rich castes must always remain rich and the poor ones eternally poor.

As proof of their abhorrence for corruption of any kind the flat owners in several colonies took out candle light processions in support of the historic movement launched by the noted Gandhian Anna Hazare, nearly two years ago. But in India tradition (such as keeping the poor in poverty) is tradition. It cannot be broken by any law. The flat owners were not even conscious that taking advantage of the extreme poverty and ignorance of law of their employees they were every month stealing a large slice of the workers' lawful salaries.

These colonies contain respectable and well to do people of all religions hailing from all parts of India. People of various professions including rich doctors, senior government officers, businessmen, editors and company executives live in almost all such complexes in NCR (National Capital Region).

My experience with the urban and semi-urban middle class, including myself in it, tells me that all of us are furiously busy with competing with our "nearest and dearest" relatives and friends in wealth and power. Husbands are competing with wives, brothers, sisters and cousins are competing with each other. It is a race in which no one is the winner but nevertheless is the sole occupation of every body. It is like an addiction: grab whatever you can from whomever you can, even if the victims of your insatiable greed are your own employees.

I have narrated this example in such detail because for me it is a case study of the way corrupt practices have crept into the lives of the Indian middle class. Most of the time we are not aware at all that there is something morally or legally wrong in what we are doing.

My case study shows that the RWAs are refusing to pay the lowest class of their workers the statutory 'minimum wage' on grounds of principles based on tradition and convention and not because they could not afford to pay. My further study shows that this is true of almost every employer in the 'unorganised' sector in the country. He has the capacity to pay but he thinks he can make better use of the money than the 'urchins' he employs. According to a report based on statistics maintained by the National Sample Survey of the Government an individual who spends over Rs. 2,886 per month in a rural area or Rs. 6,383 per month in an urban area is in the top 5% of the country (and this is using the modified mixed reference period, which gives the most generous expenditure estimates). This translates to spending Rs. 96.2 and Rs. 212.77 per day. The top 10% of the country includes anyone who spends over Rs. 2296 per month in a rural area and Rs. 4610 per month in an urban area. It is the employer's duty to make sure that the underlings he employs are paid well below that divide to keep them in their place.

Writing in the Wall Street Journal of June 28, 2013, Francis Fukuyama says that "all over the world, today's political turmoil has a common theme: the failure of governments to meet the rising expectations of the newly prosperous and educated."

"The theme that connects recent events in Turkey and Brazil to each other, as well as to the 2011 Arab Spring and continuing protests in China, is the rise of a new global middle class. Everywhere it has emerged, a modern middle class causes political ferment, but only rarely has it been able, on its own, to bring about lasting political change. Nothing we have seen lately in the streets of Istanbul or Rio de Janeiro suggests that these cases will be an exception."

"In Turkey and Brazil, as in Tunisia and Egypt before them, political protest has been led not by the poor but by young people with higher-than-average levels of education and income. They are technology-savvy and use social media like Facebook and Twitter to broadcast information and organize demonstrations. Even when they live in countries that hold regular democratic elections, they feel alienated from the ruling political elite."

"None of this is a new phenomenon. The French, Bolshevik and Chinese Revolutions were all led by discontented middle-class individuals, even if their ultimate course was later affected by peasants, workers and the poor. The 1848 "Springtime of Peoples" saw virtually the whole European continent erupt in revolution, a direct product of the European middle classes' growth over the previous decades."

In India, by contrast, the members of the new middle class are busy grabbing whatever they can by hook or by crook to enrich themselves at the cost of the poor. This is why extremists like Naxalites and Maoists find a fertile soil amongst the poor classes of India for their abominable culture of "terror".

My case study of seventeen-months of this Delhi residential complexe's stubborn refusal to pay the government—fixed minimum wage to sweepers and its gardeners made me explore more deeply the attitudes of the new Indian middle class in general in money matters. I found that we did not hesitate to bend, circumvent or ignore the laws of the nation to make the extra buck. I realized that like every one else I too had been indulging in corrupt acts without even for a moment thinking they were illegal. The impact of our actions done individually or collectively on the poorer classes, in the absence of any government worth the name to protect their interests, did not count in our calculations.

The case study I made of these colonies shattered all my life long dreams of some day ushering real socialism in India. After all, I said to myself, these are the very same self-seeking people who will hold the reins of power in a socialist society. They (and I include myself among them) are incapable of looking beyond their noses to causes outside their immediate personal objective of making money for themselves and their families, relations and friends. They can never change their attitude to life. I remembered my interview with Ashoke Mehta, the famous socialist leader of the freedom movement.

In the late Nineteen Sixties when he became deputy chairman of the Planning Commission, I asked him why the cooperative experiment which had been so successful in Maharashtra and Gujarat could not be introduced in backward east U.P. and Bihar, "Lal, I have staked my whole political career trying to do just that and failed. You can take a horse to the water but you cannot make him drink," he replied.

That in this country the poor must always remain poor, no matter how much the country progresses, was also stated in different words by the great socialist leader Ram Manohar Lohia. I was present in the Lok Sabha press gallery when, in 1963, Dr. Lohia threw his famous and historic "three-anna challenge" at Nehru. "Panditji," he said, shouting at the top of his voice and interrupting Nehru's speech "for all your talk of progress, the average income of the Indian farmer is still three annas (nineteen paise) per day. You can ask your officials to check their figures. I shall resign my seat in Parliament if I am proved wrong." The government never refuted Lohia's figure.

In India caste is supreme One's status is determined by caste. In North India it is symbolized by the hookah (bubble bubbler). I discovered this while covering the Parliamentary elections in 1962 in the outer Delhi constituency which was then entirely rural. Only people of the same caste can smoke from the same hookah. Half a century later the picture remains the same today. The hookah has been augmented by stronger stimulants like drugs and country liquor. In this social mileu the lower castes must be kept low, no matter what laws you pass to improve their lot.

It suddenly dawned on me that at last I had got the biggest scoop of my life as a journalist. What I had studied was not just the story of one housing colony but the real story of the whole of India and Indianness. So why not write about it, I thought.

At this point it may not be a bad idea to take a look at what foreigners think of us and our character. Corruption is a recurring theme in reports on India in almost all foreign newspapers and magazines.

Some years ago New York's *Wall Street Journal* in a frontpage article by Peter Wonacott said "few countries, however, can match India's numbers of alleged criminals in Parliament and state assemblies. Following the 2004 election, almost a quarter of the 535 elected members of India's national parliament have criminal charges registered against them or pending in court, according to the Public Affairs Center, an Indian elections watchdog. Half of those with charges pending against them face prison terms of at least five years if convicted . . ."

Nine years later the number of alleged 'criminals' in our Parliament and legislatures has increased. Revelations made in newspapers on July

11, 2013 show that 30% or 162 out of 543 Lok Sabha MPs and 31% of 1258 of 4,032 MLAs in India have criminal cases pending against them. Almost half of them are of a serious nature.

The phenomenon of rampant corruption that we see at all levels in Indian society has a reason. We are living in an era of competition that envelopes the whole of humanity and manifests itself in different forms in different cultures and societies depending on their past traditions.

A schizophrenic epidemic of competition among the upper castes has gripped India in its most virulent form. Just as a man in a lunatic asylum will never admit he is mad, the entire human race is unaware that it is afflicted by this disease. Of course there are rare exceptions of wise men who are conscious of the phenomenon. But they are helpless spectators of a tragicomedy being enacted before their eyes. I call it so because I am also aware that the same tools and neuro-scientific processes that wrought this havoc. The same tools can and will have to be used to fully control it.

According to Dr. G. Ramakrishna, a Sanskrit scholar from Bangalore there are various references in our scriptures which enjoin upon the shudras to do their caste duty which is menial labour and nothing else. Different punishments were prescribed for committing the same crime for different castes.

Following are some example that he gives of this rule.

May the pani-s (a shudra caste) lie in darkness, unenlightened's may the be confined to an uninviting abode.—(Rig Veda)

From the shudra shall be extracted labour either by paying wages or by not paying any wages.—(Menusniri)

The duty of the Shudra is to serve those of the upper Varna-s.

(Bhagwat Gita and Apastamba Dharmsutra)

Dr. Ramakrishna who has been a member of the senate of the Bangalore University and Secretary of the Federation of All India University Teacher's Associations also says that by commercializing education we have ensured that the poor man always remains poor. "Where is a poor man going to get Rs.1.5 crores for an MD and MS degree in medical science or even pay Rs.30,000 to pay for admission to a simple B.Com course?" he asks. Commercialization of education was the best way to eliminate the great mass of people from the competition for highly paid professions, he thought. According to Wikipedia says that "As per the available information, the private out of pocket expenditure by the working class population for the education of their children in India has increased by around twelve times over the last decade." At this rate there is no hope for an ordinary person's children to expire for highly paid professions.

Dr. Ramakrishna also agreed with me that our sense of caste superiority was not easy to erase. Himself a Brahmin, he is a signatory to an appeal filed in the Supreme Court against a judgement of the Karnataka high court refusing to stay an obnoxious practice in the Kukke Subramania temple near Mangalore, the famous port city in the state. Every year a large number of priests are feasted at a special ceremony. After they have eaten the upper caste devotees of the holy shrine roll their bodies over the left overs of the feast on the palm leaf plates. Thousands of devotees flock to the shrine to participate in this practice which is supposed to bring them rich rewards. The auto-rickshaw drivers' union of the city has supported the priests' case because the annual ceremony brings them so many customers.

Dr. Ramakrishna asks "with this kind of mindset how can you ever eradicate caste prejudice from this country which is many times stronger than the race prejudice in Western Countries?"

With my own experience I can assert that British times were better in the matter of education for all. Even a poor man's son could aim to become an I.C.S. Officer. Today it is all gone. Our ways of thinking are entirely feudal. We do not think of the poor man when we plan for progress in any field. I once met a senior Nepali journalist who ran his own English daily from Kathmandu and was the Nepal correspondent of several foreign news agencies. I asked him why was it that Nepalis sought only menial jobs in India and other countries while Indians who went abroad worked in higher class positions like those of doctors, scientists lawyers and so on?

"This is so" he replied with candour "because we won the war when British forces tried to capture Nepal. Had we lost in the war we would be like you. The story is current that when our late King established a university in Nepal around the year 1920, he came to the palace and wept. 'Today I have lost my kingdom. These people will get education and get ideas against my monarchy' he told his wife."

It must be noted here that while Chinese Government spends $357 billion on education every year the combined expenditure on education by the Central and State governments in India is only $74 billion, or 20% of what the Chinese central government alone spends.

There is nothing wrong with human nature. But everything seems to be wrong with human behaviour. We falsely attribute all criminal acts and obsessions of man to human nature. Apart from endowing it with the instinct of self-preservation nature has left every species free to chart its own course.

In India the story is often told of a child who opens the door to a visitor who asks him to call the head of the house, say Mr. X. The child goes in and after a minute comes back with the reply "Mr X says that he is not in the house and has gone out on some business."

As we grow into adulthood and wiser we learn to lie and conceal the truth to gain advantage over other people. Lying is not human nature. It is a behavioral trait acquired by man from his social surroundings.

But we must never forget Lord Krishna's prophetic words to Arjuna in the Bhagwat Gita. "Thou seest Me as Time, Time who brings all to doom, the slayer Time". What we are seeing today is a passing phase. Like all things born the pervasive corruption in India will also meet its ultimate doom. Carlyle once said "the darkest hour of the night comes just before dawn". Our 'dawn' may not be far away.

20

An Unforgettable Lesson from Darul Uloom

Two months after joining the Statesman in October 1957 as a staff reporter I was asked by my news editor, P.W.J. Crosland, an Englishman, to take a random tour of U.P. and adjoining areas of Rajasthan and Madhya Pradesh to look for stories for the paper. "Go where you like", he said. I was to take the office car, a Baby Ford, to nearby areas and travel by train for longer distances. "You can stay at the best places", he said in parting.

For the next six months I was my own master. For me it was like a holiday in royal style. It was a good opportunity to revisit places familiar to me, like Mussoorie, Hardwar, Allahabad, Benaras and Agra and take a look at others that I had never visited like Gwaliar, Jhansi and far away Gorakhpur from where, if possible, I could make a quick trip to Lumbini, the birth place of of Lord Buddha.

The universities, where The Statesman was then widely read and respected, were my special area of interest. During my tours of places within 150 miles of Delhi by car I chose new routes to cities I had lived in and was surprised by the wealth of story material that lay hidden here and there in the countryside.

It was thus that on a cold afternoon of January 1958 I came to be in Darul Uloom, the holiest of holy seminaries of Islam in India in the tehsil town called Deoband in Saharanpur district of U.P. It is claimed to be only next importance to the Al Azhar university of Islamic culture at Cairo. I arrived there in the afternoon and was taken around its modest campus by an official of the institution. Since they were all dressed alike in simple Islamic style, it was difficult to make out which of them was the boss. They all had designations in Arabic or Persian language of which I could make out nothing. The place was then a structure of small galleries and domes and uneven but clean terraces. At the end of the hour long tour of the place followed by discussions with a few teachers and students I asked my guides.

"Can I see the head of this institution?"

"You mean the Vice-Chancellor?" asked one of them.

This was the first designation that I heard pronounced in English.

"You see ours is regular university with a full-time Vice-Chancellor," he said proudly and added, "if you like one of us can take you to his house."

There was nothing distinctive about the residence of the Vic Chancellor which lay in a wide street packed with houses on both sides. He received me in the front room with a window opening on the street. He was a stout elderly man with a black beard and wore an embroidered woolen jacket over his dress of Salwar and Kamiz which was perhaps the standard uniform of all residents of Darul Uloom. The settee on which he sat was covered with a thick carpet, possibly Persian, and a rug was spread on the floor on which a few easy chairs were placed for visitors. I do not remember anything about the hour long discussion I had with him but for a vague notion that besides Islamic studies the curriculum of the institution included all other subjects taught in Indian universities. He also told me that he was a regular reader of The Statesman. At the end of the interview he said politely "It is dinner time. Would you care to have a meal with us?" The Maulana made this request with such courtesy that I found it impossible to refuse.

"I would love it", I said.

He ordered his attendants to arrange to serve us food in the very room where we sat. The chairs were pushed aside and a thick parabolic mattress was spread on the rug. After the food had arrived my host looked out of the window and said to an attendant "I notice there is a driver in his car. We should feed him also."

I felt relieved. It would save me a half hour wait in the market to enable Bhagwan Singh, the driver, to have his meal in an eatery or dhaba. But I was not prepared for what happened next. I had thought that the driver would be served food in the car or in a servants' quarter. Imagine my surprise when Bhagwan Singh walked in and the V.C. said to him. "Please come and join us at the dastarkhwan." The two attendants and a male member of the family also sat down on the carpet around the dastarkhwan.

This experience of a driver and attendants taking food with the master, a person of high rank in society, kept bothering me for ten years till I happened to be in England in 1968. I was selected by the Thomson Foundation for a three—month course in Advanced Agricultural Journalism at Cardif. One great advantage of this training was that it gave us the opportunity to tour the rich, green, undulating and highly forested countryside of England and Wales. Almost every week-end we were dumped into a bus and taken to visit modern cow stables, poultry farms, grazing grounds and rural markets. We passed through and stopped at places like Stratford on Avon, Shakespeare's birth place by the river Avon, the bridge on the river Wye on which Wordsworth wrote a famous ode and the city of Birmingham.

On each trips the driver of the bus had all his meals with us, paying his bill himself and sitting at any table be liked regardless of whether the head of our course, a member of the staff or some of us were sitting at the same table. We were staying at the International Hostel in Penarth, a sea side holiday resort five miles from Cardiff, in rooms overlooking a big golf course and the sea coast. The woman who came to clean our rooms was equally chummy with Mr. Fields, the hostel Superintendent. She gave me a bound book on Penarth to read. It came as a surprise to me since from books and novels England had always appeared to me to be a hierarchy bound country where class mattered and birds of the same feather had no choice but to flock together.

In my own house, before my father retired from service in 1954, the driver of his car was treated as part of the domestic staff. Though he was drawing twice the salary of the cook he was considered inferior to him because the cook was a Brahmin and the driver a member of the lower castes.

When motor cars first came to India no owner could manage a car by himself because to start it needed to be cranked from outside by a long iron rod inserted in a hole below the radiator fitted at the end of its long bonnet. It involved manual labour which the Brown Saheb loathed. Sometimes, if the battery was low or carburetor over full with petrol, the car wouldn't start even with a crank and had to be pushed. A horn which looked like a bugle and fitted with a rubber balloon was also fixed outside the front door near the driver's seat, along with a back view mirror. The first motor cars were of sturdy build but were prone to numerous mechanical faults which could be easily mended but needed some physical exertion by the driver. For all these reasons any one who owned a car hired some one to drive it. In the beginning cars were few and slow moving and the roads empty. It did not need much skill to know driving. Anybody could learn to drive a car in two days. Drivers were low paid and made to do other domestic duties like cooking and washing plates. Self-starting cars which needed no cranking to start came to India towards and end of Nineteen Thirties. They were expensive, large and consumed more petrol. It was only after World War II, and more so in the early Fifties that self-starting came in vogue in all cars. Most people started driving their own cars and only rich people hired drivers. With more vehicles on the road drivers required better training and their salaries increased. They became conscious of their status and started refusing to do domestic chores.

Though car driving is recognized by all wage boards as a skilled profession, Indian society still does not give it the respect it deserves. They are branded as suspected thieves, criminals, drunkards, gamblers and drug addicts. People who make these allegations forget that the description by and large fits the middle class on much as the lower classes. Modern civilization of globalised consumerism has made many of us commit illegalities unthinkable in the past. There are today black sheep in every profession. Using them as examples you can scandalize a whole profession howsoever respectable its public image. The contempt with which the Indian middle and upper classes look upon the blue collar worker is an international scandal. It betrays the caste prejudice embedded deep in the psyche of Indian society since most members of the working classes belong to the lower castes or the weaker sections of minority communities.

I have always looked upon the driver as our second line of defence. I cannot forget the bravery of Arjun, who served us for eight years as a driver, in chasing a man who had lifted a laptop from the back seat of our car and was running away with it in a crowded market where criminal gangs of all types operate. Arjun was helping my son carry some bags when looking back he saw the thief picking up the computer. At the risk of being beaten up by members of a gang he ran after the man and retrieved our property. Or take the case of Moti Ram, a quiet plump man and driver of The Statesman car in which I was touring a flood affected area. We were traveling over a narrow muddy and slushy earthen bund about fifteen feet above a river. He stopped the car, asked me to get down, and drove through the dangerous stretch. If the road had caved in the car would have gone down into the river with Moti Ram in it. To my shame, I did what he asked me to do and walked behind the car till it had crossed the earth filled muddy patch.

My case is that no one hires a driver without checking his credentials. No thief can enter houses in a street where drivers are standing near their cars. Some residents do not appreciate this simple fact and instead suspect them to be mixed up with thieves. They forget that car drivers are one of the most upcoming status conscious class in India. When I was in The Statesman the whole community of drivers there was proud of the fact that the son of one of them had got an engineer's job in America. Chanda, daughter of another member of the tribe, worked with me as my secretary in my post-retirement job of editor of a weekly magazine. I attended her wedding in a church to another white collar employee of a firm. Earlier, her better looking younger sister had married a young man well employed in the film industry in Bombay.

Her father Kewal Ram, was one of the best drivers in The Statesman because he was also a mechanic. I always took him with me on official tours as well as during my holidays when he would also take leave to drive my car. Once we took him to Mt. Abu via Jaipur and Udaypur. While returning our car broke down near Sirshi. He managed to bring it to Sirohi before night fall where we had it repaired under his supervision. Throughout my service with the newspaper I could afford only second hand cars and that too by taking loans.

Take the case of Bhagwan Singh, the driver who, along with me, had the privilege of dining with the Vice-Chancellor of Darul Uloom. He was Jat farmer from Munirka village adjoining lands on which IIT and JNU came up later. During my drives to neighbouring areas he had once taken me to his house, a small building with a wide open courtyard in front of it. Soon, as the city expanded the Government acquired all the village land. Though the price of the same land has risen at least a hundred thousand (1,00,000) times of what the Government paid the farmers then, Bhagwan Singh thought the money he had received was enough to enable him to quit his job and enter the politics of the village. He soon became a sarpanch and dropped in to see me and his friends in The Statesman, dressed in his new attire of a local neta, which included a dhoti, kurta and a dupatta tied around his head with its foot long tail falling on his back. You can imagine my surprise when a decade later I saw him driving the car of my cousin Sat Prakash who lived in Green Park, close to his village. He had blown up all the money he had got from the government and taken a job again on less than half the salary he would be getting had he stayed in The Statesman. If he had any regrets for his hasty actions it did not show on his ever cheerful face. Thus, incidentally, is also a reflection on the government's policy of reckless land acquisition without proper rehabilitation of the dispossessed farmers. Some car owners do not allow their drivers to enter their homes and hand over the car key to them at the door. Very few offer them a cup of tea during their ardous day-long duty, or give them over time or meal money when they go to parties. During my whole career as a journalist I have enjoyed the hospitality of several car drivers in their homes.

To cap it all comes the welcome news from Mumbai that Prema Jayakumar, daughter of an auto rickshaw driver, has topped the nationwide examination for Chartered Accountancy, and her younger brother, Dhanraj has also cleared the same examination with her. It is one of the most difficult professional examinations in India.

I have dwelt at length on the case of drivers as an illustration of the silent revolution taking place in India among the whole class of blue collar workers. In my old age I have a lot of time to discuss with them the personal lives and problems of the masons, carpenters, plumbers, mechanics, nurses, postmen, electricians and others of their class who come to work in my house. Every where it is the same story. All of them are keen to give their children a better life by educating them upto their utmost paying capacity and proudly announce it to their familiar customers when their progeny outshine others in their school and college exams. Even house maids have entered the race and many of them have children in college and one or two have daughters employed as computer operators in call centres.

About two years ago one of our maids panicked when her daughter who is enrolled in a Delhi University College came home one evening sporting bobbed hair and bereft of her foot-long pony tail which she had got cut at a beauty shop. "Before she elopes with a boy and spoils the reputation of the family I must marry her off to a boy in my village," she declared. Some friends, including my wife, dissuaded her from her hasty resolve. The girl is about to finish her graduation this year.

The children too are conscious of the need to build their future and despite the constraints of shape for study and cost and quality of education they receive they sometimes do better than the children of the middle and upper classes who are prone to getting drawn into too many distractions of modern life. To achieve this ambition of improving the lot of the next generation they have to suffer unimaginable hardships, privations and insults from those who try to take the maximum labour from them for the least pay. The government turns a blind eye to their pleas that the minimum wages due to them under the law are no being paid by 90% of the employers. For centuries the upper castes in Hindu Society has been accustomed to extracting virtually free labour from the lower castes. That mindset cannot change.

The only crime of the poor in the eyes of the gentry of India is that they belong to the lower castes who must remain lowly in morals and behaviour. They are the first to be suspected whenever a burglary or theft occurs. They are used to being rounded up by the police on false suspicious only to be let off after they have given their pound of flash to the custodians of law.

In Western countries denial of the Minimum wage fixed by the Government is a serious crime punishable by imprisonment. Even Indonesia, a poor and backward country, rigidly follows the same law. In India all the people who deny the minimum wage to their workers can afford to pay. The boot is clearly on the other leg. While we suspect our workers to be thieves it is we who are stealing or robbing each worker of Rs.2000 to Rs. 4000 of his due salary every month. Cumulatively, the amount the middle class quietly filches from the poor in this manner would be many times more than the thousands of crores allegedly grabbed illegally by our top politicians and bureaucrats. All this wealth stolen from the poor worker turns into black money and is invested in property, thus setting off a vicious circle and making the life of the poor more difficult. Despite such open loot in this and other matters the privileged members of this class claim to be honest and respectable citizens of India who have every right to point an accusing finger at the country's rulers. As explained earlier in this book success of a society or civilization depends on equitable sharing of the wealth generated by it amongst its different classes. Once that balance is disturbed it can only lead to social chaos. But then, as Gunar Myrdal said "India is soft state". It can easily by subjugated and tamed to submit to injustice of any kind.

It is claimed by the Pandits of the philosophy of our nouveau riche middle class that the lower castes and classes have to be shunned and socially boycotted because they drink, gamble and steal. While claiming for themselves the privilege of experiencing all the liberties and enjoyments of the 21st century they wish to apply standards of 19th century morality while judging the lower classes. Don't we drink? Are some of our dearest friends not alcoholics? Don't we gamble? Don't many of us play cards with money at stake? Don't we proudly proclaim as a great achievement our visits to the casinos at Las Vegas and Macau? I am a gambler myself. Almost all my income comes from my wife's substantial earnings from gambling on the stock exchange, which according to my way of thinking is home of the Devil himself. One of the first things that Jesus Christ attached was the "realto" the ancient counterpart of the modern stock exchange. The rest of my money comes from the rent I receive for my extra flat which has quadrupled in eight years through my adherence to the prevalent practice of illegally changing tenants every two years turning them into gypsies. And lastly, quite apart from our other activities, black or white, are we not moving in the reverse gear when we pilfer Rs.2000 to Rs.4000 from every worker's salary by paying them much less than their due prescribed by law in Minimum Wages Act? The onus of committing thefts should fall on us.

Only on December 15, 2012 The European Parliament passed yet another resolution condemning the atrocities perpetrated by the upper castes on the dalits and adivasis. Amnesty International has on numerous occasions pointed to the crimes against dalits and minorities. Yet, with the so-called economic growth the persecution and dispossession of the poor by the upper classes grows stronger. We have a democracy "of the rich, by the rich and for the rich".

Not for nothing has Gunar Myrdal, the Swedish Nobel Laureate, in his famous book The Asian Drama called India "a soft state", which means a country where law enforcement and social discipline are low. The Asian Drama was written fifty years ago in the Fifties and Sixties when Myrdal's wife, Alva Myrdal, also a Nobel laureate was Sweden's Ambassador to India. Today, if he were alive, Gunar would perhaps have coined a new word for India as a totally "non-governance" state whose only function is to make laws which are never enforced. It is a laissez faire society where every one is free to do what he likes so long as he can keep the police in good humour.

There is nothing good or band, high or lowly, about a professon. As an assistant editor in the Statesman two of us had to share the services of a secretary. For a year or so the person who served as our secretary was the middle aged wife of an officer of the air force who later became an Air Marshal and chief of the Indian Air Force. While working with us as the spouse of an area commander she had also to function as the head of an organization set up to help in the welfare of families of the lower ranks. The equally efficient person who succeeded her as our secretary was the daughter of a clerk in The Statesman.

When I joined The Statesman in 1957, the editor's secretary was Mrs. Buckman, a portly Anglo-Indian. She was a for middle looking middle aged woman who would talk to no one but the boss. Every morning an office car would go to her house to pick her up and drop her back home in the evening. Others entitled to this facility had to travel in groups. During Christmas week Mrs. Buckman and her husband were invited to have tea or dinner at the house of the editor, an Englishman.

Peons had their own protocol. By the standards of those days they were the richest people among the junior staff. I know a colleague, a bachelor but alcoholic, who would some times borrow small amounts from Asghar, the reporters' room peon, towards the end of the month. The reason of their comparative richness was that in the mornings they earned more than their salaries by hawking newspapers. They all lived single in joint chawl like quarters built for them by The Statesman, enclosed on all sides by a high compound wall, free of charge since they had to pack the paper after it was printed, wrap it in bundles and deliver it in vans to newspaper hubs all over the city and even to nearly towns upto Dehradun, at a distance of 250 kilometers every night.

A peon will not touch a glass of water or a cup of tea for your consumption though he would gladly rush across the street to bring you hot pakoras or other eatables. If our Editor wanted a glass of water he would press the call bell for his peon who sat on a stool glued to the Keyhole outside the room and ask for water. The peon would salute him and walk with a majestic gait to the senior staff canteen, a nearly 200 feet walk down corridors and verandahs and tell the Chief Khansama (Chef) that Saheb wanted water. The Chef who had three assistants under him would give up everything, polish a tray with a cloth, place a glass of water on it and walk to the room of the burra sahib (big boss). Though they normally came to office in informal dress Englishmen liked to flaunt their authority through their underlings. The editor's peon (name unknown) and driver Budh Singh and the Chief Khansama Abdul were the only three persons in the huge organization who were entitled to tie pagris around their heads with their long tails falling on their backs behind the neck. The pagris would conform to the freshly starched uniforms they wore down to the boots.

The Statesman peons celebrated the festival of Holi in grand style. It being a holiday for the paper the whole campus was at their disposal. They would fill a small drum with canabis juice (called bhang in Hindi) and get drunk with it before starting the Holi revelries of spraying colour on each other. In the evenings they held a devotional meeting after which 'prasad' (sweets offered to the gods) was distributed. The top bosses made it a point to put in an appearance on this occasion. Sometimes they came with their wives who found it very interesting to find the pons dressed in their best clothes, their faces reddened by gulal.

When Asghar, the reporters' room peon retired he settled down in his village in East U.P. and bequeathed his post in the newspaper to his son Ibrahim. The Statesman was packed with sons and daughters of retired employees at all levels). Imagine my surprise when in 1975, accompanied by a friend, Asghar walked into my bungalow in Lucknow carrying in one hand a long double-barreled gun. After exchange of pleasantries over a cup of tea he came down to the purpose of his visit which was to obtain a license to keep the gun he had purchased at a high price from an ammunition dealer in Lucknow.

Why do you need a gun? Do you have enemies to fear for your life?" I asked him.

"Are saheb, bina bandook ke gaon men koi ijjat nahin Karta (no one respects you in a village unless you have a gun) Asghar owned a small farm and a pukka double storey house which he had built out of sewings from his earnings in The Statesman, and was regarded as a man of substance in his community.

Likewise when I visited Benares (now Varanasi) where we had no correspondent I went to the shop of our agent in the main market. The enthusiasm with which he entertained me was surprising. He told me that he had served The Statesman throughout his life and when he retired as the head peon . . . . saheb (he named an Englishman under who was the general manager when he retired) made me an agent for Benares where the paper was selling poorly. "Slowly I changed everything and now the paper is selling all over the city, specially in the Benares Hindu University. We get both, Delhi and Calcutta editions. Bengalis prefer the Calcutta edition. Saheb allowed me to take an agency of other newspapers also. So I am a happy man". I later found that his son was running his business with the help of about half-a-dozen hawkers while he devoted most of his time in visiting temples and singing bhajans.

He was respected in business circles as a religious man and was an active member of a devotional group.

I happen to know the general manager of a software export company which today has more than hundred engineers, some working with clients abroad, besides other ancillary staff. He is the same person, who twenty years ago was sweeping the floors, washing dishes and cooking staff lunch for this company for a paltry salary when it was started by a fresh IIT graduate with only three engineers. Today this manager has a brand new car and a flat of his own and his children go to good public. His successor recruited a few years later as an all purpose peon now heads a critical division of the company and owns a car. Meanwhile, the company has grown from strength to strength. This disproves the widely held theory that only MBAs can run and develop a company based on the latest technology.

I have given these numerous examples of drivers, maids and peons as illustrations of my point that every profession has a "dignity" of its own and we have no right to deride it. Even the Supreme Court has defined the fundamental right to life as the right to life "with dignity". Many of these examples relate to my experiences in The Statesman, a British company owned newspaper because Englishmen respected "the dignity" of each profession. We don't. This is how a handful of them governed a sub-continent of two hundred million people and adjoining countries too. This is why the Sun never set on the British Empire. Even a scavenger in an Englishman's house had the same privileges as a driver or a cook. They gave each person a space, an area of autonomy where no one could interfere. Even the "untouchable" sweepers living quarter was as spacious as the adjoining quarters of the Brahmin driver or cook, with some space outside to rear hens or breed honey bees.

Releasing its survey of 162 countries where slaves are found, the Walk Free Foundation, an Australian NGO, said in October 2013, that it had found that 30 million people were registered as 'slaves' in the World. Of them half were in India, which means that the number of slaves in India was equal to the combined total of 161 countries. Which is not surprising when you consider that of the combined total of Black Money deposited in Swiss Banks by people all over the world half comes form India alone. We in this country has a long tradition of treating as slaves the lower castes and tribals who together constitute 40% of the population. The phenomenon is now being repeated with renewed vigour. The only solution is too fold. One, demonetization and making of all financial transactions digital as has already been done in Scandanairan countries and two, launching of a non-violent movement against this new brand of slavery that Martin Luther King launched in America against this evil.

One thing I like most about Dr. Bindeshwari Pathak, founder and director of Sulabh International, is that he has not only liberated ten of thousands of scavengers from their drudgery but also given them dignity by dinning and feasting with them, taking them on delegations to UN bodies, educating their children in schools and hosting them in his plush headquarters in Delhi where he introduces them to Indian and foreign VIPs. He gave the same treatment to Vrindavan widows. Pathak does this because he has not forgotten his humble origins which many of us of the newly rich middle class have obliterated from our minds. If you want the best out of them you have to give your workers "dignity" first.

21

Drop by Drop

In the prepaleolithic geological era when the Earth was formed it is said that it rained continuously for forty thousand years. This is how the oceans were formed. Likewise, the ocean of corruption and untold misery that we see all around us the world over with a few islands of prosperity and straight-forward dealings has also been filled up drop by drop by a torrential rainfall of the greed and lust for power and wealth of billions of people ever since homo sapiens appeared on the globe in a remote corner of Africa. The Indian epic Ramayana has a reference to this phenomenon unique to human beings. Lord Rama's father king Dasrath had died of grief after being forced to banish Ram to the forest for fourteen years under a vow he owed to Kaikayi, Ram's step mother, so that her son Bharat may become King of Ayodhya. Sumantra, the King's chief advisor, told the royal rishi Vasishth that without a king to rule the kingdom there would be complete anarchy, rule of dharma (religion) would disappear, people would take to looting and even women's honour would not be safe. So Vasishtha sent the fastest horse riders in the Kingdom to far away Kandhar (in today's Afghanistan) to fetch Bharat who was holidaying in his maternal grand father's kingdom, so that he could be crowned king of Ayodhya. This shows that man was the same five thousand years ago as he is today, greedy and lawless. Kautilya's 'arthashastra' written two thousand years ago prescribes various punishments for corrupt acts. Chaucer's classic Canterbury Tales have references to similar acts of misdemeanour in Britain in its early days.

Corruption was prevalent in ancient China too. The sage Lao Tsu once said. "Those whose virtue exceeds their rank are honored, those whose salary exceeds their virtue are accursed. The nobility of virtue involves no aggrandizement, a just salary is not too much. Those who are ennobled without virtue are stealing rank, those who take unjustly are stealing wealth." Lao Tsu also said in his classic book Tao Te Ching "What is firmly established cannot be uprooted". Crime and corruption are more firmly rooted in the vast landmass of India than anywhere else. Why is it so? And why have they taken such deep roots in this country that there seems no apparent remedy against it?

Since this book is an autobiography I presume I should begin with my own example to illustrate how these vices have taken deep roots amongst all of us. My own actions show how we have become totally insensitive to the pain we inflict on others by the illegalities we commit every day. The real reason for this, which I found out by a thorough introspection into my own life's record of eighty-five years, is that we are not even aware that we are corrupt. Being corrupt is our way of life. By all normal standards I have always been looked upon by all those who have dealt with me as an honest and straight forward person. But the standards they apply in judging me are the same that they apply to assessing their own behaviour which they consider to be above board. This is where all of us go wrong. If only we would care to look at what people of other nations think of us we would know the truth. We claim to be modern but do we really act like responsible citizens of a modern democracy?

Take the case of my cook, Marie(name changed). She came to us over seven years ago as a girl of about twenty through a Christian society that supplies tribal girls from Eastern States to work as house maids in Delhi. Marie belongs to a village in Assam, about five hours drive from Gauhati, the state capital. She had already worked in Delhi for about two years when the agency sent her to us on a salary of Rs.2,200 per month. Back home her mother was dead but her father lived with her two brothers and one younger sister. One day a group of Bodo militants who are fighting for a separate Bodo state came to her house and asked the elder brother to join them in the struggle. Upon his refusing to comply they shot him dead on the spot. A few years later her father also died. Then the younger sister moved to a nearby town to work as a beautician and her brother drifted to Bangalore and took up a small job there. Now Marie has no home to go back to and has to fend for herself. This winter, after a gap of three years, the three siblings had a reunion in their house in the village which is now occupied by her father's sister and her family. Towards the end of her vacation I called her home severals times to find out when she would return. Each time she was away visiting relatives and friends but her female cousins who took my calls always sounded cheerful and giggled everytime I called. Normally she encashes her month's leave every year which brings her emoluments to nearly Rs.8,000 a month, or 7500 when she does not encash her leave. This amount includes her overtime payments for working on Sundays and generous tips from house guests. To earn this she has to work from seven in the morning till ten in the night with brief breaks totaling not more than three hours. Her duties are cooking for a family of six and going shopping for milk and groceries three times a day. In between she gets time to watch her favourite TV serials. She is assisted by two part-time maids who are paid Rs.30 an hour for various other jobs like washing utensils, sweeping and dusting the house and other odd jobs. Marie has given up membership of the Christian tribal society, which charged her Rs.75 month, but acted as her home away from home. It looks after unemployed and sick members and takes them out to church and picnics every Sunday. With no place to go to Marie now works on Sunday too and her allowance of Rs.100 for each Sunday, fixed seven years ago, remains unchanged simply because she cannot complain. The primary condition of her service is that she has to be available to us on call all these fifteen hours a day. We have installed a call bell and also an intercom phone in the kitchen which she has to attend instantly throughout the day. She answers the door bell about fifty times a day and serves tea about twenty times to all and Sundry who happen to visit the house. She has our large guest room to herself when there are no house guests visiting us.

Now, by Indian standards I would be considered a benign employer. But if I were living in America or any West European country I should be cooling my heels in a prison for torture and wrongful confinement of a girl, for grossly underpaying her and misappropriating the money due to her. Even by the Indian Minimum Wages Act her salary should be double of what she is getting. (My only defence is that I give her board and lodging as well). For all practical purposes she is my 'slaves'.

The truth is that India has a long tradition of master-slave relationship and every one quickly tends to fit into this pattern. A herd of elephants or a bee-line of ants has only one leader. The rest follow. But in India every one is a master or slave. There are no equals except amongst slaves. And a slave has no voice. Marie has to accept her lot as a 'slave' girl. The invention and spread of the mobile phone has given her access to the outside world. She can occasionally talk to her brother in Bangalore and sister in Assam and relieve her emotions. She has also made several local friends amongst servants of the colony, mostly house maids but may be one or two boys too, with whom she keeps talking about various things that their mistresses talk about. Being a TV addict she spends most of her money on dresses and cosmetics. This weakness of hers suits us. We can exploit it by throwing at her crumbs by way of tips ranging from Rs.20 to Rs.100 to do extra work thus making her miss her brief outings to movies and cheap eateries with her friends to movies and cheap eateries. She is absolutely honest and does all our shopping without ever pilfering a penny. But, all the same because of her craving to look smart she needs money all the time. Amongst other fads, Marie must visit her beautician once a week. Recently she went through a full treatment to straighten out her protruding front teeth at considerable cost. Like a good Christian she goes to Church on Christmas and Good Friday. But hers is a poor church for low-caste Christians tucked away in a slum not too far away. Her main problem is that she has to stifle her emotions for which there is no outlet. She has to work round the clock (fifteen hours officially) and round the year with no Sundays or holidays. On festival days when everybody is enjoying a holiday she has to work harder to make special dishes and sweets for the family and guests. If she has a headache and wants to lie down for a few hours, all hell breaks lose in the house, we are all so accustomed to her services, specially old people like me and my wife. On one occasion she was late by half-an-hour in returning from her shopping spree. My wife got panicky and remarked "I hope she has not run away with a boy like another girl in the colony". I admonished her for saying such a thing. "Marie is too nice for that," I told her.

In her own way the girl seems to be quite attached to all of us. She looks upon me as her godfather, though she has to slog all day to keep her job all the same. It is not that she is on her feet all the time. She has plenty of time to watch TV serials and talk to her friends on her mobile phone and above all always keep cheerful and smiling. In her own way she thinks her life of slavery is normal to her class. When she came to us seven years ago she had to send part of her meager salary to support her father and younger brothers and sister. Now, relieved of those responsibilities she has plenty to spend on herself which keeps her happy.

Marie is illiterate. She can barely read the letters of the English alphabet though she can read the numerals very well. Her predecessor Leena (name changed) a Christian girl from Jharkhand, was always sulking and angry with her lot. She was a matriculate, could write tolerable essays but we gave her practically no time to study. Of course in between work, like Marie she too avidly watched television serials. Leena wanted to work as a receptionist in an office, a secretary or at least take a job of looking after a well-to-do patient, which she finally got when she left us.

I have given so much space to the lives of Marie and Leena because there are millions of Maries and Leenas in India for whom life is perpetual slavery. When they marry, more often than not, their husbands are alcoholics who leave the task of care of the children, besides earning money for the family, to their wives. We had such a woman working for us for ten years as a second house maid. Her husband was a sweeper in a big organization receiving a good salary. But he spent most of it on country liquor. She educated her children in their ancestral village with their grand parents and got them settled. The family's joy knew no bounds when her eldest son became a car driver, one step up the social leader and gave them some relief from the extreme drudgery of their lives.

Some of these girls get lured into the flesh trade as a side business. An educated girl we had hired over ten years ago used to tell us that she had joined a coaching class. The "tutor" would suddenly call her at an odd hour of the day or night. While going to him instead of books she would always carry in her bag her finest dress which she would evidently put on at her tryst, we believed. Watching television and keeping in touch with friends and family in different parts of the country have given these poor people the same desires and aptitudes as those of the middle class elite. Marie belongs to the luckier class of the poor in India. However hard her life, she has food, shelter and a vocation for which there is always a thriving market. She can watch the glamour and glitter of Delhi and vicariously share in its pleasures. Back home in her Assamese village they cook one meal of corn or coarse rice with salt and condiments but no vegetables and use a local herb for black tea without milk and sugar. Most of the time they remain idle with no work in sight.

The Indian middle class takes this extreme deprivation of the poor classes in its stride as an act of God in the same calm spirit as it takes a case of rape, kidnapping of a poor man's child, a dead body lying on the roadside because no passerby with a vehicle cared to take the victim to a hospital, negligence of teachers and doctors appointed to serve the weaker sections of society, a custodial death due to ruthless beating by the police and a thousand other injustices that the common man in India faces every day. His food and water are routinely poisoned and all that he can do is to develop an immunity to these poisons in course of time or succumb to them.

I am as much a participant-spectator in these offences as any one else. Marie's weekly working hours are two and a half times those of her counter parts in any civilized Western country. We are forcing her into this drudgery because she has no option if she is to survive. We are a democracy alright but we are democracy of the days of Demosthenes, its founder, when it was first introduced in Athens. It was only meant for 'citizens', or masters, not slaves who were more numerous and had no rights. We are a democracy of "Masters", which means the middle class elite, not slaves or the poor classes.

For the past 25 years I have been living in a housing complex in the national capital. We count ourselves, and perhaps rightly so, as a middle class elite of intellectuals and executives belonging to various professions. The worst aspect of the true character of the Indian middle class shows up when it is acting as a group and I am as guilty of it as the others. Take the case of any group housing society or residents' welfare association. The flat owners may be lording in luxury, have two to three cars per flat, travel only by air, spend their holidays abroad, send their children to America and other foreign countries for study, routinely spend a few lakhs a year in check ups in five star hospitals, think nothing of spending a few thousand rupees over a meal in a restaurant, have fine gardens and lawns within or outside their bungalows and flats, but you will hardly find any of these "societies" paying its sweepers, gardeners and directly appointed security guards the "minimum wage" of around Rs. 7,500 per month fixed by the government.

Shop keepers and other businesses like small industries sitting on properties of tens of crores and having sales of several lakhs a day are even more mean in treating their workers. Hardly anyone of them pays the Minimum Wage and if he does, he makes them work twelve hours a day, often seven days a week.

The government turns a blind eye to all these violations of its own laws because the officials and politicians who run it are themselves loathe to part with even a fraction of their ill-gotten wealth to be given to their own workers. They are firm believers in the master-slave theory which forbids slaves from voicing even a meek protest. Doesn't matter if the rents of a room or jhuggi in a slum has risen to Rs.5000 per month, prices of food and everything else are shooting up and even drinking water has to be paid for. Doesn't matter if the fees in the meanest of schools are rising, medical care is becoming almost inaccessible to the poor, transport costs are touching the ceiling. All these hardships and more faced by the poor members of the "slave" class mean absolutely nothing to the class of 'masters' because according to Indian tradition all 'slaves' are 'shudras' comparable to animals. The 'slave' class in India is truly and metaphorically a species apart, animals whose mouths must remain tied to stop them from speaking so that their limbs could be used to their maximum capacity for "productive" work. The Indian middle class spends at least twice as much on keeping a dog as a pet as it does on keeping a maid in its homes or a delivery boy in its shops. Dogs never bark at their owners' nor do maids and delivery boys ever say a word against the treatment they receive from their masters. If they do they are out. I have seen this merry-go-round in my own grocer's shop whose shop assistants and delivery boys leave him every two months. One of them who left him a few years ago was more enterprising. He started delivering vegetables to his master's customers. Then he bought a cart and parked it in a corner of the street, paying the weekly "hafta" (bribe) to the beat policeman. Gradually he called two relatives to join him. The three of them have a thriving business. But such lucky breaks are available only to a few. Most of them have to slog twelve hours for which they are paid at half or two-thirds the minimum wage of around Rs.7,500.

The current wave of urbanization has created a new class of "gentlemen slaves" (the term includes women also) who have money but no homes of their own. 'Masters' like me prey on them. In the last nine or ten years my income from my extra flat in the adjoining colony has shot up four times. Like every house owner, I have performed this miracle by changing tenants every two years. Tenancy laws exist only on paper. In Delhi a salaried executive, however high his or her salary, is a gypsy who must shift to a new house every two years. It makes him rootless. The phenomenon is described in detail elsewhere in this book. But suffice it to say here that single young working women are its worst victims. I had two such girls as my tenants who had to leave my house, as per the unwritten law, within two years. Unless the government enforces its tenancy laws firmly and most rigorously, so that a flat owner who turns out a tenant without needing it for his own occupation and use goes straight to jail, the safety of working girls, who include all classes of them from nurses to senior executives, will remain in jeopardy. They must be allowed time to build their roots in the locality where they hire a flat. Greedy landlords like me look for 'soft targets' like young working boys and girls who would rather move to another house than go to court on this issue. Even the clause of an automatic annual increase of ten percent in the rent provided in every lease agreement with a tenant does not satisfy our lust for money.

The lower classes are equally to blame for their misfortunes and the hardships they face in their life. They try to imitate the rich middle class elite in every way and vie with each other in splurging money which they do not have. If the richest man can spend over a hundred crores ($20 million) on a wedding, a poor man or woman earning only a few thousand rupees a month must spend at least a few lakhs on the wedding of a son or daughter. They cannot save so much money in 20 years. Beg, borrow or steal, but you must be 'one-up' on your neigbour. They love brawls at drink parties which they arrange at short notice. They go on pilgrimages to distant shrines which they cannot afford, put their children in expensive schools beyond their means, visit beauticians for hair cuts and work themselves to death to satisfy their ego in this manner.

A crime ceases to be a crime if everybody does it. It is like Adam's fall from the grace of heaven on eating the forbidden apple upon being tempted by Eve. We are all fallen angels. Everything we do we do it in the name of God. We have so many gods, goddesses, godmen, babas, saints, pirs and gurus to protect us from any harm that we can do anything and everything with impunity. In olden days before a dacoit, brigand or raja or nawab went on an expedition to loot and plunder his own or the neighbouring domain he would offer prayers and gifts or chadars to his chosen deity and obtain his or her blessings. Honour killing is sanctified by all religions of the world. So is killing of infidels (a name for people who do not belong to the King's religion). Even saints turned a blind eye to horrendous acts committed in the name of religion. Some even cited them as examples of the most ideal conduct. Saint Kabir, whom I worship like a god, eulogized the practice of 'sati' (burning of widows on the pyres of their dead husbands) in several of his poems as an act of extreme devotion. Saint Tulsidas placed women and shudras (outcastes) in the category of animals and drums that deserved a sound beating every now and then. Burning at the stakes was justified punishment in Europe for any one who differed from the edicts of the Vatican priestly class in matters of belief, philosophy or knowledge.

Kings were accepted world wide as the chosen representatives of God. Hence the universally accepted theory of "Divine Rights of Kings" which prevailed all over the world till the Nineteenth Century and is still venerated in various forms in backward regions including India. From this proceeds the right of the rich to exploit the poor under a Master and slave relationship, which gives the Master all the rights and his slaves none. Women were the worst victims of this system. A realistic account of the treatment of women through the ages has yet to be written. They were taken for granted as slaves of men. The poor were poor and the rich were rich by the will of God. In India this belief was perfected and sanctified to its utmost limits by creating the four castes. In Bhagwad Gita, the song divine, portions of which I have been reading for sixty years almost every day, and which was written by sage Ved Vyas a few centuries later, Lord Krishna, the incarnation of God, is supposed to have said:

"I created the four castes". He exhorts Arjuna, the warrior king, to do his duty as a member of the Kshetriya caste which was to fight and kill his enemies. The Gita treats the vast caste of Shudras (untouchabales) highly disparagingly, and barely tolerates the Vaishyas (traders), but places on the highest pedestal Brahmins and Kshatriyas and forbids inter-mingling of castes through marriage. Thus the caste of untouchables must remain untouchable through eternity. In some tribes whom we call 'savages' eating of the flesh of people belonging to enemy tribes is a common practice. The genocides that occurred in the Twentieth Century are a reminder that even people who call themselves the most civilized are prone to resort to such practices when it suits them. The mass slaughter of Jews by Hitler and wholesale killing of millions of Hindus and Muslims by each other when British India was partitioned into India and Pakistan, are reminders that everywhere man has remained a barbarian at heart and would not hesitate to kill, loot and plunder his fellow men when it suits him. The unprovoked Iraq war is another instance of the same phenomenon. Fortunately, in this case there were internal protests against this outrage all over America and Europe, something unthinkable in the past.

All these brutal practices did not spring up overnight. They have evolved and become part of what we call our "character" over tens of thousands of years. The principal among them is the evolution of Master-Slave relationship among human beings. The master enjoys all the privileges and the slave none. You either belong to the class of masters or slaves. There is no middle ground. In India this phenomenon is more distinct than anywhere else in the world. This is so because of our abhorrent Hindu caste system which all other communities in this country—Muslims Christians and Sikhs—have adopted wholesale because it suits their elite and also because most of them are converts from Hinduism and old habits and attitudes die hard.

This master-slave relationship has many aspects. A man is master in his own house is an old adage. It simply means that the right of a person to do whatever he likes in what he considers to be his own territory is inalienable. No one can question him howsoever brutal his acts might be. This right of the 'master' established by long tradition is not something new or unique to one country alone. It is a universal right of the 'master' in the exercise of which no one can interfere, howsoever violent his conduct might be. In India caste has given this inhuman tradition the permanence of a class of slaves who can never emerge from their slavery.

I am writing this in my autobiography because I am as much a communalist and casteist as anyone else. If you scratch almost any Indian, beneath the skin you will find in him the deep rooted emotions collectively shared by his community or caste. To some extent it is true of human beings anywhere on the globe, even amongst "enlightened" people. But in India it is out in the open. As the so-called "development" projects are executed all over the country, they are apportioned to different classes of "slaves" such as OBCs, Scheduled Tribes and Scheduled Castes. What actually happens is that quickly there spring up masters and slaves in each community, with masters gobbling all the benefits meant for the whole community. A correspondent of Outlook magazine who is an Assamese, visited far off North Lakhimpur city in his state after a lapse of fourteen years. It had looked like a sleepy hamlet during his previous visits. He was startled to see so many cars on the streets and was told the apparent prosperity he was witnessing was due to the leaders of each community grabbing all the development funds for themselves and flaunting their new found wealth, thus leaving the masses high and dry. No one can dare to raise a little finger against this loot by the 'masters' because the culture of protest is alien to our age-old traditions. Since infancy we are trained to "obey" our superiors who are our masters, right or wrong. We are also taught since childhood that our "Sanskars", (age-old family traditions) must precede the laws made by foreigners and imposed upon us.

Tradition alone is the Law. If a woman has to burn on the pyre of her deceased husband or if a young couple must be lynched for marrying outside their castes, it will only enhance the glory of our great religion. In such an atmosphere of extreme submissiveness the "masters' have a field day and the masses—all of whom are mere 'slaves—must submit to every act of injustice and exploitation.

This master-slave relationship, which is peculiar to Indian society, has given rise to a new class of 'masters', called slave drivers. They hold all the power of the 'masters' and loot and plunder the masses as a matter of right. They go by various names like dadas, chamchas, dalals, agents, extortionists and so on. They are given glamorous designations in government and private offices.

I am particularly interested in this class of "dalals" because I belong to it. I am essentially a "slave driver". The kings and rajas of olden times used bards to weave songs describing their imagined glorious acts and sing them before the public with beat of drums. We, members of the media, are their exact replica as drum beaters of the masters of the day. We drive the masses into absolute obedience by singing praises, day in and day out, of the new order that goes by the name of "consumerism", which is another name for the vice of possessiveness, Our brain washing is so total and complete that there is no rival to this theory left in the field to challenge it. The entire intellectual community throughout the world is bending over backward to acclaim this grand theory as the saviour of humanity. Institutions are springing up across the world, ostensibly to train 'talent' but actually to train breed a race of 'masters' that will rule the rest of humanity, chiefly in backward regions like India, China. Africa and Latin America. In time to come an atmosphere will be created by 'bards' like me so that whosoever opposes this 'master-slave' theory is dismissed as a brainless idiot.

I am a direct beneficiary of this avalanche of propaganda by nearly all the intellectuals of the world which is heavily financed by the forces behind the philosophy of "consumerism" and controlled by a few 'super-masters'—the billionaires and trillionaires spread throughout the world. However, I see a ray of hope. The famous historian Thomas Carlyle once said "the hour before dawn is the darkest". In our scriptures it is called "the dark night of the soul", just before the moment when a saint is on the verge of attaining enlightenment. I am hoping that internal forces are at work within the soul of man which will sweep away this darkness of ignorance and submissiveness to the forces of evil and release all mankind from the chains of 'slavery' that have bound us hand and foot. In the Gita Lord Krishna says that "whenever there is a complete eclipse of righteousness in society, I (God) take birth as a human being and put virtue back on its seat". Our epic, Ramayana, depicts tyranny as the ten-headed monster Ravana, to kill whom God had to take birth as Ram. Ravana's greed and lust for power was so strong that it needed ten heads to contain it. Lord Krishna says in the Bhagwat Gita "who wealth and power do most desire, least fixity of soul have such."

Likewise, Christ was born to emancipate humanity from the curses of wealth and power. In my opinion, Christianity has done more for the uplift of the poor than any other religion in the world. It has liberated women from the curse of polygamy that plagued the world. This act alone has brought untold relief and honour to the female half of humanity in the Christian world. This religion has exalted the poor by its preaching that service of the poor is the highest form of service to God. Mother Theresa is a shining example of this belief in recent times. Gandhi, who took his cue from Christ, is another. 'Daridra Narayan', poorest of the poor, was his God. He had said that before he took any step he first considered how it would affect the poorest man in India. Christ is the only 'incarnation' of God who said that "it is easier for a camel to pass through the eye of a needle than for a rich man to enter the kingdom of heaven". I hope good Christians throughout the world will some day listen to Lord Jesus Christ's prophetic gospel.

We in India need a truly capitalist democracy of the West European type. European capitalism generates enough resources for the government to maintain a welfare state and protect human rights and contribute large amounts to various charities. Indian capitalists, on the other hand, sponge on state subsidies and loot public money through devious means to become bilionaires oversight with the active connivance of politicians and bureaucrats. In India there are no Bill Gates and Warren Buffets who can give tens of billions of dollars to noble causes throughout the world. There is no dearth of such people in Western democracies.

In the West Fundamental Human Rights are fully protected. So are the rights of labour to a decent wage comparable to the professional classes. Unemployment benefits, health care and free education for all are guaranteed. And above all people are free to speak their minds. This is definitely superior to anything that any socialist country has achieved. The West European model is so far the best form of government. But to get it in our country we have to get rid of all the flab of the past that goes by the name of tradition, which in essence means the master-slave theory, that it seems to be an impossible task.

22

Gangloot of Mother India by "aam aadmi"

One of my great regrets in life has been that my father refused to send me to our Nobel Laureate poet Ravindra Nath Tagore's open air university in Santiniketan to be an artist when I became a matriculate in 1943. Had he conceded my request this copious book on the state of Indian society would not have been necessary. Instead, I would have just drawn a caricature of it as the fattest man on earth with the restless head of a monkey, showing the leadership hungry for power, and the feet of a crane depicting the lower classes. He has to move about on a wheel chair because his feet and knees cannot support the weight of his burgeoning stomach which represents the nouveau riche middle class and is prepared to absorb everything that comes its way, from a pie or cent to a million dollars or more, to satiate its hunger for money to which there seems no end in sight. The more it receives the more it wants, laving nothing for the poorer sections who constitute the feet of the body and who have been reduced by it to the status of its 'slaves' with no wants of their own and denied what another Nobel Laureate Amartya Sen calls their minimum "entitlement" or wage.

The countrywide protest demonstrations against the gang rape of a hapless girl in a moving bus have yielded nothing because it was essentially an elitist movement. For a time it appeared to resemble a mini Arab spring, Indian style, that almost brought the administration to its knees. Ultimately, as usual, the Government got away by making many promises which it had no intention to fulfill. The police, its executive arm, remained as indifferent to this heinous crime as it had always been, and very often sided with the rapists. As I have already reported in an earlier chapter during the Parliamentary elections of 1967 the late Dr. Ram Manohar Lohia, the great socialist leader of olden times, had told me that Parliamentary democracy could succeed in bringing social welfare policies in India only if it was backed by street demonstrations. Nowhere in the world had Parliament been an instrument of social change. At best it maintained the status quo. Dr. Lohia's prophesy has come true. The complete inaction of the common people (specially our intellectuals and professionals who were very active in the freedom movement) euphemistically called "aam aadmi", on social issues concerning their own neighbourhoods or the whole nation during the last sixty five years since Independence, has resulted in the near collapse of governance.

People in authority from the smallest level to the highest are engaged in the exercise of the instinct of self-agrandisement by whatever means. This trend would not have continued had we been more alert in watching the interest of the nation. Dr. Lohia's vision of India as a socialist state, which I shared at that time, has turned out to be a pipe dream though great leaders like Jawaharlal Nehru strived hard to attain it. In the Indian version of socialism, where ever it has been practised, political leaders become "masters" (owners) of public property and the common people their slaves with no right to speak or protest. Greed of leaders enjoying power without responsibility has destroyed even the thought of socialism as an option from the people's mind.

I have the highest respect for Anna Hazare, Arvind Kejriwal and members of their teams for reviving the forgotten culture of Satyagraha in India. But with all due respects to them I would like to submit that they are barking up the wrong tree. As Gandhiji had often said and practised "Reform begins from below, not the top". He also insisted that a person's duty came first, not rights which had a secondary place in the Mahatma's scheme of life. The money and national wealth embezzled by ministers and top bureaucrats is a miniscule portion, perhaps only one percent of the money illegally grabbed by the so-called "aam admi", that is, common people like you and me.

What I liked about the recent street protests all over the nation was that they were aimed at the misdeeds of the "aam admi"—and not our political leaders and top officials and businessmen. The perpetrators of the heinous act for which the most stringent punishment was sought, including death sentence for all the six culprits in this case, were common people. Those whose negligence was blamed for the tragedy were again middle class people belonging mainly to the police and judiciary. The callousness and indifference of the so-called respectable male members of the middle class to such happenings was ruthlessly attacked by the young participants in these mass rallies. Girls and women among them were even more vocal in condemning such hypocricy of the gentry.

In saluting the young women who joined these protest rallies I find I am in the most honourable company of Justice Altamas Kabir, the present Chief Justice of India. He said "I salute those who were moved enough to come out, protest and demand justice for the December 16, Delhi gangrape victim. The public upsurge after the incident was justified and necessary".

However, sexual relations are a complex issue. It has several interconnected strands which must be addressed together. I would have been happier by these demonstrations if the young women had simultaneously campaigned for a few concrete reforms like a complete ban on dowry in any form, cash or kind, lavish expenditure on marriage parties in posh hotels and clubs. Event organizers should be barred from arranging marriage parties.

What was most heart warming to my passion for mass protests against injustice were the huge demonstrations by street vendors of Delhi and Bombay against what they described as "police terror", but what I know to be a move by our Congress party governments to pave the way for Walmart and its likes under its plan to induct FDI (Foreign Direct Investment) in multi-brand retail. This is a battle that the poor man in India must fight till all Indian jails are over full with protestors to force the government to retreat from its suicidal path. It is specially designed only to pander to the tastes of the luxury loving new middle class and spells the doom of millions of poor bread earners in India whose legitimate earnings will now be siphoned off to fatten the pockets of rich foreign investors. Once again the Supreme Court has come to the aid of the small man. A bench consisting of Justice Lodha and Justice Mukhopadhyaya has lambasted the government on this issue and asked it to show what steps it has taken to protect the small trader from these big sharks who use all kinds of foul practices to eliminate the small man in the field, before allowing FDI in retail trade.

I would be the happiest man on earth the day workers in the unorganized sector, which constitutes the bulk of India's work force, rise up and demand with one voice strict enforcement of the minimum wages act. What is the use of enacting a pro-poor law if the government has decided in advance that it will "never, never" implement it, except in the organized sector which accounts for a miniscule fraction of labour in India? And this applies to governments of all political partie3s, including the communists.

We should be grateful to Anna Hazare and his team for reviving the Gandhian weapon of Satyagraha, non violent protest against injustice. Our myopic government should read the writing on the wall. Driven to the wall the poor man in India will have no choice but to turn to Maoists or Naxalites who are already active in forty percent of the country. According to a Union Home Ministery report they have already infiltrated in big cities through various human rights organizations with leftist leanings. India should stop projecting itself as a big power until the last poor man in this large nation of 1.2 billion people has been provided with "roti, kapra aur makaan" (bread, clothing and shelter).

Using my own life and experience of 85 years as an example, this book is an effort to show how the epidemic of corruption in India has spread from the bottom upwards. We have only ourselves to blame for this state of affairs and not our leaders and top bureaucrats. I have not the slightest hesitation in admitting that all my life I have thrived on practising corruption while enjoying the reputation of being 'an honest man', because I am sure my critics would be sailing in the same boat with me. People sitting in glass houses cannot afford to throw stones at others. This book should be read as confessions of a man on whom it has dawned a bit too late in life that he has wasted all of these years pandering to the whims and fancies of the Devil while claiming to be a saintly soul.

As the saying goes, I have tasted the water of many rivers. In between long spells of journalism I have been a tourist guide, a representative of a publisher of a Who's Who directory, a school teacher, a college teacher in the early Nineteen Fifties before returnig for good to the "world's second oldest profession", journalism, in 1955. Even in that halcyon era of the first flush of freedom, in every profession I joined dishonest practices were flourishing and in each of them I was an active participant. The only difference between then and now is of scale. What looked like a sewerage channel has now grown into the polluted Ganga. The dessert has become the main course of the meal. As late as the Eighties the Bofor's scandal worth Rs. 64 crores appeared to be a big scam. Now to produce the same impact on the public mind you have to add three zeroes to the figure of 64. Take any area of activity the figures of amounts illegally grabbed by the "common man" that is, the middle class, would cumulatively add up to five to seven figures in crores, that is, fourteen to sixteen figures.

The milk you drink often acts as a slow poison. It is synthesized with all kinds of white stuff that gives it the right colour and thickness. India is the largest consumer of milk in the world. You can yourself imagine the amounts involved in this operation which covers all sectors, public, private and cooperative. It has become fashionable these days to drink bottled water though filtered or boiled water is much safer. The samples examined by experts were mostly found contaminated and injurious to health.

Pirated software is provided free to customers by vendors of computer hardware. Besides there are several shops in the cities of India including Delhi and other Metros who sell only pirated software. It is widely used in almost all 'respectable' establishments some of whom buy only one licensed copy and make copies for use by other computers in their company.

At any given time you will find a large number of manholes over sewers along the roads removed by thieves, mostly belonging to the same department which replaces them. Often people fall and even die in those pits. Telephone cables are routinely stolen resulting in a closure of the service to a whole colony for weeks at a stretch. The thieves are usually known to members of the staff. In the old days when telephones were scarce I have obtained additional telephone lines through touts. Garbage heaps abound all over the cities of India amidst the glamour and glitter of malls, theatre halls, five star hotels and wide fly overs. Nobody gives a thought to them. The health department which is supposed to look after sanitary conditions in hotels and restaurants is non-functional in almost every city except for the purpose of collecting its share of the resulting loot from these establishments. Power thefts by common people and industries, small and big, alone cost the government many times more revenue than the alleged loot by our big politicians. I have got additional power meters fitted without proper permission through linemen. I declined their suggestion that they could "sell" it cheap without the meters. Every body gets a share of the loot by the buildings industry, except the workers who actually build the projects. Architects, engineers, contractors, sanctioning officers of DDA and similar agencies and municipal authorities, all have a slice of the cake. I have added rooms to my flats and made other illegal alterations through these techniques. For getting your flat converted to free hold the most preferred route is a tout. So also if you get a flat you have bought transferred in your name in municipal records. Taxi meters seldom work. And, above all these activities, the police is the presiding deity to which every one must pay a tribute. Its makes sure that its ubiquitous, if brutal, presence is never missed by any of these gentlemen criminal.

About the medicines you swallow the less said the better, because it involves the highest professions in the world, scientists, doctors big multi-nationals and, of course, producers of fake drugs which account for nearly half the medicine market in India. And it applies to Ayurvedic and Yunani medicines too.

The loans you take from banks need never be repaid if you grease the palms of agents and bank officials. Rajiv Gandhi is credited with saying as early as the Eighties that 85% of what government spends on its development programs is consumed by the establishment and only 15% reaches the beneficiaries.

Aid given by international agencies is swallowed up by the officials who operate it. In the late Seventies I was asked by my bosses to do a cover up the story of scandals involving a reputed International aid organization's shipments of blankets and other aid meant for cyclone victims in Bangla Desh and routed through India, being sold in the market. The idea of the story was to absolve 'friends' in the Indian branch (who included high officials of the government of India) of any wrong doing in the matter. I met the person concerned and asked for documentary proof of his team's innocence. Another appointment was fixed. We were to meet in the Central Hall of Parliament for the purpose. The gentleman developed cold feet and never gave me the records that would have proved the innocence of the Indian side. Starting NGOs for social service is another racket that has spawned exponentially in recent years. Even aid to widows is not spared. To get it the poor illiterate women have to part with half or a third of the money due to them.

Raising the tuition charges of government run educational institutions sky high so that no poor man afford to pay for it is against India's objective of establishing an egalitarian society. It at once creates a new caste system where only the rich can send their children to professional institutes and the poor can never dream of joining that class. This is a fundamental issue to which our intellectuals are paying no attention at all. Both my sons have been to IIT in the Seventies and Eighties. The elder one also went to IIM Ahmedabad. Both are doing extremely well in their chosen fields. If the extortionist fees being levied today were in vogue then I could only send then to a polytechnic and no more. Were education a commercial proposition we could never have had a K.R. Narayan or Abul Kalam as President and Lal Bahadur Shastri as Prime Minister of India. Instead of sending me to the Allahabad University for higher education my father would have bought a small tractor for me and made me a gentleman farmer to plough our family farm lands and tend cattle. Commercialisation of education and abandoning government run schools to the whims of teachers' unions is the biggest single damage the government could have done to our ideals of establishing a socialistic society where everyone has equal opportunity to rise. Even in the most die-hard capitalist countries education upto the college level is available to all at government expense and there are enough government Colleges of the best quality available to accommodation to poor students, if necessary with easy long term loans. Who benefits from this? Only our nouveau riche new middle class. To add insult to injury and compound the offence against the common man the three-year degree course has been raised to four years so that no person of limited means can ever dream of putting his son or daughter in a degree college. I am not against private educational institutions run by entrepreneurs. They are rendering useful service too. But the state must invest much more on education and at the same time maintain strict discipline and, if necessary, a hire and fire policy, in dealing with the teaching community as was done during British rule when education was virtually free and teaching standards high.

Trade unions are yet another menace to our social structure. Only about six percent of the work force is covered by them but they get a large slice of the national cake for their members without doing much work in return. Teachers don't teach but draw their salaries sitting at home. Bank employees give fake loans and make money. Railway and power workers go on lighting strikes and bring the country to a halt. Unions of truck and bus drivers, taxi and auto drivers and a host of others behave like bullies who can get away with anything including murder of the system on which they thrive. By all standards the ordinary unionized "worker" in the organized sector in India is a middle class person, involved in grabbing as large a slice of the national cake as possible, by fair means or foul, without giving commensurate returns in terms of work. Their salaries keep rising by leaps and bounds, every six months, at the cost of the poor man of India.

The unorganized sector which covers 94% of the work force is the worst victim of this loot of national wealth by the middle and upper middle classes who live in decent flats and every other house has two or more cars. The workers are never paid the minimum wage fixed by the government. This again is covered by a separate chapter in this book because the economy would at once revive if only the government would enforce the minimum wages act and put money in the workers' pockets so that they can buy things and thus generate employment.

Even Indonesia, a backward and less developed country, is rigidly enforcing the minimum wages act.

In this respect also I and my family are as much at fault as any other middle class family. Our resident cook and house keeper gets for being on duty for about fifteen hours the minimum wage fixed by the Government for an eight-hour shift. She has been with us for seven years. Her two part time helpers also get proportionately less than the minimum wage. I know I can afford to pay more but if I can get away by paying less, why not? The money grabbed by the middle and upper middle class by denying the minimum wage to workers would be at least ten times more than what has allegedly been embezzled by our top politicians, bureaucrats and industrialists.

Sales tax is another area of enormous loot of the nation's treasury. Hardly any body pays sales tax nor do the shopkeepers demand it since it would mean showing higher returns from their trade and, therefore, paying many times more income tax. I had a shopkeeper as my neighbour for about a year. He lived on the ground floor and we were on the first floor. Every day when I and my wife returned from our morning walk we would find him seated at his desk which he would pull out of his drawing room into the small lawn along the passage way, furiously making fake receipts of the previous day's sales.

Even more interesting was my encounter once with a deputy commissioner of sales tax at Ghaziabad with whom a close friend had made an appointment for a matrimonial alliance of his daughter with the D.C.'s son who was studying in IIM Ahmedabad. He sat on a chair near the entrance of a small longitudinal room, a few feet away from two long benches facing each other across a table with supplicants coming and going. His son and wife were also there. But the main negotiator on his behalf was an inspector of his department. Throughout the hour long visit the D.C. kept mum like an emperor presiding over a durbar where his courtiers do all the talking. We came away without exchanging one word with him. When the inspector called my friend on phone to continue the discussions he simply hung up the receiver.

If only every body paid sales tax where it is due, the national exchequer would be richer by several lakh crores through not only this levy but also income tax. In nearly all cases both buyer and seller belong to the middle and upper middle classes, like us. We are like birds nibbling a ripe crop before it is harvested. In China they had to shoot all birds to save the harvests from being thus nibbled away. I frankly admit that, loyal to my class, I never pay sales tax whenever I can avoid it and prefer shops which do not charge it.

One can go on and on in this manner to discuss the variety of ways in which we cheat each other and yet think highly of ourselves. We started with promises of banning dowry. Today middle class marriages can cost anything between one crore and ten crore rupees. Even a poor man, a mere labourer, ends up spending about a lakh on his daughter's wedding. Any family will beg, borrow or steal to get its sons an MBA degree. When it comes to the charges of hospitals and nursing homes the sky is the limit. Doctors insist on getting even a simple flue patient admitted to a seven star hospital and force him to go through all the tests, ending up with a bill of anything between a lakh and ten lakhs. Organ replacement is now a common every day occurrence. What else can the doctors to do if to get an MD degree they have to pay a capitation fee of Rs. 2 crores per person? They have to recover this money some how and make more. Despite computerization of the entire process railway touts operate freely. The driver of a school van recently took a party of eighteen of his friends from Delhi to Shirdi by train by using a tout.

Statistics show that sex crimes committed by "respectable" people are rising. The fact is that in India they are as old as history. In my school days in the early Forties there was the famous Bilasia murder case. An Indian ICS officer was keeping a maid as a concubine. To hide the affair he murdered her and threw her body in a river. Quite apart from this case, it was common in those days in the families of the super rich to send "bandis" (bonded slave maids) with the bride as dowry. They were sometimes used by the groom as his concubines. The silent "sexual revolution" is happening in India today and changing the place of women in this country from dependents to wage earners.

I am happy to report that landlordism, the old Zamidari system, is back with a vengeance through the backdoor. My ancestors owned lands of whole villages and loaned money on what then seemed to be usurious interest but would appear to be quite normal by today's standards of money lending by banks and authorized institutions. I and my wife are now back in the same business again. Between the two of us we have a sizeable income from the stock market, in which she has developed a special expertise, and my own receipts of rent from an extra flat which I have divided into two tenancies. Thanks to our pro-landlord laws, I keep turning out tenants every two years. By this process my rent earnings have multiplied four-fold in eight years. In the old Zamindari system the money we gave as a loan to the poor was used by them to meet their needs and the rents paid by tenants on our lands were fixed. In the new system of urban landlordism the rents of the tenants of our houses keep shooting up and the money we lend to the stock market circulates only among the middle and upper classes and the poor derive no benefit from it. In fact a substantial part of the earnings from the stock market is siphoned off abroad for the benefit of foreign collaborators of Indian companies. I have noticed by today's standards I am only a small Zamindar. It is all a matter of chance as the old Zamindari was. The only difference is that while in the old "feudal" order incomes remained fixed for decades, in the new Zamindaris our income grows exponentially at the expense of the unpropertied class. This phenomenon of unearned incomes is spreading like an epidemic and creating a new consumer class with its own no-holds-barred laws of morality and ethics. Unearned incomes are fast increasing while the real value of those earned by hard labour decreasing proportionately. But the biggest loot is in the areas of income tax and excise and customs duties. We are all involved in this game. Assisted by powerful chartered accountants who devise ingenius ways of helping us to hide our wealth officially, there is absolutely no count of incomes we conceal privately. We indulge in this anti-social, anti-national and illegal practice by concealing our illgotten wealth in properties by grossly undervaluing them in a ratio of one (white) to four or eight (black). We do the same with jewellery. The over rich also deposit their loot in foreign banks.

With the shifting of more and more activity and development outlay to the private sector, in many industries almost everybody from the rank of CEO to peon demands a cut (call it commission if you like) for services rendered. Huge scandals have emerged in multi-national banks of repute, international NGOs and other major commercial organizations and social institutions.

Recently the Hindu devoted a full page to the issue of missing children. In one story it said that "lakhs of Children" are kidnapped or reported missing in India every year. It also published a letter which I wrote in response to its coverage giving an example of how if the police wanted it could not only check but eradicate the crime altogether. In my view it is as heinous an offence as rape or gang rape but in many cases the police don't care to even record it. Imagine for a moment what you would do if it was a case of your own child being raped or kidnapped. I have dedicated my novel "Vanaloore Shining" to more than 2500 children who are kidnapped from the streets of Bangalore city every year. The book is a satire on the fast growing metropolis, the symbol of the slogan of a "India shining". Is modernization worthwhile if we have to pay such a heavy price in the form of a complete break down of the social structure of our culture bred over several thousand years? Instead of playing a leadership role in this crucial debate the entire media is silent over such tragic developments because it is one of the main beneficiaries of the gangloot. It is highly gratifying to me that at last a Supreme Court, bench headed by Chief Justice Altamas Kabir himself has now issued a number of directives to the states on the subject of child kidnapping. But who cares? The states will merely go through the familiar motions of filing a status report and then forget about it. Only the media networks can force the government's hands to do something about it. But the newspapers and TV channel's have no time for such "trivialities", being too busy titillating the public with ravishing pictures of movie stars and making huge fortunes in the bargain.

Imagine for a moment how you would feel and what you would do it your own child was raped or kidnapped. Is not kidnapping worse than rape because in it you lose your child for ever and will never see it again? Thoughts of what might be happening to your child will torment you throughout your life. Is total toleration of such horrific crimes not a symptom of moral decay of our middle classes who are supposed to be custodians of our social conscience? In this case is silence not worse than bribery or corruption?

About fifty years ago a peon in The Statesman brought to me one of his neighbours from a slum dwellers' colony whose nine year-old son had been kidnapped from the train his family was traveling in at night. I could not help him because even in those proletarian times when socialism was the nation's goal, a case of rape or kidnapping in a poor man's house did not make news for a national daily. Later, I learnt from the peon that the boy had been found in a village about a hundred miles away with the help of a soothsayer who lived in a village near the ancestral home of the afflicted family in Eastern U.P. This miracle man had a geo-positioning system (GPS) of his own by which he could tell the rough location of the village or town where the boy might be found, but he could not tell the precise name and address of the kidnapper. Though rare, such miracles can only happen in India or similar "backward" countries. "Developed" societies would call it witch craft or hoodoo art. They have no space for intuitive knowledge.

As one who has been a crime reporter of a national English daily for several years I can assert with confidence that if the police really girds up it's loins to attack child litters with the same vigor which it shows in dealing with terrorists it could not only reduce this crime but totally stamp it out even without DNA samples of the children and their families.

23

Waves of Spirituality

In this environment it is only natural that empire builders should have spread out all over the country in the name of gurus and sadgurus and holy shrines. They operate on sound business principles with all the parapheruclia of foreign trained executives and institutions designed to spread their business on corporate lines. They thrive on the gullibility of the middle class each of whose members must have a guru to help him to achieve his material objectives.

I wish them good luck. (I would say in parenthesis that they should not forget the famous case of Asa Ram Bapu who is languishing in jail on a charge or raping a girl who was an inmate of his ashram and till the other day was hailed as a messiah by the masses.) In this age of commercialism no institution can survive unless it serves some useful purpose of its members. A senior manager in The Statesman once told me that his insomnia which the best doctors had failed to cure had disappeared completely on the first day of his stay at Baba Muktananda's ashram. Such stories of miracles done by modern day saints abound. That is why people flock to these godmen and holy mothers. A distant relative had all his domestic and career problems solved by falling at the feet of Nirmala Devi and adopting her Sahaj Yoga as his faith. I have also a few friends and relatives who have joined a Buddhist cult of Japanse origin who report immense benefits from their daily chants of its prayers. Many of my friends and relatives are Radhaswamis who have combined service with devotion in their fast spreading cult. A friend recently donated his huge mansion in a posh area in New Delhi to the Radhaswami mission (Agra) of which he is a member. Such examples abound. Then there is the Art of Living movement which has attracted many elitist followers who claim to have attained supreme please at its camps. An enormous list can be compiled of the various organizations preaching spiritualism of various varieties. There are the Brahma Kumaris, the followers of Rajnesh, Saibaba of the South who died recently, the Nirankaris, Hare Rama Hare Krishna movement and scores of other well known groups. Amritanandmai Ma of Kerala has made a great name world wide for launching numerous institutes of higher learning and her holy presence. Recently some members of my family touring the state waited for four hours for her familiar hug and felt amply rewarded.

I respect all of them because they would not have survived had they not served some useful purpose of their devotees. I wish them well even as I applaud the numerous gurus, who include many foreigners, who have set up their "ashrams" in America and Europe. Visits to the holy shrines of Tirupati, Vaishnav Devi and Shirdi have also become very popular these days. Except the Radhaswamis, most of these shrines and cults either did not exist or were not very popular in the days of my childhood and youth in the pre-Independence era. When I joined a journalism class at Hislop College, Nagpur, in 1952, we were told by our American teacher, a Fulbright professor, that the largest circulated among newspapers and periodicals in India was Kalyan, a religious Hindi monthly published by Gita Press, Gorakhpur. Its sale was four lakhs and almost every middle class family including ours subscribed to it. Today, the honour would undoubtedly go to a movie, TV and fashion magazine. But this has not diminished the rage for gurus amongst well to do people.

Accordingly, all our national leaders spoke of religion. Gandhi, Rajagopalacharya, K.M. Munshi, Maulana Azad, Tagore, Subhas Bose, B.G. Tilak, Aurobindo were all devotees first and freedom fighters next. They took to the fight for freedom as their religious duty. The legacy of great saints like Swami Vivekananda Sister Nivedita, Ramakrishna Paramhans and Ram Mohan Roy was already there. Great men launched great religious movements. Pandit Madan Mohan Malviya established the Benares Hindu University. Kashi Vidyapeth came up as a institute of nationalist instruction. Men like Ramana Maharishi radiated a spiritual aura over the whole country. Swami Dayanand had earlier started the Arya Samaj which grew in the 20th century as a great force in the fields of education and religious reform. Annie Besant, a portly English woman of high descent, sought to combine Eastern and Western mysticism and became one of the founders of the Theosophical Society at Madras. J.Krishnamurti was her discovery whom she declared to be a divine born to head the "Order of the Star" which she created for him to lead. Standing on a Californian beach Krishnamurti had a genuine revelation of The Truth which he called "a pathless land". He disbanded the "Order" and broke away from her. I have benefited a great deal from his numerous books and speeches in Delhi which I never missed.

Towering over the scene was the image of Mahatma Gandhi whose Ramdhun reverberated throughout the country. He placed more emphasis on means than ends. Greed, even for freedom, had no place in his vocabulary. God, he said, had provided enough for every one's need but not for everyone's greed. Freedom, if and when it comes, must come through non-violent methods. Though faint, his edicts pervaded the whole atmosphere. In the cities wearing Khadi clothes alone became a symbol of defiance of foreign rule. In the villages, of course, most people wore home spum rustic dresses. Most males could not afford even that and went about their business bare chested and bare foot with only a lungi to cover their nakedness.

Gandhi always thought of this section. Daridranaryan, the poorest of the poor, was his God. He always used to say that before undertaking any action he would ask himself whether it was going to help the poorest of the poor in India. If not, he would not do it. Before plunging into the freedom movement he spent long periods in the villages of Bihar, living eating and sleeping in their huts to understand their problems.

His experience told him that to achieve the greatest good of the greatest number village based cottage and small industries were the only way to solve India's problem of poverty and unemployment. He was a firm believer in socialism and wondered why no past saint had preached it. But his socialism had to be achieved by peaceful means, not wars and violence of any kind. He was convinced that socialism could be achieved through Satyagraha and not by beheading the rich as they did in the French and Soviet revolutions.

To me he appeared to be a re-incarnation of Jesus Christ whom I regard as the greatest socialist ever born. Jesus alone among all the great avataras and prophets declares categorically that "it is easier for a camel to pass through the eye of a needle than for a rich man to enter the kingdom of heaven." He also said that "blessed are the meek and poor for theirs is the kingdom of heaven". Though Krishna also says in the Gita that "who wealth and power do most desire least fixity of soul have such", meaning thereby they are not fit for heaven. But then Gita also preaches rigid adherence to the wretched Aryan caste system, a "sexual hierarchy" which I have described as a Hitlerite Philosophy of cruelty and oppression in my book "Manikpur Junction". (Hitler had declared himself an Aryan and adopted the Aryan Swastika as the national emblem of the Nazi state). Though Jesus also said "Give unto Ceasar what belongs to him", he had not anticipated that there would be one billion Ceasars sponging on the remaining six billion human beings. To me spirituality and truly democratic socialism are synonyms.

It is a community in which every member has an equal share of the nation's resources and is free to speak his mind. One cannot survive in our hearts without the other. You cannot be spiritual without the feeling of being united with the rest of humanity by the same soul force that resides in all of us as one Unity. You have to feel as your own the anguish of the poorest man for whose sake Christ sacrificed his life at the altar. When Gandhi could not stand the way Hindus and Muslims were slaughtering each other after our so-called Independence, he asked God to take him away from the world and He did. It is obvious that in the present selfish social environment such socialism is impossible to attain in India. I have, therefore, opted for the West European model of a Welfare State which is a via media between rank feudalism that prevails in India Today and ideal socialism of Gandhi and Jesus Christ.

So while the hundreds of gurus and cults that have mushroomed in India preach their followers meditation on peace and joy. I can only contemplate, like the great Buddha, on human suffering and the way to relieving it. Their privations and miseries inflicted upon them by the 'haves' of society like ourselves haunt me. Some gurus ask their disciples to meditate on death. I meditate on the living death that the bulk of humanity is living. I have discussed all these matters in a long chapter on religion in this book.

The difference between spiritual socialism and Marxism is that while the Gandhian variety is need driven, Marxism, like global capitalism, is market driven. Ultimately, as Galbraith said in his book The New Industrial State, in essence there is no difference between the two Both, Marxism and Capitalism treat human beings like robots for the benefit of the market, (which in essence means those who operate the market)

In the Lord's prayer Jesus says "Give us this day our daily bread". He asks for no more. In spiritual socialism the operating power is soul force. In the other variety it is brute force which will ultimately lead to human beings to engaging in a war of attrition that can only destroy all mankind and Nature too which includes all life on 'earth'. Anatole France, the famous French writer, was once asked to name three principles of good writing. He replied, "Clarity first, clarity second and clarity last." I am only a small man but if some one were to ask me to name three principles of life for the happiness of all mankind—the greatest good of the greatest number—I would reply "simplicity first, simplicity second and simplicity last." That is how Jesus Christ of my vision would have dealt with the question. For 90% of the people of India the slogan demanding "roti, kapra aur makaan" (bread, clothing and shelter) for everyone is as relevant today as it was before Independence. Even drinking water and fresh air is no longer free.

Belief in God is not necessary in my concept of spirituality. Mahatma Gandhi repeatedly said that he did not believe in God as a person. "God is not a person. He is the all pervading, all powerful, spirit" he declared. For him Truth was God. Nehru also said he did not believe in a "personal God". For Tagore Mind was supreme. Even Ramana Maharishi said God is a creation of the mind. A serious devotee could behold a vision of God in any form that he worshipped. The Great Buddha advocated search for "mind essence". Adi Sankaracharya was dubbed as a Buddhist or atheist by orthodox brahmins of his day. His Vivek Chudmani talks of submergence of the ego or jiva in the "Infinite Absolute Self". To me his "Vivek", Buddha's enlightenment through "mind essence", the super "I" of Ramana, Valmiki's "Consciousness" in his Yoga Vasistha, Christ's "Kingdom of heaven" and J. Krishnamurti's "Awakening of Intelligence" are all one and the same thing. The thing we call God is our own self, a force beyond and behind the mind. Gandhi also called it "soul force". Athiests would call it Nature perhaps. The Central idea beneath all these semantic deviations in the nomenclature of God is that of the unity of all creation. Modern science is slowly coming to the same conclusion. As Fritjof Capra has lucidly explained in his landmark book "Tao of Physics", published about forty years ago, modern sciences of quantum physics and relativity have proved what our seers and mystics perceived intuitively thousands of years ago, that this objective world we operate in is an illusion (Maya) created by our faculties of sense perception. While in this sense world we see separate objects and individualities in reality they are one whole. It is this unity of all mankind that we have to translate into action. In it there can be no one high or low. All have to be equal partners in this 'relative' existence. People like Binayak Sen, Medha Phatakar, Anna Hazare, Arundhati Roy Bindeshwari Pathak and hundreds of others who feel the common man's anguish are driven by the same sense of unity which Gandhiji has called "soul force". Compassion of Buddha cannot be taught by a revered monk in the georgeous seminar halls of New York and Washington but has to be learnt the hard way by living and breaking bread in with the poorest of the poor for whom people like Gandhi, Mother Theresa and Vivekanand worked. St. Paul is said to have shared his blanket with a leper and slept with him. That is true compassion. Only a person who feels the spiritual unity of mankind in his veins and bones can behave as St. Paul did. People who pursue wealth and power through their spirituality with the help of 'gurus' are, in my opinion, worshipping the wrong God. True spirituality of my conception lies in service of the poor and fighting in the continous ongoing Mahabharata war against injustice done to them at any level by modern day Ravanas and Duryodhanas.

Mr. S. Sivadas, whom I have already introduced in an earlier chapter, gave me two priceless books "the Way of The Pilgrim" and "Philokalia". Together they have a toxic effect on the mind. They seem to open up a whole new vista of the wilderness of Russian Tundras which have their own spiritual message and the mysticism of the Greek Christian monks in the early centuries when their influence stretched over the whole Caucasian region. It reminded me of B.G. Tilak's Arctic Home of the Vedas, there being a similarity, if not identity between earliest Christian and Vedic perceptions of The Truth and it recalls warmer times long long ago when there might have been a civilization and vegetation in the Arctic zone. The Gita also has a reference to it when it recalls the worship of the "old world's far light". There are innumerable mysteries to fathom about the hoary past, beyond the range of history and mythology. With modern tools of deciphering the past the real treasures of the spiritual revelations of the pre-historic era may be possible. As Tilak has pointed out references to the several months long dawn and sunset in the Rig Veda are pointers to a lost civilization which we must strive to find.

These days I am having a running dialogue with my old friend and critic Mr. Vinod Dhawan, a former News Editor of The Hindustan Times and currently an expert in modern day Western mystics and gurus. I met him first in 1982 when he was running the books counter of the pandal erected for a series of lectures by J. Krishnamurte in the lawns of Vallabhai Patel house in Rafi Marg in Delhi. In those days he was Krishnamurti fan and had traveled to Varanasi to join him in his meditation camp there. But he is man who has tasted the waters of many streams of spirituality and is now a master of nearly all of them. He and I differ on many crucial points on this subject. His current obsession (if I am using the right word) is with "non-duality" which is very popular with Western mystics these days. Nearly all of them claim to have derived their inspiration from Ramana Maharishi. But Dhawan may be ultimately right. The Truth is so elusive and so is deep meditation upon it that it is impossible to over-estimate their powers.

I am myself a devotee of Ramana Maharishi in so many ways. But I feel that to practice his beliefs without his austerity and compassion is like visiting Kashmir or Switzerland in a dream. It is not a real experience of the soul. Further I have a strong belief that non-duality cannot be practiced without feeling the anguish of the poorest man on earth: Yashoda Ma, one of the greatest saints of the last century who lived in a cottage in a pine grove in her cottage near Mitrola in Almora district of Uttrakhand with her well known disciple Krishna Prem, an Englishman, and a few others, used to sleep with a stray dog lying by her side in her bed. One day while shoeing it away with a stick for stealing her 'prasad' (devotional offerings of sweets to the image of a god) she saw her Lord, Baby Krishna, in the body of the dog, crying. Similarly, Gandhi saw "Daridranarayan", the poorest of the poor, who is kicked about like an animal and untouchable by Indian society, in whose service he spent all his life in the hope of "seeing God face to face". The last word on the subject was said by Jesus Christ or whoever wrote it in the Lord's Prayer in the phrase "Give us this day our daily bread."